FINANCIAL INCLUSION GROWTH AND GOVERNANCE

Dr Deepali Pant Joshi

GYAN

Financial Inclusion Growth and Governance
Dr Deepali Pant Joshi

Price: ₹ 750
ISBN: 978-81-212-1305-9

First Published, 2016

Gyan Publishing House
5, Ansari Road, Darya Ganj, New Delhi-110002
Phone: 9811692060
E-mail : books@gyanbooks.com

Printed at: G. Print Process, Delhi.

Contents

For my father

Shri Jagdish Mohan Pant

(Former Administrator General Official Trustee of the State of Uttar Pradesh)

"whose blessings make all things possible".

"Jo Sab tab Pratap Raghurai,
Nath na Kachu Mor Prabhutai"

HANUMANJI

Extract from the Sundarkand.

This work has been achieved through the benevolence and Grace of the almighty; to him alone I attribute the successful achievement of this task.

—Ramayana

Acknowledgements

I thank with gratitude the good Lord Hanumanji for his beneficence and favour Ta Kahun Kuch Agam Nahin Ja par Tum Anukool. Nothing is difficult for him whom the Lord Blesses.

Most things in my life have been possible only due to the blessings and inspiration my late and beloved father Mr Jagdish Mohan Pant who always believed in me to him I dedicate this work.

I acknowledge the many debts of gratitude owed to my family my encouraging mother Professor Chandra Pant. My husband Rajeev and my affectionate sons Paritosh and Kunal who support and encourage all my endeavours.

The views expressed are personal and do not reflect the views of the institution with which I am associated for a little over three decades.

I extend sincere thanks to Gyan Books the publishers of this work and anticipatory thanks to the prospective readers of the book.

Dr (Smt) Deepali Pant Joshi

Reserve Bank of India

Preface

This book highlights the importance of Financial Inclusion Growth and Governance; inalienably linked to each other and integral to fostering financial stability. Rapid Financial Inclusion will lead India to a trajectory of exponential economic growth with Equity allowing India to take its rightful place in the comity of nations and to take a leadership role in South, South East Asia and the world.

This book explores in depth the subject of Growth and Governance Financial Intermediation for all especially for women and the weaker, and most vulnerable sections. This insightful and analytical book explores the many facets of the multiplier effect on economic growth which the possession of a Bank account and of being linked to mainstream financial institutions can have on the vulnerable sections of society. It shows how Linkage with the Financial System will help the poor, the weak, vulnerable, the underserved, build financial capability by accessing saving, credit, remittance, Insurance, and Transaction facilities at reasonable costs from the financial system. This will load to sustainable, scalable, income generation allowing them to work their way out of poverty. The book explores the moral and economic arguments for financial Inclusion which are both equally compelling. The book showcases the macro policies which have driven Financial Inclusion and brings out the importance of the Prime Ministers Jan Dhan Yojana as an effective delivery model of financial inclusion. It explains how financial intermediation for the masses will help unleash the forces of economic growth. This book addreses an issue which has high priority on the National

Agenda and will be a valuable source of reference on the subject for Economists, bankers, policy makers, teachers, civil society, multi lateral institutions engaged in development, Civil servants, researchers analysts, social scientists and the thinking person. With this book the author has made another substantive contribution to the field of development economics.

Introduction

This is on Financial Inclusion it discusses Financial Inclusion, Financial Literacy and Customer Empowerment. These are three facets of Financial Inclusion. A neglected aspect integral to securing these and attaining the overall goal of financial Inclusion is good governance. Hence, I have chosen to title this book Inclusion Growth and Governance. There is a causal linkage between economic growth and good governance by governance is meant the quality of public administration and the integrity of the function to ensure desired virtuous outcomes. There is a strong positive effect between better governance and outcomes. Governance than becomes a line function which leads to the translation of overarching macro policy to, quantifiable measurable outcomes, and concrete deliverables on the ground. This process enables incremental change, to take place slowly, but surely at the base level. Programs suffer not through lack of vision but due to improper monitoring and translation to outcomes at the base level where changes have to happen catalytically over a slow process of continuous monitoring and handholding. Thus, good efficient governance is an imperative. The dimensions of governance begin with political stability, quality of Governance, Rule of Law, control of corruption through institutions of accountability all these translate to effectiveness of Government Governance thus is defined as "the processes of interaction and decision-making among the actors involved in a collective problem that lead to the creation, reinforcement, or reproduction of norms and institutions." It is narrowly summed up as effective monitoring of attainment of objectives at every level. Governance as defined by the World Bank is the manner in which power is exercised in the management of a country's economic and social resources for development. The project of the World Bank,Worldwide Governance Indicators defines governance as the traditions and institutions by which authority in a country is exercised. This considers the capacity of the government to effectively formulate and implement sound policies and the respect that citizens have for the state of the institutions that govern economic and social interactions among them. The inalienable link between growth and governance has been established through several empirical studies. The concept of good governance emerged at the end of the 1980s, first at the World Bank and was further developed upon by International Development Aid agencies and organisations such as UNDP and OECD. According to the World Bank, good governance entails sound public sector management (Efficiency, Effectiveness and Economy), Accountability, exchange and free flow of information (transparency), Legal framework for development (Justice, respect for human rights and liberties)(World Bank, 1994). UNDP lists nine major characteristics of good Governance: Participation, Rule of law, Transparency, Responsiveness, Consensus Orientation, Equity, Effectiveness and Efficiency, Accountability and Strategic Vision. Good governance can spur the processes of economic growth and lead to gains, which are tangible, equitable and inclusive. The compelling link between growth and financial inclusion an is due to the pivotal role the banks play as financial intermediaries, both at a macro and a micro level. At a macro level, banks contribute to growth through mobilisation of savings and allocation of credit towards optimal deployment avenues available in the economy; while at a micro level, banks provide households and businesses an opportunity to realise their economic goals and improve their financial position through a range of financial services, thereby contributing to overall growth. Banks are constrained in this function as they are unable to access a large segment of the population due to financial exclusion. Financial inclusion and the consequent increased penetration of banks to the hitherto unbanked segments, thus, have strong linkages to economic growth.

Inclusion therefore is inalienable with Growth and Governance, particularly relevant at this juncture. Across the globe, especially in the wake of the financial crisis, there is a clearer understanding that sustainable growth and financial stability become achievable on a wider base of participatory development attained through financial Inclusion. Indian policymakers have pursued polices for moving towards equitable development over the years.. There is some progress on the ground however; the quality of Financial Inclusion that we have achieved over these years leaves much to be desired. When we say quality, we do not imply anything esoteric we mean that although a number of accounts are opened, the number of transactions in these accounts continues to be minuscule. Progress is not commensurable with potential. The larger question, therefore, is what is holding us back. Can this be attributed to poor governance of our Financial Inclusion processes and the framework which can lead to lack of accountability at the highest policy level i.e. Board and at the level of senior management.

Good Governance: An essential pre-requisite

The vision of Inclusive Growth and Governance dictates the need to broaden and deepen access to development finance for all. Only well functioning and efficiently governed financial institutions can provide financial services to meet the growing needs of the economy. Despite early recognition of the need for universal financial inclusion, a large cross-section of the population, remained financially excluded. Measures initiated by the Regulator/Government in the post-independence period resulted in impressive gains in rural outreach and volume of credit, the structure suffered from inherently weak governance. The achievements were 'quantitatively impressive, but 'qualitatively weak'. Over time and especially, in the wake of the adoption of the RBI encouraged structured Financial Inclusion Framework adopted by banks over the last few years, there has been substantive development in the architecture and thinking on financial inclusion. There has been a growing realisation that there is no "one-size-fits-all" financial inclusion strategy which can be cloned over the length and breadth of our country, although few core conditions are essential to maximize the benefits derived from such a strategy. Effective Governance is the most predominant of these conditions and is, in fact, a *sine qua non* for achieving financial inclusion.

Effective financial inclusion is not attainable until good governance supports the entire structure of the financial inclusion programme. Good governance under the financial inclusion programme is achievable through a planned and structurally integrated framework, supported by a policy vision. It is essential to calibrate and continuously monitor the entire governance structure of the financial inclusion programme, the progress achieved so far and issues and challenges that need to be tackled to make it a success.

Governance Deficit

The need for effective governance implies that the underpinning of all processes, through norms that define our actions, allocate power and prescribe a matrix against which we can calibrate our performance. Lack of effective governance has been one of the major reasons for slow progress in implementing our Financial Inclusion initiatives.

Ownership and Accountability

Why is the pace and progress of Financial Inclusion slow is Financial Inclusion not happening even after the infrastructure is in place? It is clearly due to lack of accountability and a problem of attitude. Many of the banks still have not developed an appropriate, cost-effective delivery model for Financial Inclusion and therefore, they are not thoroughly convinced that Financial Inclusion is a profitable business opportunity. Resultantly, they still perceive it to be a social/ regulatory obligation and consequently their efforts are half-hearted. The inadequacy of Management Information System (MIS) creates further complications. The cost for setting up the intermediate brick and mortar structures and developing the (BC) Banking Correspondent network has to be seen as future investment. Obviously, it cannot be revenue accretive from day one. Still, if one were to logically work out the mathematics of serving the customers in a brick and mortar branch and through a BC, keeping the fixed and variable cost in mind, certainly the BC model would work out much cheaper in the medium term. Therefore, for the Financial Inclusion model to work, the banks need to take ownership of the model and ensure continuous and full support to the Business Correspondents at the ground level. There is need to punish the non-performers in the system and the governance system has to be improved for ensuring buy-in from the Top as also ensure Management commitment and accountability from the rank and file of the bank.

Delivery Model Pradhan Mantri Jan Dhan yojana (PMJDY)

The PMJDY will ensure provision of Universal Access to attain scale. It aims to put in place stripped down versions of bank branches which can be set up with lower overheads and capital costs while subserving the purposes of extending penetrative reach in the hitherto unserved and underserved areas.

Viability Issues

Inclusion metrics need to morph to focus more on the number of transactions in Bank accounts opened and whether graduated upscaling is taking place or not. The Access-Usage conundrum has to be clearly understood (DBT) Direct Besefit Transfers will act as a natural enabler of this process. While access to financial services has improved, the usage of the financial infrastructure continues to be tardy. While impressive banking outlets are available across the country, the number of transactions in many accounts opened by the BCs, remains unimpressive. This not only restricts the potential benefits that could accrue from increased financial access but also reduces the viability of Financial Inclusion activities for banks and BCs. The reduced viability, in turn, impacts the scalability of the model and, in the process, retards the Financial Inclusion efforts.

CGAP-CAB National Survey of Banking Agents 2012-13BC operations

The first national survey of banking agents taken up by CGAP in conjunction with the Reserve Banks College of Agricultural Banking pointed to serious impairment hampering the scaling up of the BC model. At present there is only a Quantitative focus on increase in the number of agents rather than increase in the depth of banking operations through the BC. A viable Bank BC model will emerge if banks change the nature of the relationship with the BC and give up the restrictive Cash Management Systems adopted. In this model BCs fully prefund their business operations in terms of cash limits and security obtained from BCs; Non-insurance of cash held in transit by BCs; Low or untimely remuneration received by BCs/CSPs; allowing transactions only in limited products through the BC channel. These have restricted the involvement and effectiveness of the BCs as a vital peg in the financial inclusion jigsaw.

Best Practices

Reviews have shown that different banks are adopting different practices. The time has come for banks to come together and identify best practices for the scaling up of the BC model. Banks need to work under the aegis of IBA and come up with "Best Self Regulatory Practices for BC Operations" based on industry best practices. Banks need to standardise operations under the BC model.

CGAP-CAB 2013 Transaction activity by Business Correspondent Agents

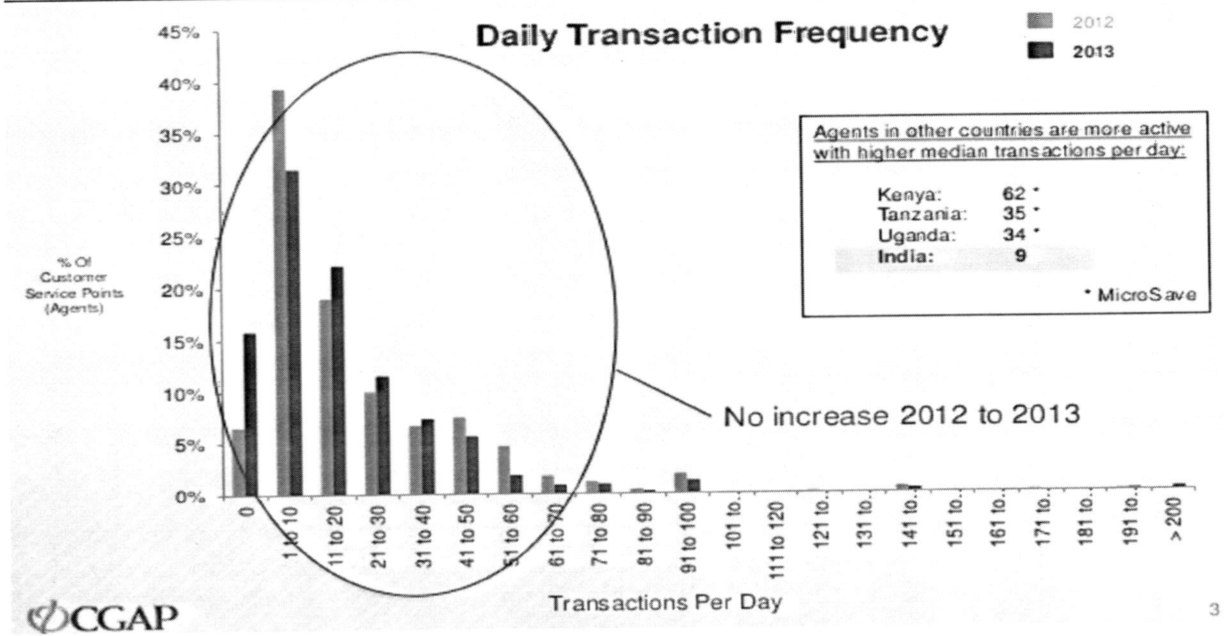

CGAP-CAB Comparison between surveys in 2012 and 2013

Particulars	*2012*	*2013*	
CSP agents who had never transacted	5 per cent	16 per cent	Worsened
Agents with technical capability that allows clients to transact at other CSPs	65 per cent	48 per cent	Worsened
Unprepared to transact	11 per cent	25 per cent	Worsened
Median account opening time	10 minutes	10 minutes	Same
Median account activation time	4 days	9 days	Worsened
Median CSP income	Rs. 2700	Rs. 2700	Same
Visited by Bank/BC in prior Month	82 per cent	89 per cent	Improved
Visited by Bank/BC in Prior week	60 per cent	72 per cent	Improved
Those Paid on time	50 per cent	48 per cent	Same
Received training	90 per cent	85 per cent	Worsened
Positively viewed Bank's/BC Support	64 per cent	58 per cent	Worsened

Banking Activity in India

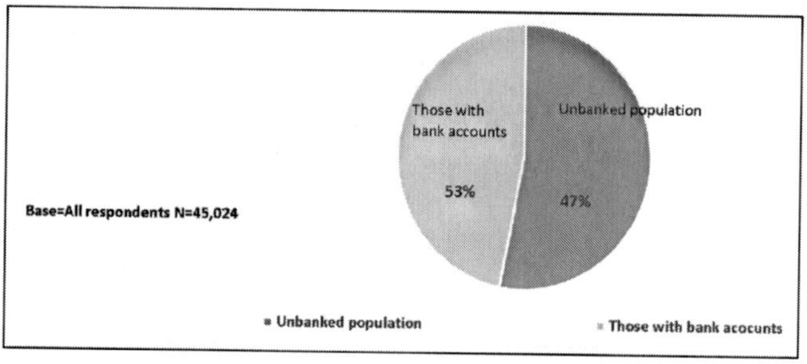

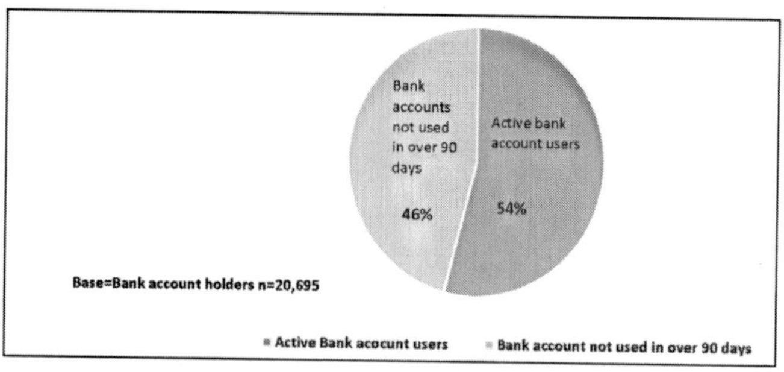

Trust in Financial Service Providers

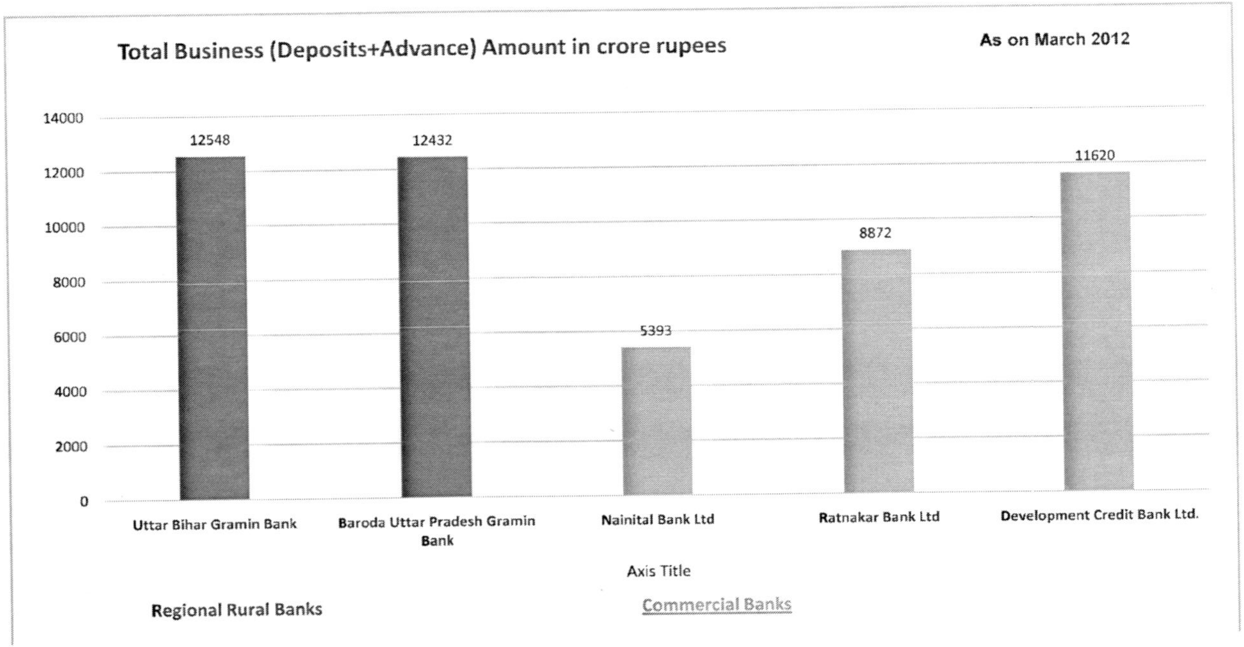

Higher variation in active banking by gender and location, within certain states

Percentage for both charts:percentage of bank account holders in each group who use their account actively (in the last 90 days)

States with highest gender gap in active bank use among bank account holders

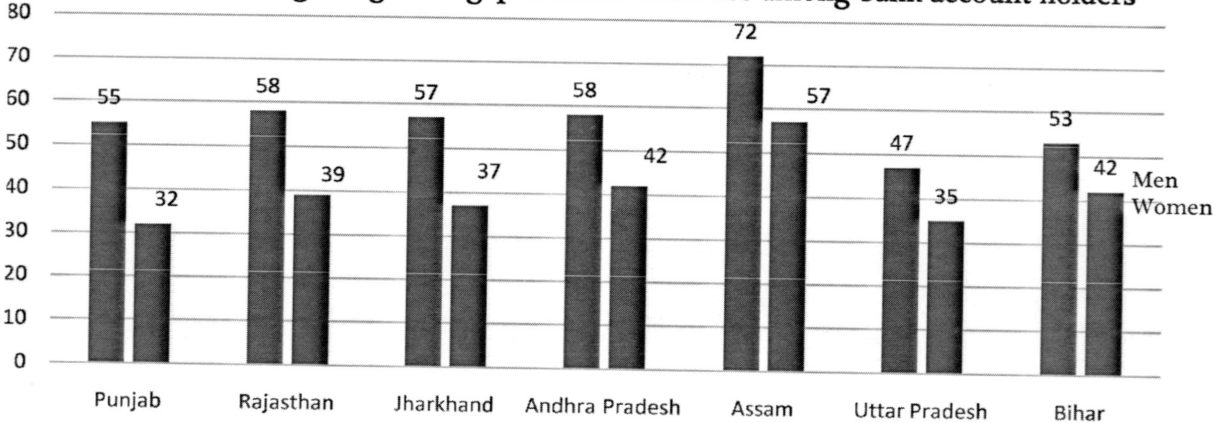

Base: Punjab (Male= 286, Female=305) Rajasthan (Male=576, Female-411), Jharkhand (Male=260, Female=196), Andhra Pradesh (Male=977 Female=542), Assam (Male=202, Female=173)

Men Women

Technology issues

While banks have innovated on technology, the same has not resulted in significant reduction in the cost of providing financial services. Beneficiaries/stakeholders often complain of constraints in digital/physical connectivity. This, coupled with delays in issuance of smart cards, reliability issues in hardware infrastructure such as hand held devices, etc. have impacted the quick roll out of financial services across the country. Over dependence on vendors and the resultant problems is a serious governance deficit which needs to be overcome for effective rollout of our Financial Inclusion initiatives.

(E) Regulatory Governance to Self Governance

The primary role of the regulator is to issue broad guidelines to ensure standardised practices across the banks at the national level. In line with these broad guidelines, it is the responsibility of the bank management to develop their own internal processes, structures and governance framework based on their business model and overall business strategy. The internal governance should ensure that a robust system is developed to keep a check on adherence to rules and regulations.

Presently, there is a top-down approach to implementation of regulation and regulatory controls at all levels. Financial Inclusion delivery models also operate in similar ways where top-down approach is followed by banks while deciding the operational aspects of Business Correspondents and other delivery channels. It is this approach which needs a fundamental change. We need to move from forced implementation to willing participation to facilitate achievement of Financial Inclusion goals. Effective governance at all levels within banks would ensure that regulations are seen as an essential element of business and are not adhered to merely for compliance the sake of tick box. Banks' policies should evolve from best practices and ground level realities. The regulator should not be required to micro manage the principles on which Financial

Inclusion models operate. This can be achieved in following ways:

i. Alignment of business plan with all micro policies

ii. Self regulation

iii. Bottom up and participatory approach

iv. Robust internal checks and control

v. Knowledge sharing at industry level

In general, Governance is administered in three ways viz. through market forces, through governing body or through network. In an organisational set up, it is the rules and regulations that guide all activities. Regulatory governance reflects the emergence of de-centered and mutually adaptive policy regimes which rest on regulation rather than service provision. From the perspective of the Governance framework guiding the financial inclusion process, banks need to devise their own strategies to ensure that an effective and conducive governance regime is in place to ensure attainment of Financial Inclusion goals.

Conclusion

Good governance is at the core of improving the delivery of public services. Good governance provides a mechanism for linking inclusion, decision making, and accountability. Problems in infrastructure, critical for building an inclusive India, can often be traced back to lack of ownership and poor governance. Many of the initiatives launched over the years for achieving the objective of rapid growth coupled with poverty alleviation and inclusiveness have failed to achieve their goals because of lack of ownership, ineffective governance and insufficient accoun-tability at various levels. Without effective implementation, even substantial government expenditure results in limited success.

The success of banks cannot be measured simply in terms of profit their banking operations generate. Banking services success of banks, lies equally in addressing the financial needs of various stakeholders. Not only is this about making the system more inclusive, it is also about protecting the financial consumer, through improved awareness and better grievance redress mechanisms. The mantra of good corporate governance, there-fore, does not just encompass ethics and business practices followed by the bank or its personnel; it has to go beyond compliance with regulatory directives. It must consider fair and acceptable behaviour, among others, to those who are more vulnerable, even if it is at some cost to Bank bottom lines.

For Financial Inclusion initiatives to succeed, it is important for banks to craft new policies on governance and compliance, wherein good governance is the primary responsibility of the bank's board of directors and its senior management. While the mandate of the leadership of each bank to make strategic decisions is to be respected as, it is these choices, that differentiate one bank from another, as a business proposition; however, the governance perspective that is sought needs to be fundamentally entrenched as a core competency across all banks.

There is a causal linkage between growth and good Governance. The deficit of governance can impair and impede development. I am often asked why the BC model is not scaling up as it should to meet the humungous credit needs of our population. The answer is simple. The model lacks effective governance at every level. There is inadequate supervision of the banks' frontline staff. The vision of the Board room is not transmitted to the frontline manager. Governance failure is also reflected in the vendor dependence in the usage of technology. We have to chart a clear path and change this dependence into efficient and effective systems which are scalable and sustainable. So, the overarching theme here is a persistent and immediate need to address the governance deficit to ensure financial inclusion and concomitant growth.

In sum, good governance and accountability at different levels of bank management is the key for the success of the financial inclusion programme. Maximum attention needs to be paid to firmly showcase the virtues of financial inclusion to the banks' boards and to ensure acceptance of these at the highest level. It is also important at the same time to make the Boards accountable to deliver the results on the mandate of financial inclusion. The acceptability and accountability at lower level of management will automatically follow. We also need to improve governance mechanism for delivery of banking services through BC network by ensuring better co-ordination Collaboration commitment and governance amongst all stakeholders, including the technology providers, vendors, etc. Up until now, we have followed a carrot and stick policy to ensure the success of the financial inclusion programme with the carrots being used more predominantly. Having created a flexible and friendly regulatory environment for financial inclusion for inclusive banking practices, the time has come for us to use the stick more often, albeit judiciously, to make financial inclusion an integral part of banking operations and ensure its acceptability as a strategeic objective at bank board level. This has to be supported by good governance at every level of the management. What remains key is record keeping, transaction monitoring and reporting; one of the biggest concerns in India today is putting the systems in place associated with the delivery of the financial inclusion programme. When it comes to financial inclusion in India, the crux, therefore, is that we need to address the basic risks while opening up the sector fully i.e. allowing more players and modes into the mission, and for this, we need to have much more coordination and collaboration, not just between industry participants but also between the various arms of policymakers. The international practices and guidelines are there for us to use, to close with an extract from Robert Frost:—

"The woods are lovely, dark and deep,

but I have promises to keep

and miles to go before I sleep".

Though a lot has been achieved in our journey towards universal financial inclusion we still have distance left to travel Financial Inclusion is a moral imperative as much as an economic necessity.

Financial Inclusion Growth And Governance

1

Role of Banking in Development

Commercial Banks contribute much to the growth of the economy through financial intermediation by promoting savings and extending loans to agriculture, trade and industry, by helping in physical and human capital formation and by transmitting the monetary policy signals formulated by the Central Bank of the country.

In terms of Section 5 of the Banking Regulation Act, 1949, "banking" means the accepting, for the purpose of lending or investment, of deposits of money from the public, repayable on demand or otherwise, and withorawable by cheque, draft, order or otherwise.

Branch-wise Network of Commercial Banks – December 2013

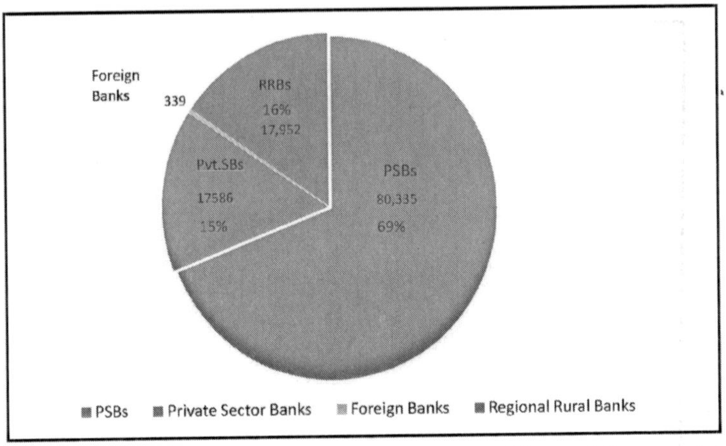

Source: Bank Group-wise Number of Functioning Offices of Commercial Banks report on DBIE (http://dbie.rbi.org.in) updated from MoF database of DSIM, RBI.

Rural Branch Network of Commercial Banks – December 2013

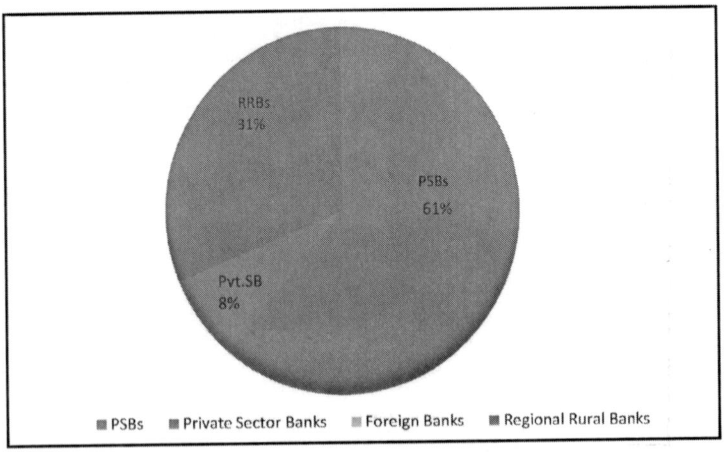

Source: Bank Group-wise Number of Functioning Offices of Commercial Banks report on DBIE (http://dbie.rbi.org.in) updated from MoF database of DSIM, RBI

Urban Branch Network of Commercial Banks – December 2013

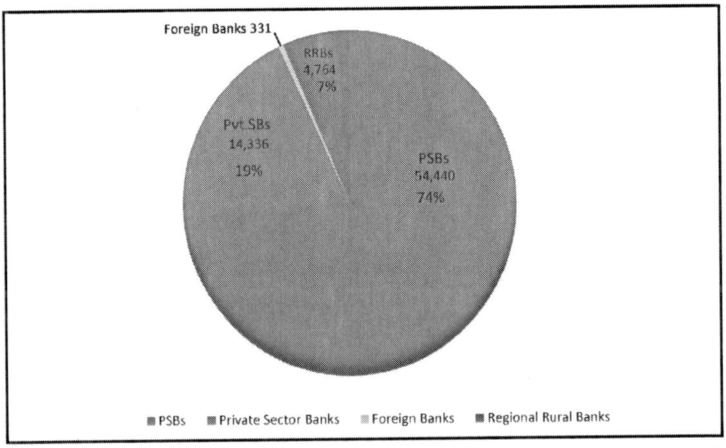

Source: Bank Group-wise Number of Functioning Offices of Commercial Banks report on DBIE (http://dbie.rbi.org.in) updated from MoF database of DSIM, RBI.

Bank Group-wise Branch Network –March 2013

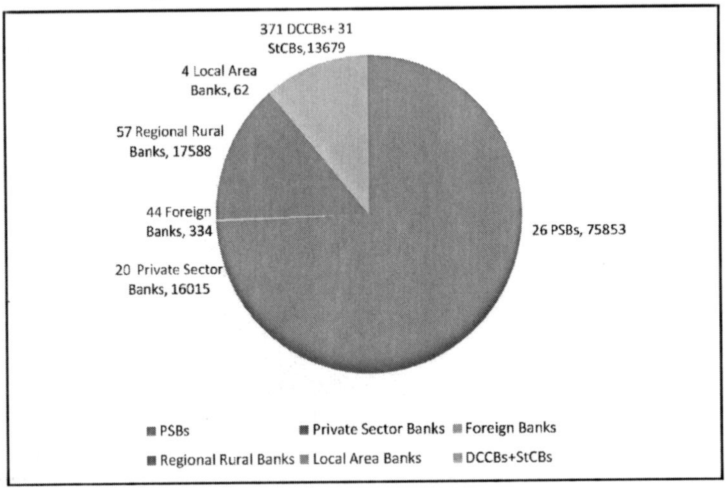

Source: Bank Group-wise Number of Functioning Offices of Commercial Banks report on DBIE (http://dbie.rbi.org.in) updated from MoF database of DSIM, RBI.

Development Initiatives by RBI

RBI, as the regulator of banks has played a pivotal role in development of banking in India and has taken several initiatives to promote development and Social banking as follows :

- In addition to the core functions..., RBI took proactive steps in extending banking facilities to rural and semi-urban areas, Adoption of lead bank scheme, Establishment of specialised financing agencies. Deposit Insurance Credit Guarantee Corporation, Industrial Development Bank of India, Unit Trust of India, National Housing Bank, National Bank for Agriculture and Rural Development etc.
- In terms of Section 54 of the RBI Act, 1934, RBI maintains expert staff to study various aspects of rural credit and development to tender expert guidance and assistance to NABARD and conduct special studies in areas for promoting integrated rural development.
- Prescription of priority sector lending norms.
- Ensuring better banking customer service, Financial Inclusion and Financial Literacy initiatives, etc.

Lead Bank Scheme – Need–Features

The Lead Bank Scheme was introduced by RBI in 1969 to develop a structure so that the benefits of banking reach the poor, to allow grass root functionaries of banks and Government agencies to work together. Nationalisation of 14 Banks and the Green Revolution in 1969 created a requirement of timely, adequate institutional credit and the supply of quality inputs to spur agricultural growth and industrial and economic development.

Lead Bank Scheme envisages credit planning, coordination of activities of banks, financial institutions and Government Departments. It overseas flow of credit to various sectors in rural areas, implementation of Government sponsored poverty alleviation and employment generation schemes.

Under this scheme a district has been choosen as is aunit of development and one bank is assigned Lead Bank responsibility for one district viz. One bank in each districtlead Bank. Initially it covered only rural and semi-urban areas. Now this scheme covers 671 districts including 16 districts in metropolitan areas of Kolkata (1), Hyderabad (1), Chennai, Mumbai (2) and Delhi (11) to address urban financial inclusion.

Lead districts in India

Committees Under Lead Bank Scheme

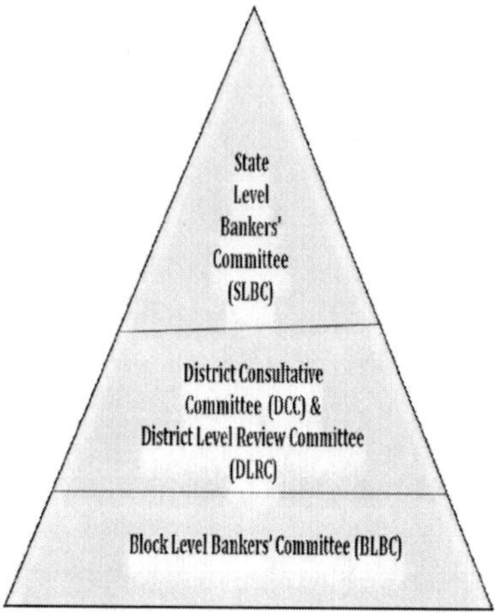

SLBC Convenor Banks and Lead banks

SLBC Convenor banks (16)	*Lead Banks (26)*
• Andhra Bank	• Allahabad Bank
• *Bank* of Baroda	• Andhra Bank
• Bank of India	• Bank of Baroda
• Bank of Maharashtra	• Bank of India
• Canara Bank	• Bank of Maharashtra
• Central Bank of India	• Canara Bank
• Dena Bank	• Central Bank of India
• Indian Bank	• Corporation Bank
• Indian Overseas Bank	• Dena Bank
• J & K Bank Ltd.	• Indian Bank
• OBC	• Indian Overseas Bank
• Punjab National Bank	• J & K Bank Ltd.
• State Bank of India	• OBC
• Syndicate Bank	• Punjab & Sind Bank
• UCO Bank	• Punjab National Bank
• United Bank of India	• SBBJ
	• State Bank of Hyderabad
	• State Bank of India
	• State Bank of Mysore
	• State Bank of Patiala
	• State Bank of Travancore
	• Syndicate Bank
	• UCO Bank
	• Union Bank of India
	• United Bank of India
	• Vijaya Bank

Functionaries under Lead Bank Scheme

Forum	Banks/FI	Govt. Authorities
SLBC **Convenor:** SLBC Convenor Bank of the State **Chairman:** CMD of SLBC Convenor Bank and Addl. Ch. Secretary to co-chair **Invitees:** CM/FM, National Comm. for SC/ST, State Minorities Fin. Corpns., NGOs, select LDMs	Regional Director-RBI, CGM-NABARD, State-In-Charge-SIDBI, Industrial Financial Corporation of India, PSBs, Pvt. SBs Chairmen- RRBs, MD-State Cooperative Bank, State Cooperative Agriculture & Rural Development Bank, MD-SFC	Secretary-Planning, Finance, Ag., Rural Devp., Poverty alleviation, industries, Director, Inst. Finance, Registrar Cooperative Societies
DCC & DLRC **Convenor:** Lead District Manager of lead bank **Chairman: Dist. Collector/ Dist. Magistrate/ Dy. Commissioner** **Invitees:** Issue based, other Govt. Depts., Corporations **Invitees: in DLRC:** Public representatives-MLAs, MPs, ZP President	RBI-Lead District Officer, NABARD-Dist. Devp. Mgr., RMs of 5 or 6 big PSBs in district, In-charges of RRBs, Pvt.SBs, GM-DCCB, Representatives of Primary Cooperative Agriculture & Rural Development Bank, SFC, KVIB	CEO-ZP, Project Director-DRDA, Dist. Planning Officer, GM-DIC, Exec. Officer-SC, ST, BC Corporations, Dist. In-charges of Agri., Animal Husbandry and Industries, Dist. Dy. Registrar-Co-operatives
BLBC **Convenor:** Manager of the branch of lead bank in the block HQ **Chairman:** Lead District Manager of lead bank	RBI-Lead District Officer may attend selectively BMs of all commercial banks, RRBs, DCCBs and Primary Cooperative Agriculture & Rural Development Bank	BDO, Tahsildar, Line Departments Officers of , Other Govt. Depts.

Implementation–Planning at Grass Root level

- State Level Credit Plan
- District Credit Plan
- Block Credit Plan
- Branch Credit Plan
- Bottom Up Approach

LBS – State Level Bankers' Committee

The State Level Bankers Committee (SLBC) is the apex forum under the Lead Bank Scheme (SLB). Its Meetings are held at quarterly intervals as per an annual calendar. At present there are 35 SLBCs (29 SLBCs and 6 UTLBCs). Sub-committees of the SLBC are also formed for various purposes to address the issues in achievement of set goals under the Lead Bank Scheme.

Major Functions of Lead Bank Scheme are:

- To address impediments of development of banking system in the state with the State Govt. authorities.
- To discuss issues, problems and arrive at solutions in the field of agricultural and rural development, banking development, financial inclusion and evolve consensus for action.
- To undertake critical analysis of the progress of the implementation of Annual Credit Plans (ACPs), credit linked programmes / schemes of Government and other agencies in various districts.

Mechanism of Grass Root Level Development Planning

LBS–DCC, DLRC Fora–Role of District Collectors-Issues

District Consultative Committee (DCC) forms many need based sub-committees such as on CD (Credit Deposit) Ratio, financial inclusion, financial literacy, education loan, credit flow to MSE sector, Bank-SHG linkage/Joint Liability Groups (JLGs), etc. DCC & District Level Review Committee (DLRC) meetings are held at quarterly intervals and DLRC is held in the month subsequent to holding of DCC. For the DLRC, public representatives—MLAs (Member of Legislative Assemblies), MPs (Member of Parliaments), ZP (Zila Parishad) President are invited.

As chairman of DCC & DLRC, the District Collectors play a vital role in the economic development of the district. District Collectors guide and lead the functionaries towards achieving the development goals under Lead Bank Scheme.

Issues:

- Preparation of DCC & DLRC Calendar and holding of meetings as per calendar and effective utilisation of the fora for achieving social good for grass roots level planning
- Support from all stake holders
- Popularising Bankers Committee (BC) model
- Appropriate level of participation in meetings
- Data submission by banks to lead bank.

High Level Committee to review the Lead Bank Scheme

Over the four decades since the introduction of the LBS, several changes have taken place in the country, especially after 1991 with the beginning of globalisation and liberalisation of the Indian economy. The reforms have encompassed all sectors including the financial sector. The Commercial Banks are much more focused today on their financial position and have improved their competitiveness and efficiency. Their capital adequacy ratios and provisioning standards are as per the best international standards. Although priority sector obligations continue to be in force for both private sector and public sector banks, attention has increasingly been drawn to the fact that large sections of the population remain outside the formal banking structure and the real and financial sectors continue to lag behind in certain regions. While policies are in place to facilitate flow of credit to the more vulnerable sectors/sections of society, there is a need to ensure greater dissemination and effective implementation of these policies at the grass root level, besides reviewing timely information and for better assessment of outcomes.

A need was, therefore, felt for a comprehensive review of the Scheme. Accordingly, as announced in the Reserve Bank's mid-term review of Annual Policy for the year 2007-08, a Committee was constituted Chief/finance seeretaries of State Governments with CMDs/ senior functionaries of banks and others as members to review the Lead Bank Schemes (LBS) with a focus on financial inclusion and the recent developments in the banking sector.

Recommendations of High Level Committee

The Committee held wide ranging discussions with various stakeholders viz. State Governments, banks, development institutions, academicians, NGOs, MFIs, etc. and noted that the Scheme has been useful in achieving its original objectives of improvement in branch expansion, deposit mobilisation and lending to the priority sectors, especially in rural/semi urban areas. Therefore it recommended the following:

- One of the main objectives of LBS is to enable the banks and State Governments to work together for inclusive growth.
- LBS aims at comprehensive Financial Inclusion using multiple channels, intermediaries and Information Technology.
- To draw up a roadmap for provision of banking outlets in unbanked villages with population of more than 2000 by March 2012 and to give an impetus to financial inclusion in the hitherto neglected areas.
- Strengthening role of State Government: Providing infrastructure and facilitating financial inclusion.
- Strengthening role of SLBC: Addl. Chief Secretary of State Government & CMD (Chairman and Managing Director) of SLBC bank to co-chair SLBC meetings; Chief Minister and Finance Minister of the concerned state to be urged to attend at least one SLBC, SLBC to steer financial incunsion and other program. Strengthening District Consultative Committee (CDCC) & Lead District Manager (Lead Development Manager) machinery–Appropriate it is necessary that officials at senior level

are appointed to helm these institutions so they possess necessary delegated devision making and financial powers to execute and implement decisions at the graps root level scale official with adequate powers, support staff, infrastructure.

- Capacity Building of stakeholders assumes importance for their effective functioning.
- Credit Plus Activities are important.
- Monitoring of credit plus activities of banks/ State Govt. Capacity/ skill building of farmers/ small entrepreneurs.
- Access to new technology and practices.
- Facilitate setting up of Financial Literacy Cells (at present 896 FLCs are functions in the country).
- Setting up Rural Self Employment Training Institutes (RSETI) as per plan projections of the Government. Number of RSETIs as on 31st March 2013 – 578.
- **Grievance Redressal :** Quarterly district level grievance redressal meetings by lead bank.

Issues and Challenges

- Augmenting credit flow to various sectors of the economy
- Fulfilment of Priority sector lending
- Credit Deposit Ratio
- Meeting Financial Inclusion Goals
- Meeting Financial literacy Goals

Priority sector : refers to those sectors of the economy which may not get timely and adequate credit in the absence of this special dispensation. Typically, these are small value loans extended to farmers for agriculture and allied activities, micro and small enterprises, poor people for housing, students for education and other low income groups and weaker sections. Those sectors which are able to get timely and adequate credit would not qualify for status of priority sector.

Categories under the Priority sector are: Agriculture, Micro and Small Enterprises, Education, Housing, Export Credit, Others. Priority Sector targets are allocated bank wise on pan India basis.

Targets under Priority Sector

Category	*Domestic banks/ Foreign banks with 20 and above branches*	*Foreign banks with less than 20 branches*
Total Priority Sector	40 per cent of ANBC	32 per cent of ANBC
Agriculture	18 per cent of ANBC	No specific target
Micro & Small Enterprises (MSE)	No specific target	No specific target
Advance to Weaker Sections	10 per cent of ANBC	No specific target

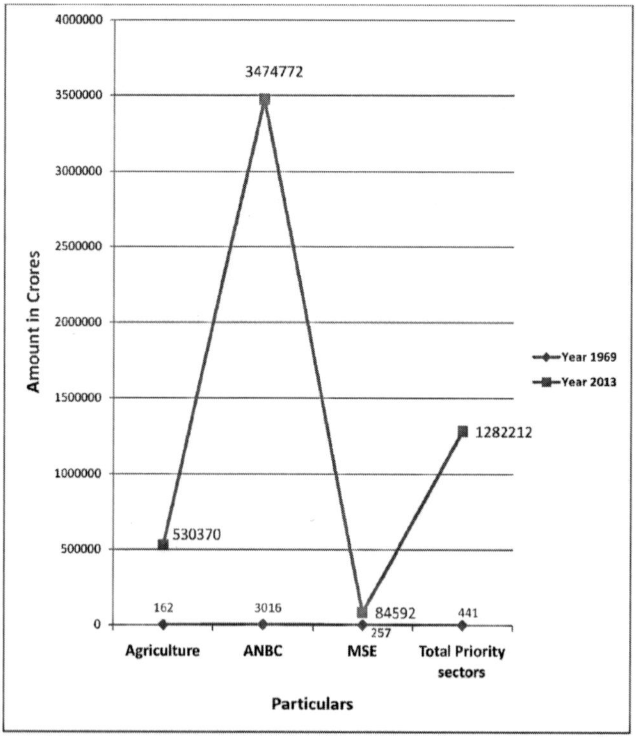

Status of Lending under Priority Sector

Government Sponsored Schemes

Reserve Bank of India monitors the flow of credit under the following credit linked Government Sponsored Schemes implemented by various ministries of the Government of India.

RBI issues guidelines/instructions to banks periodically on proper implementation of Centrally Sponsored Schemes and collates Bank-wise/State-wise data on achievements made by the banks these Schemes on the basis of returns submitted by them:

1. National Rural Livelihood Mission (NRLM): formerly Swarna Jayanti Gram Swarozgar Yojana (SJGSY) implemented by the Ministry of Rural Development, GOI through Scheduled Commercial Banks, Regional Rural Banks, Co-operative Banks.
2. National Urban Livelihood Mission (NULM) formerly Swarna Jayanti Shahari Rozgar Yojna (SJSRY) implemented by the Ministry of Housing and Urban Poverty Alleviation, GOI through Scheduled Commercial Banks (excluding RRBs).
3. Self Employment Scheme for Rehabilitation of Manual Scavangers (SRMS) implemented by the Ministry of Social Justice and Empowerment, GOI through Public Sector Banks.
4. Differential Rate of Interest (DRI) Scheme implemented by the Ministry of Finance, GOI through Indian Scheduled Commercial banks.

Bank credit's extended to the beneficiaries (weaker sections) under the above Schemes comes under Priority Sector lending.

Issues and Challenges – Credit Deposit Ratio

CD Ratio is the ratio of outstanding credit to outstanding deposit at a particular point of time. It is a function of credit absorption capacity which is dependent on the development level of the States in the form of availability of necessary infrastructure facilities required for development of industries, agriculture and service sector etc. This is a regular item of agenda discussion in SLBC and DCC meetings and these fora identify measures to enhance CD ratio and to increase credit absorption capacities in the region. In 1980, RBI advised Public Sector Banks to achieve a CD Ratio (CDR) of 60 in respect of their rural and semi urban branches, separately, on an all India basis. In 2005, Banks advised to set up Special Sub-Committee (SSC) of District Consultative Committee (DCC) in districts with CDR < 40 in order to monitor progress and draw up Monitorable Action Plans (MAPs) for improving CDR on a self set graduated basis.

CD Ratio Analysis–Region-Area wise.

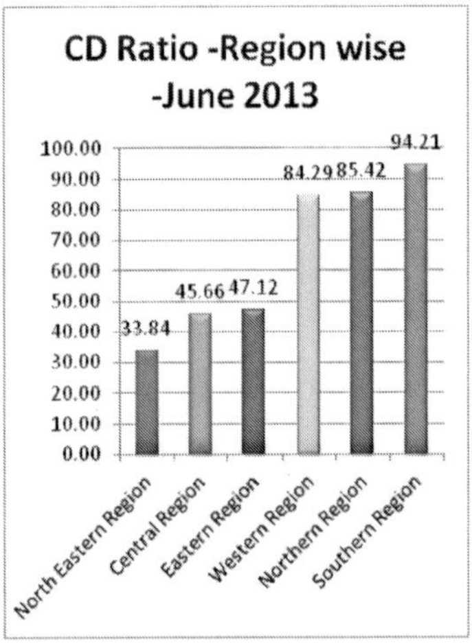

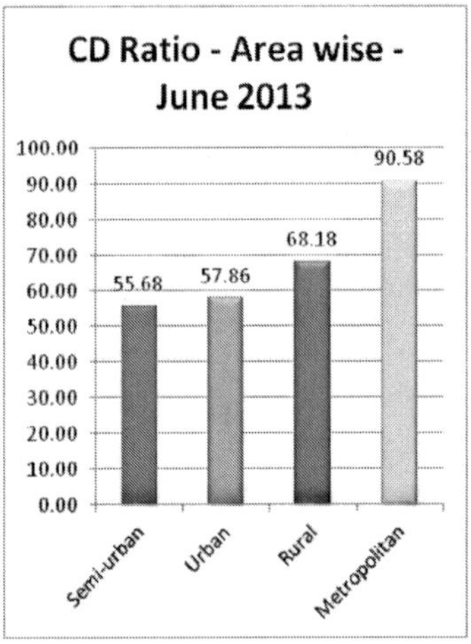

Issues and Challenges – Financial Inclusion

Financial Inclusion is the process of ensuring access to appropriate financial products and services needed by all sections of the society in general and vulnerable groups such as weaker sections and low income groups in particular at an affordable cost in a fair and transparent manner by mainstream institutional players.

Institutional Framework for Achieving Financial Inclusion

Government of India and Reserve Bank of India
Financial Stability & Development Council-Technical Group on Financial Inclusion & Financial literacy
Financial Inclusion Advisory committee of RBI
17 offices of RBI spread across the country
46 Public and Private Sector Banks, 67 RRBs, 35 SLBCs, 644 LDMs
Partnership with other stakeholders UIDAI, NABARD, State Governments

Financial Inclusion – Approach

Reserve Bank is furthering financial inclusion in a Mission mode through a combination of strategies ranging from

- Technology LED Model Leveraging the triumvarite of Jan Dhan Aadhar Card Mobile Telephony
- Branchless modes of delivery of banking services
- Moving the focus from growth to inclusive growth
- On the assumption that the poor are bankable
- Importance given to sustainability, viability and scalability
- Financial Inclusion comprehensively defined- Financial Inclusion Plans and Roadmap
- Adopted a Bank - led model.

FI initiatives of RBI to encourage spread of banking in rural areas

- **BCs:** Permitting banks to engage Business Correspondents.

- **Simplified branch authorisation:** Domestic Scheduled Commercial Banks permitted to freely open branches in Tier 2 to Tier 6 centres (with population of less than 1,00,000) under general permission, subject to reporting.
- **Opening of branches in unbanked rural centres**: 25 per cent of the total number of branches to be opened during a year, in unbanked rural centres.
- **Special Dispensation Scheme for opening of bank branches in (North Eastern Region)**: Under the Special Dispensation Scheme of RBI for NE Region Banks enables to open bank branches in unbanked and under banked centres, a total of 34 branches have been opened at identified centres in five North East States of Meghalaya (4), Tripura (5), Arunachal Pradesh (8), Manipur (11) and Nagaland (6). RBI is reimbursing the one time capital cost and recurring cost for five years in respect of branches opened under this Scheme upto June 2012.
- **Phase-wise approach** to provide door step banking. facilities in all the unbanked villages in the country.
- **Phase-I:** A roadmap for covering all unbanked villages with more than 2000 population was prepared by various banks through State Level Bankers Committees SLBCs for coverage of Unbanked Population through various modes either through Branch or BC or Other modes. All the 74414 such villages already covered comprising 2493 branches, 69589 BC and 2332 other modes.
- **Phase-II:** Roadmap for covering all unbanked villages with less than 2000 population has been prepared by various banks through SLBCs. SLBCs reportedly identified and allotted about 4,90,000 such unbanked villages to various banks for provision of banking services in next three years.
- **December 31, 2013 Progress:** 137865 villages covered comprising 8954 branches, 121845 BCs and 7066 other modes.

Roadmap Progress in villages with more than 2000 and less than 2000 population villages

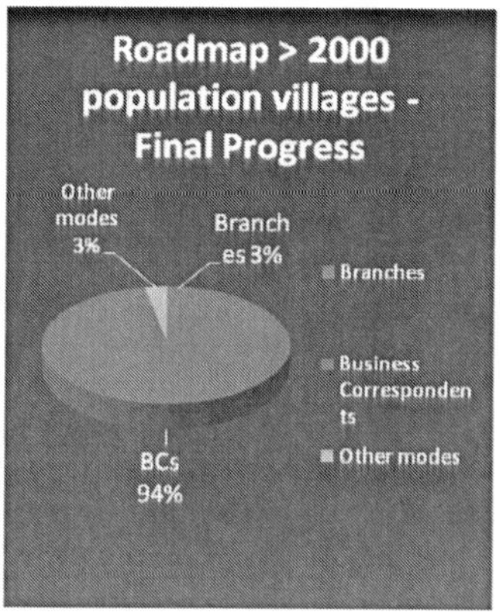

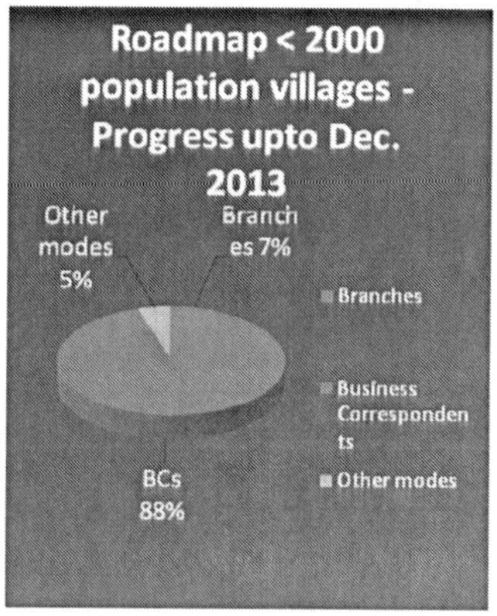

Financial Inclusion Plans (FIPs)

- Board approved three Years FIPs were prepared for providing banking services in villages with population of more than 2000 during April 2010 to March 2013. Thereafter, Financial Inclusion Plan was prepared for villages with population less than 2000 during April 2013–2016. To be reviewed in SLBCs.
- FIPs of Regional Rural Banks – Prepared after migration to Core Banking Solution (CBS) migration.
- Self-set targets – 46 Parameters–FIPs to be integrated with Business plan of the banks.
- Basic Accounts, Electronic Benefit Transfer, Kisan Credit Card, General Credit Card accounts to be opened including through Business Correspondent model.
- Specific products to be designed to cater to the financially excluded segments.
- Close Monitoring by Reserve Bank of India–Monthly Reporting–Annual Comprehensive Review.
- FIPs Disaggregated – Regional Offices of RBI to review state level FIPs.

FIP Achievements upto December 2013

- Banking connectivity extended to nearly 3,28,679 villages from 67,694 villages in March 2010.
- Total No. of Basic Saving Back Deposit Accounts (BSBDAS) have gone up to 229 million of which 108 million are Information Communication Technology (ICT) based accounts.
- Credit to farm sector households has touched 39 million households while credit to non farm sector households has touched more than 6 million households.
- About 238 million transactions carried out in ICT based accounts through BCs during the nine months period ended December 2013 as against 250 million transactions recorded during the year 2012-2013.

Financial Literacy initiatives of RBI – Use of various Channels Initiatives

- Financial Literacy material in the form of simple Question and Answers on Banking prepared.
- Distributed to all banks for use during financial literacy sessions conducted by them.

Channels

- Holding, News exhibitions, Quiz Competitions
- Town Hall Events - Interaction of RBI Top Management with public
- Outreach visits to villages by RBI Top Management.
- Visits to Schools and Colleges by Bank Officials.
- Visits by School and College children to RBI.
- Inclusion of Financial Literacy in School Curriculum.
- Distributing Books and Pamphlets on financial literacy.

Conclusion

It is expected that the Banks State and Central Government take proactive role at all levels for ensuring conducive credit culture. Availability of infrastructure especially rural connectivity, capacity building, publicity and awareness, better coordination between Government and Banks with wholehearted participation of Government officials and block development officials functionaries etc., official in various Lead Bank Scheme is also expected.

References

1. RBI Annual Report.
2. Report of the High Level Committee to review Lead Bank Scheme.
3. Ministry of Finance, Government of India.

2

India Securing Economic Growth With Equity

It is now evident that Emerging Market Economies EMEs as Australia and India can buttress global economy. This has been clearly demonstrated by our experience of the recent global economic crisis. The Great Recession, for example, has been less deeper than what it would have been because of the growth contribution of EMEs, particularly China, India and Australia. At the current juncture, when advanced economies are still experiencing a demand recession, it is the import demand from the EMEs which is helping them make the necessary adjustment. However, in order to maintain their growth momentum, we will need to address huge challenges and put in place both collective and individual country strategies. Significantly the most important way in which these countries can contribute to global economic prosperity is by doing more of what we have been doing so far–that is by maintaining our growth momentum. The second area where we can contribute to global prosperity is through ensuring that multilateral fora as the G-20 forum remain meaningful and effective and academic collaboration, People to People exchanges increase. India has remained relatively insulated from these developments and our impact analyses suggest that our exposure to troubled sub-prime assets and related derivatives is negligible in comparison to many other economies. Whereas this may be regarded as fortuitous, it is perhaps our nuanced approach to financial sector reform and development that has served us well; our approach has been marked by conscious gradualism with the implementation of coordinated and sequenced moves on several fronts predicated on the preparedness for change of the financial system in particular, and of the economy in general.

We have built in appropriate safeguards to ensure stability, taking due cognizance of prevailing governance standards, risk management systems and incentive frameworks in financial institutions in the country. Overall, these progressive but cautious policies have contributed to efficiency of the financial system while sustaining the growth momentum in an environment of macro-economic and financial stability. The real challenge we face today is ensuring economic growth with equity and distributive justice. We have pledged to move towards Universal Financial Inclusion by 2012.

- The overarching and cross-cutting nature of financial inclusion has made it one of the main pillars of the development agenda. Distress in the advanced economies has increased vulnerability of the poor and brought the needs for safety nets into even sharper focus.
- The global financial system must be sound, stable, prudent and should combat money laundering and terrorism. It must, however, also serve the global population, seeking to reach those who until now have been unserved. Inclusive growth as a strategy for economic development aims at making products and services, including financial services, available to those who for various reasons stand excluded. The financial sector in the country has experienced revolutionary changes, but there exist a large number of people who have not been benefited by this. Financial exclusion, which is generally the outcome of poverty, ignorance and environmental factors, is also to a great extent related to supply side issues, i.e. lack of appropriate financial services for such people.

- The Reserve Bank has in its Policy Statement clarified that it will implement policies to encourage banks which provide extensive services, while disincentivising those which are not responsive to the banking needs of the community, including the underprivileged. Further, banks have been urged to review their existing practices to align them with the objective of financial inclusion. There are issues both from the supply side and the demand side which require macro level policy interventions and operational issues. At the level of policy we have in the recent past initiated several measures to create an enabling environment to give a boost to financial inclusion. Operational issues require the commitment of all stakeholders and of implementing agencies at the grassroots level to ensure that policy initiatives are translated to concrete progress on the ground.

As per the estimates provided by the G-20, more than two billion adults continue to lack access to financial services and the millions of micro, small and medium sized enterprises (MSMEs) face difficulties in accessing finance. Financial inclusion is fundamental for improving the livelihoods of the poor and in supporting MSMEs, the engines of economic growth and job creation, to start, grow and thrive.

The G-20 has developed an Action Plan for improving financial inclusion, which provides a set of six concrete and pragmatic action areas to advance financial inclusion for individuals, households and MSMEs and promote the application of the G-20 Principles for Innovative Financial Inclusion. We have been playing a part in the G-20 and I am the India expert on the Financial Inclusion Expert Group which is co chaired by Australia.Together we have cobbled together the Principles for innovative Financial Inclusion which we hope will shape the initiative in days to come.

G-20 Principles for Innovative Financial Inclusion

These principles formulated by the G 20 aim to help create an enabling policy and regulatory environment for innovative financial inclusion, which will critically determine the speed at which the financial services access gap will close for the more than two billion people currently excluded. They reflect the conditions conducive to spurring innovation for financial inclusion while protecting financial stability and consumers. They are not a rigid set of requirements but are designed to help guide policymakers in the decision making process with regard to their own country context. The principles are as under:

1. *Leadership*: Cultivate a broad-based government commitment to financial inclusion to help alleviate poverty.
2. *Diversity*: Implement policy approaches that promote competition and provide market-based incentives for delivery of sustainable financial access and usage of a broad range of affordable services (savings, credit, payments and transfers, insurance) as well as a diversity of service providers.
3. *Innovation*: Promote technological and institutional innovation as a means to expand financial system access and usage, including by addressing infrastructure weaknesses.
4. *Protection*: Encourage a comprehensive approach to consumer protection that recognises the roles of government, providers and consumers.
5. *Empowerment*: Develop financial literacy and financial capability.
6. *Cooperation*: Create an institutional environment with clear lines of accountability and co-ordination within government; and also encourage partnerships and direct consultation across government, business and other stakeholders.
7. *Knowledge*: Utilise improved data to make evidence based policy, measure progress, and consider an incremental "test and learn" approach acceptable to both regulator and service provider.

8. *Proportionality*: Build a policy and regulatory framework that is proportionate with the risks and benefits involved in such innovative products and services and is based on an understanding of the gaps and barriers in existing regulation.
9. *Framework*: Consider the following in the regulatory framework, reflecting International standards, National circumstances and support for a competitive landscape: an appropriate, flexible, risk-based Anti- Money Laundering and Combating the Financing of Terrorism (AML/CFT) regime; conditions for the use of agents as a customer interface; a clear regulatory regime for electronically stored value; and market-based incentives to achieve the long-term goal of broad interoperability and interconnection.

India Scope

The country has registered impressive growth in the last couple of years which could be attributed to the policy stance taken by the Government and the Reserve Bank. The GDP growth rate which was 4.4 per cent in 2001 was 7.4 per cent during 2009-10.

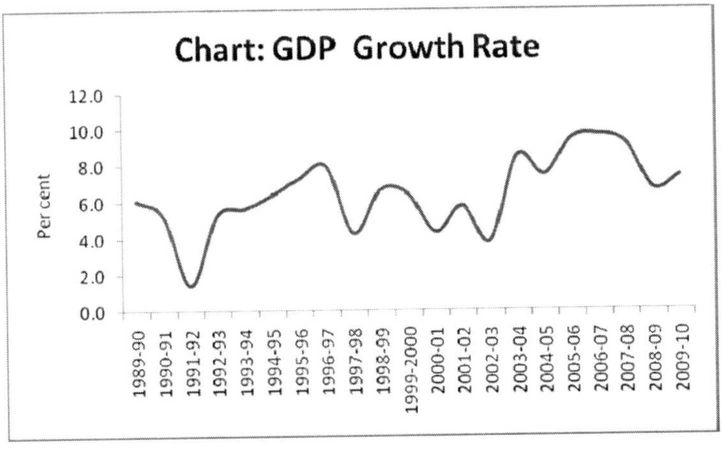

GDP Growth Rate

Year	*Growth rate*
1989-90	6.1
1990-91	5.3
1991-92	1.4
1992-93	5.4
1993-94	5.7
1994-95	6.4
1995-96	7.3
1996-97	8.0
1997-98	4.3
1998-99	6.7
1999-2000	6.4
2000-01	4.4
2001-02	5.8
2002-03	3.8
2003-04	8.5
2004-05	7.5
2005-06	9.5
2006-07	9.7
2007-08	9.2
2008-09	6.7
2009-10	7.4

It could be seen that the growth rate has been consistently higher from the year 2003-04 when compared to the earlier years. and decelerating with the rest of the world adfter the rubicon of the Global financial crisis of 2007-08.

Economic growth has meaning only if the benefits of growth are equally shared. 'Inclusive growth' as a strategy of economic development received attention owing to a rising concern that the benefits of economic growth have not been equitably shared. Growth is inclusive when it creates economic opportunities along with ensuring equal access to these opportunities. Apart from addressing the issue of inequality, inclusive growth may also make poverty reduction efforts more effective by explicitly creating productive economic opportunities for the poor and vulnerable sections of the society. Inclusive growth by encompassing the hitherto excluded population brings in several other appurtenant benefits to the economy. The concept of "Inclusion" should be seen as a process of including the excluded as agents whose participation is essential to the very design of the development process, and not simply as welfare targets of development programmes.

Banking statistics in India

No. of Scheduled Commercial Banks – 170

of which RRBs – 82

Total number of Branches – 80547

No. of Rural Branches – 31667

No. of Semi Urban Branches – 31667

No. of Urban Branches – 15733

No. of Metropolitan Branches – 14178

Dimensions of Access Problems

I could of course go on and on but time is both fleeting and limited hence a smallchart to present to you the general drift.

Standard indicators of financial inclusion, ranging from percentage of population having bank accounts, insurance protection and debit/credit cards to distribution of availability of banking business across states, across different sections of the society and between urban and rural centres, suggest the possible existence of enormous untapped growth potential, which has not been exploited, partly due to lack of access to finance at reasonable cost. 50 per cent the current level of banking penetration, measured in terms of outstanding bank credit to GDP, is significantly below the levels reached in advanced economies and several EMEs.

Dimensions of Access Problems

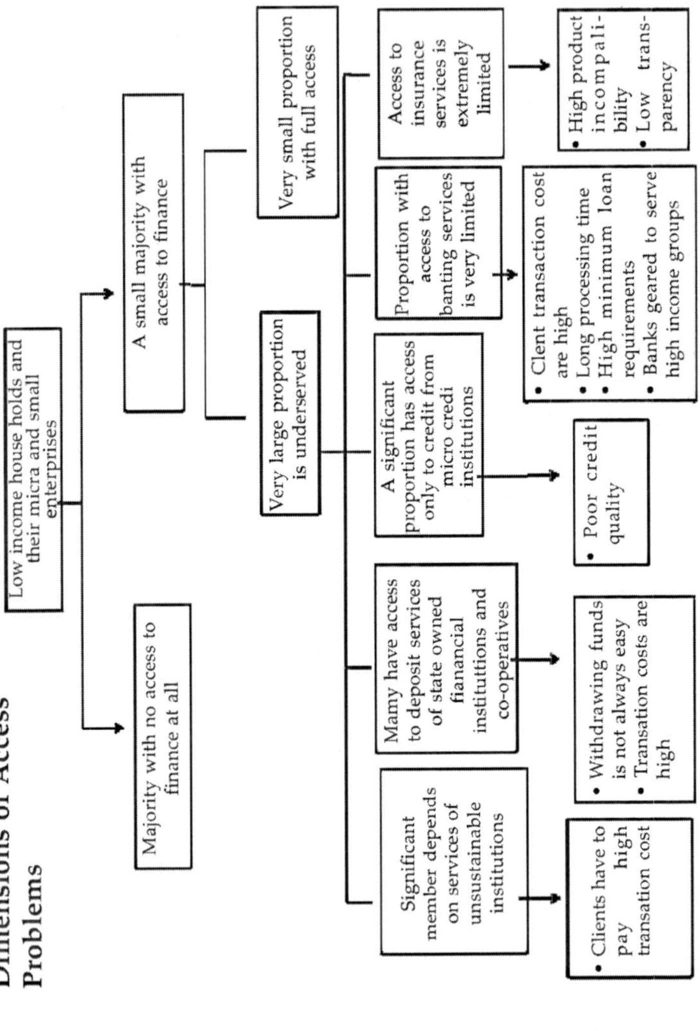

The potential of the financial system has not been harnessed fully due to the extent of financial exclusion prevailing today.

Geographic and Demographic Penetration

The approach to financial inclusion in developing countries such as India differs from that of the developed countries. In the latter, the focus is on the relatively small share of population not having access to banks or the formal payments systems whereas in India, the focus is on the vast majority who are excluded.

Financial and Development Indicators

The broad approach towards financial inclusion followed in India in the 1970s and the 1980s was more oriented towards branch expansion and meeting the credit requirements of specific sectors/segments and there was relatively less emphasis on individual/household level inclusion. The recent approach focuses on financial inclusion of individuals and households.

Extent of Exclusion

In India, despite widespread expansion of the banking sector, particularly after nationalisation of major commercial banks in 1969 and 1980, a significant proportion of the households, especially in rural areas, are still outside the coverage of the formal banking system. These households have been dependent up on the informal money lenders for their credit needs and had few avenues for keeping their savings. A visit to the bank branch often resulted in their losing their wage for the day.

The financially excluded sections largely comprise marginal farmers, landless labourers, oral lessees, self-employed and unorganised sector enterprises, urban slum dwellers, migrants, ethnic minorities and socially excluded groups, senior citizens and women.

Some of the figures for Financial Exclusion are very glaring – 45.9 million farmer households out of a total of 89.3 million households do not have access to credit either from the institutional or non-institutional sources (NSSO, 2008); one branch is catering to the banking needs of 16,000 population (June, 2007); only 17 credit accounts and 54 saving accounts are there per 100 persons with all the institutions (June 2007); only 13 per cent are availing loans from the banks in the income bracket of less than Rs 50,000; and 53 per cent people are still taking loans from the institutional and non-institutional sources only for emergency purposes. The Eleventh Five Year Plan for the country states that '*The development of rural India is an imperative for inclusive and equitable growth and to unlock huge potential of the population that is presently trapped in poverty with its associated deprivations*' (GoI, 2007).

Challenges to Inclusion

There are several challenges towards achieving financial inclusion in India. Some of these are as under:

(i) India's large size, its sheer geographic proportion and the population of the country itself make it difficult for any programme at a national level to reach out to everyone. This is one of the biggest stumbling blocks in providing access to affordable financial services to each and everyone in the country.

(ii) Poor infrastructure in many parts of the country inhibits the development process.

(iii) Availability of flexible financial products that cater to the needs of the masses.

(iv) Absence of a successful delivery model/business model for financial inclusion.

Initiatives of Central Bank

The Reserve Bank has significantly scaled up its efforts aimed at increasing the level of penetration of bank financing in the economy, using appropriate regulation as well as moral suasion.

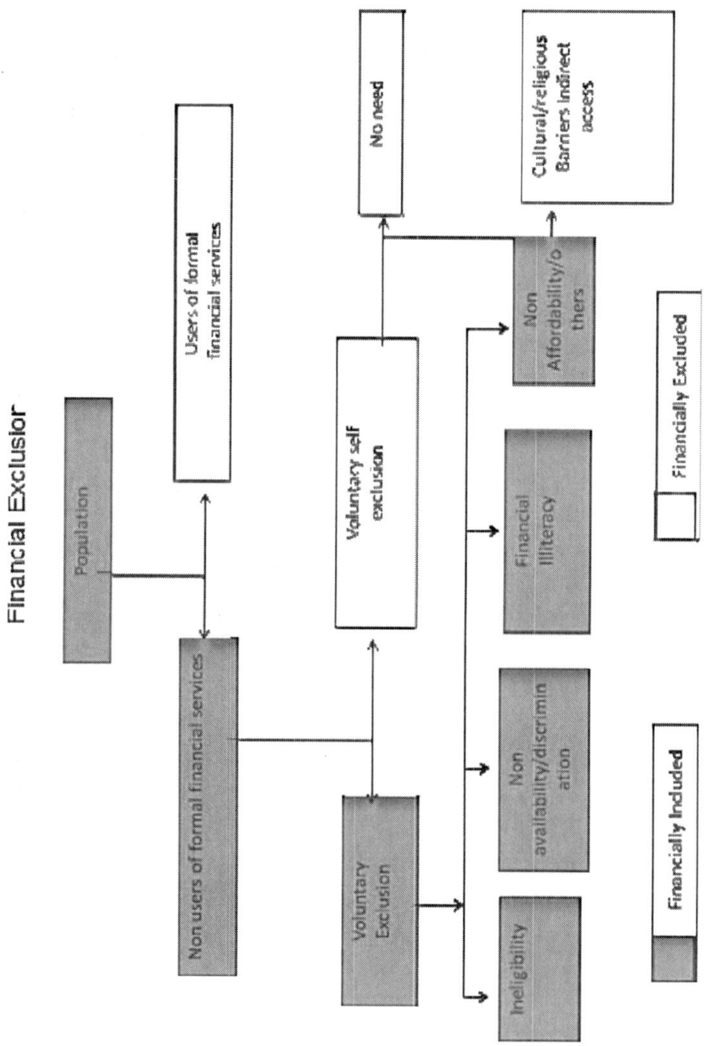

Financial Exclusior
Population
Users of formal financial services
Non users of formal financial services
Voluntary self exclusion
No need
Voluntary Exclusion
Ineligibility
Non availability/discrimin ation
Financial Illiteracy
Non Affordability/o thers
Cultural/religious Barriers Indirect access
Financially Included
Financially Excluded

There are six lakh villages in the country and the proportion of rural residents who lack access to bank accounts remains at 40 per cent, and this rises to over three-fifths of the population in the east and north-east of India while there are 33,000 rural branches hence the task of moving to universal financial inclusion is indeed formidable and clearly neither brick and mortar nor click and portal will meet the case hence financial innovation becomes a desideratum Banks have been encouraged to devise innovative solutions and leverage technology to extend penetrative outreach.

Strategies adopted for financial inclusion:

(i) *Road map for provision of banking service in villages:*

Banks have been advised to draw up a roadmap to provide banking services through a banking outlet in every village with a population of over 2,000, by March 2011. Such banking services may not necessarily be extended through a brick and mortar branch but can be provided through any of the various forms of ICT-based models, including through Business Correspondents (BCs). 73000 villages with population of more than 2000 with no banking facilities as per the 2001 census have been allocated to various banks for providing banking services.

(ii) *Simplified Branch Authorisation:*

To facilitate opening of bank branches in the villages and to address the issue of uneven spread of bank branches, since December 2009, Domestic Scheduled Commercial Banks have been permitted to freely open branches in Tier 3 to Tier 6 centres with population of less than 50,000 under general permission, subject to reporting. In the remote hilly regions of North Eastern States and Sikkim, Domestic Scheduled Commercial Banks can now open branches in rural, semi urban and urban centres without the need to take permission from Reserve Bank in each case, subject to reporting.

(iii) *Financial Inclusion Plan (FIP) of banks:*

With a view to increasing banking penetration and promoting financial inclusion, domestic commercial banks, both in the public and private sectors, were advised to take some specific actions. First, banks were required to put in place a Board- approved Financial Inclusion Plan (FIP) in order to roll it out over the next three years and submit the same to the Reserve Bank. Banks were advised to devise FIPs congruent with their business strategy and to make them an integral part of their corporate plans. The Reserve Bank has deliberately not imposed a uniform model so that each bank is able to build its own strategy in line with its business model and comparative competitive advantage. Second, banks were required to include criteria on financial inclusion in the performance evaluation of their field staff as work done in the rural areas did not earlier have the same weightage for promotions as work done in other segments which lead to direct profit accrual for the Bank.

(iv) *Relaxed KYC norms:*

The Prevention of Money Laundering is an International Concern hence there is a great stringency attached to the Know your customer norms. The Know Your Customer (KYC) requirements for opening bank accounts have been relaxed since August 2005 and simplified for small value accounts accounts with suitable deposit and transaction caps, balances not exceeding Rs. 50,000/- and aggregate credits in the accounts not exceeding Rs one lakh a year. Introduction by an account holder who has been subjected to full KYC drill would suffice for opening such accounts or the bank can take any evidence as to the identity and address of the customer to the satisfaction of the bank.

(v) *No-frills accounts:*

Reserve Bank of India, in November 2005 advised all Scheduled Commercial Banks to make available a basic banking 'no-frills' account with 'nil' or very low minimum balances that would make such accounts accessible to vast sections of the population. Banks have also been advised to provide small overdrafts in such accounts to incentivise the poor borrower to visit the bank branch.

(vi) *General Credit Cards:*

In December 2005, banks were advised to consider introduction of a General Purpose Credit Card (GCC) facility up to Rs 25,000/- at their rural and semi-urban branches. The credit facility is in the nature of revolving credit entitling the holder to withdraw up to the limit sanctioned. Based on assessment of household cash flows, the limits are sanctioned without insistence on security or purpose. Interest rate on the facility is completely deregulated.

(vii) *Business Correspondents/Business Facilitators:*

Since January 2006, the Reserve Bank has permitted banks to utilise the services of intermediaries in providing financial and banking services through the use of business facilitator and business correspondent (BC) models. The BC model allows banks to do 'cash in-cash out' transactions at a location much closer to the rural population, thus addressing the last mile problem. With a view to ensuring the viability of the BC model, banks have been permitted to collect reasonable service charges from the customer, in a transparent manner under a Board-approved policy.

The banks may engage the following individuals/entities as BC.

i. Individuals like retired bank employees, retired teachers, retired government employees and ex-servicemen, individual owners of kirana/medical/ fair price shops, individual Public Call Office (PCO) operators, agents of Small Savings Schemes of Government of India/Insurance Companies, individuals who own Petrol Pumps, authorised functionaries of well run Self Help Groups (SHGs) which are linked to banks, any other individual including those operating Common Service Centres (CSCs);

ii. NGOs/ MFIs set up under Societies/Trust Acts and Section 25 Companies.

iii. Cooperative Societies registered under Mutually Aided Cooperative Societies Acts/ Cooperative Societies Acts of States/Multi State Cooperative Societies Act.

iv. Post Offices; and

v. Companies registered under the Indian Companies Act, 1956 with large and widespread retail outlets, excluding Non-Banking Financial Companies (NBFCs). This liberalisation has been allowed recently.

(viii) *Focus on Smaller Banks:*

Given the strategic positioning of Regional Rural Banks (RRBs), the Reserve Bank has directed their sponsor banks to speedily, and fully, implement Core Banking Solution (CBS) in all RRBs and commit to firm timeline, by September 2011, by which all RRBs will become fully CBS-compliant this is expected to give a further fillip to financial inclusion efforts given the penetrative outreach of the RRBs in the rural areas. The RRBs have been requested to open 2000 branches by September 2011. As on June 30, 2010, RRBs have reported opening 153 new branches.

(ix) *Scaling up IT:*

Banks had been urged in May 2007 to scale up IT initiatives for financial inclusion speedily while ensuring that solutions are highly secure, amenable to audit, and follow widely-accepted open standards to ensure eventual inter-operability among the different systems.

(x) *Mobile Banking:*

Mobile banking has immense financial inclusion potential and Mobile banking guidelines for banks were issued in October 2008. Since December 2009, banks have been permitted to offer this service to their customers subject to a daily cap of Rs 50,000/- per customer for both funds transfer and transactions involving purchase of goods/services.

(xi) *100 per cent Financial Inclusion Drive:*

At the state level, the State Level Bankers Committee (SLBC) has been advised to identify one or more districts for 100 per cent financial inclusion. Responsibility is given to the banks in the area for ensuring that all those who desire to have a bank accounts are provided with one by allocating the villages among the different banks. As on March 31, 2010, 432 districts have been identified by SLBCs for 100 per cent financial inclusion. Of these, 250 districts in 18 States and 5 Union Territories have reported having achieved 100 per cent financial inclusion.

(xii) *Financial Inclusion Fund and Financial Inclusion Technology Fund* (FIF and FITF):

Based on the recommendations of the "Committee on Financial Inclusion" two Funds, namely the "Financial Inclusion Fund (FIF)" for meeting the cost of developmental and promotional interventions for ensuring financial inclusion, and the "Financial Inclusion Technology Fund (FITF)", to meet the cost of technology adoption has been set up at NABARD with an overall corpus of Rs 500 crore each. The corpus is shared by GOI, RBI and NABARD in the ratio 40:40:20. In the union budget for the year 2010-11, the corpus of each of these funds has been enhanced by another Rs 100 crore.

(xiii) *Financial Literacy and Credit Counseling Centres:*

Each SLBC convenor has been asked to set up a credit-counselling centre in one district as a pilot, and extend it to all other districts in due course. As on March 2010, banks have reported setting up 135 credit counselling centres in various States of the country. A model scheme on Financial Literacy and Credit Counselling Centres (FLCCs) was formulated and communicated to all Scheduled Commercial Banks and RRBs with the advice to set up the centres as distinct entities maintaining an arm's length the bank so that the FLCC's services are available to even other banks' customers in the district.

(xiv) *SHG Bank Linkage Programme:*

To give an impetus to microfinance, the same was categorised under priority sector lending and lending to SHGs was brought under the weaker sections of the priority sector. Banks have been advised to provide adequate incentives to their branches for financing the SHGs. According to the data as on March 2009, there are more than 61 lakh deposit-linked

Self Help Groups (SHGs) in the country with outstanding deposits aggregating Rs 5550 crore out of which 42 lakh-odd SHGs are credit-linked, with an outstanding loan amount aggregating Rs 22,700 crore, signifying financial inclusion of close to 10 crore members.

Conclusion

Further, there needs to be an expansion of the ambit of the financial inclusion process by moving from pure banking services to non-banking services and adjacencies such as general health and insurance services. Yet another challenge lies in ensuring the equitable distribution of banking business across regions of the country.

Financial inclusion is a win-win proposition for the people, banks and the nation. The merits of financial sector reform need to be seen through the prism of what finance could do to harness the growth potential with stability, and financial inclusion represents a critical component of the policy process that intends to make the financial system serve the needs of the real economy.

If we move towards Universal Financial Inclusion as large democracies we contribute to a more equal and a more stable world.

References

1. RBI Annual Report
2. Trend and Progress of Banking in India
3. Ministry of Finance, Government of India

3

Skill Development

The National Mission on Skill Development, under the Chairmanship of Hon'ble Prime Minister of India has set a target of preparing 500 million skilled persons by 2022. On the other hand it is expected that approximately 75 to 80 million jobs will be created in India over the next 5 years; 75 per cent of these new jobs will require vocational training to enhance the employability prospects. There is a pronounced 'skill gap' both in terms of quality and quantity; and current vocational education and training infrastructure is not geared to meet industry requirements (CII report on case for setting sector skill councils, 2009). This is a contradiction of scenarios–supply demand mismatch on the one hand and rising population of educated unemployed. At present only 2 per cent of the work force in the age group 15-29 has undergone formal vocational training and 8 per cent have had non-formal vocational training. 93 per cent of the workforce is in the unorganised sector. Vocational education and training is provided in India by several educational institutions/organisations functioning under about 17 different Ministries of the Government of India. In spite of this, of the 12.8 million new entrants to the workforce every year, the existing skill development capacity is only 3.1 million.

Skill gap

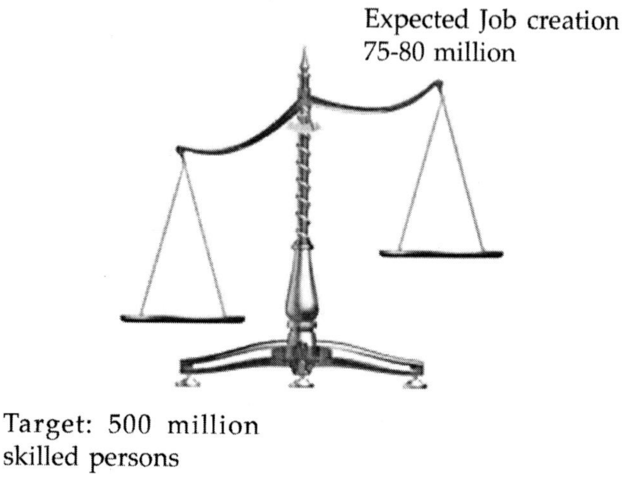

Population in 15-59 age group by 2022

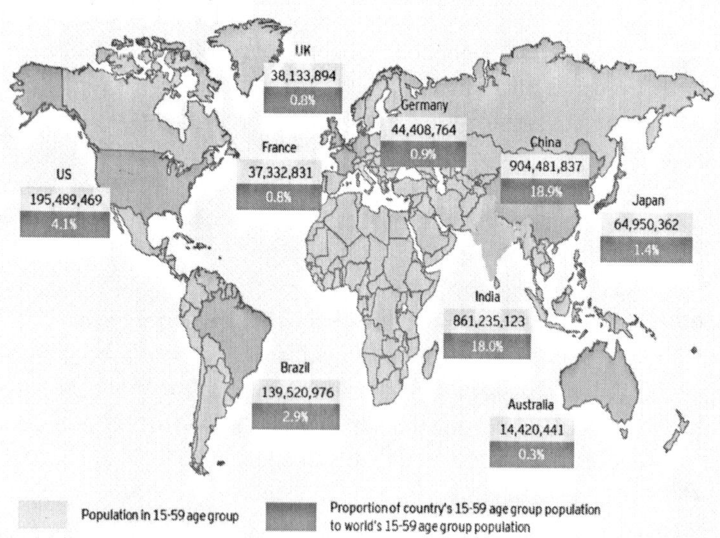

Source: Ernst & Young research

What numbers say?

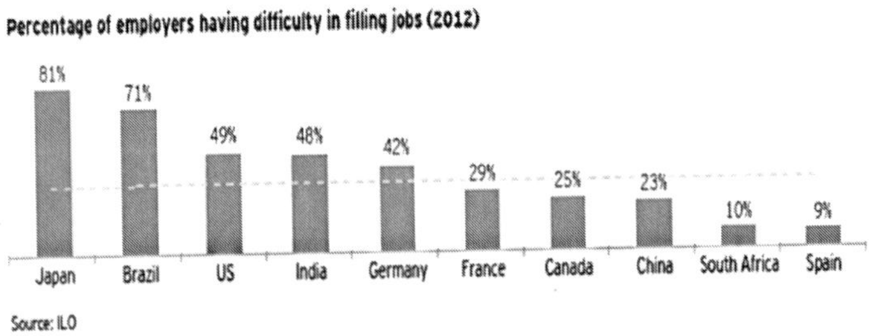

Bridging gap between Demand and Supply

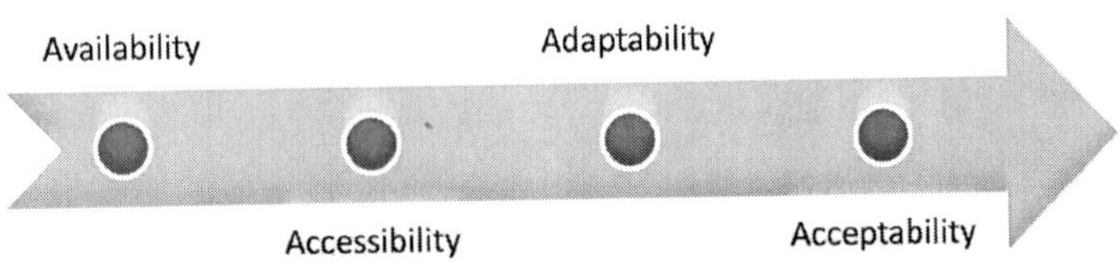

Availability: More Vocational training centers and need for change in Vocational Education (12th Plan);

Accessibility: Disparities in terms of income level, education level, geographic divide etc;

Adaptability: Focus on target group;

Acceptability: Training facilities, methods, Govt. schemes, infrastructure etc.

AVAILABILITY

Vocational Training: Vocational training programs in India fall outside the formal schooling cycle. It is institution-based with varying entry requirements as well as course durations. The proportion of practical to theoretical instruction in vocational training programs is also higher than in vocational education. It is open to students who leave school after completing anywhere from Grade 8–12.

Programs are operated by Industrial Training Institutes (ITIs) and Industrial Training Centers (ITCs). It comes under the auspices of the Ministry of Labour and Employment (MoLE) and the Ministry of Human Resource Development (MHRD). Administrative responsibility is held by the Directorate General of Employment and Training (DGET), located within the MoLE. ITIs and ITCs operate under the guidance of DGET, which formulates policies and lays down standards and technical requirements such as developing curricula, instructor training, and skills testing. It governs a number of specialised training-related institutions.

Vocational education : In India refers specifically to vocational courses offered in school Grades 11 and 12 under a centrally sponsored scheme termed 'Vocationalisation of Secondary Education'. Vocational education falls under the purview of the Ministry of Human Resources Development (MHRD).

Rural Self Employment Training Institute RSETI Highlights

- Rural Youth trained: 380070
- Employment Generated: 133378
- Banks participation in RSETI

Rural Self Employment Training Institutes, RSETIs an initiative of Ministry of Rural Development (MoRD) to have dedicated infrastructure in each district of the country for imparting training and skill upgradation of rural youth geared towards entrepreneurship development. RSETIs are managed by banks with active co-operation from the Government of India and State Governments.

Financial Progress of RSETIs

During 2009-10		*During 2010-11*		*Cumulative as on 31.03.2011*		*During Apr-Jun 2011*		*During Jul-Sep 2011*		*During Oct-Dec 2011*		*During Jan-Mar 2012*		*Cumulative as on 29.02.2012*	
No. of RSETIs	*Grant dis-bursed (■crore)*	*No. of* RSETIs	*Grant dis-bursed (■crore)*	*No. of* RSETIs	*Grant dis-bursed (■crore)*	*No. of* RSETIs	*Grant dis-bursed (■crore)*	*No. of* RSETIs	*Grant dis-bursed (■crore)*	*No. of* RSETIs	*Grant dis-bursed (■crore)*	*No. of* RSETIs	*Grant dis-bursed (■crore)*	*No. of* RSETIs	*Grant dis-bursed (■crore)*
103	29.46	102	57.80	205	87.26	22	14.29	37	19.11	8	11.55	7	3.00	279	135.21

Accessibility: Credit Delivery, Financial Inclusion and Literacy

Several anti-poverty programmes have been in operation focusing on the poor and the unemployed in the rural and urban areas. Over the years the poverty alleviation and employment generation programmes have been strengthened to generate more employment, create productive assets, impart technical and entrepreneurial skills and raise the income levels of the poor. RBI monitors the anti-poverty programmes which are sponsored by Central Government. There are two major programmes viz Swarnjayanti Gram Swarojgar Yojna (SGSY) and Swarna Jayanti Shahari Rozgar Yojana (SJSRY) meant for poverty alleviation and employment generation in rural and urban areas respectively. These programmes are implemented through credit linkage with commercial banks and subsidy allocations through the concerned Ministry's budgetary allocations. The beneficiaries under these schemes are rural and urban below poverty line people, minorities and SC/STs including OBCs. All the beneficiaries under these schemes fall under the category of weaker sections which are eligible to get credit under priority sector lending. Credit given by commercial banks under these schemes during the last three years is given in Annex I&II.

Government has approved the restructuring the SGSY as the National Rural Livelihoods Mission (NRLM), to be implemented in a mission mode across the country. NRLM's mandate is to reach out to all the poor families, link them to sustainable livelihoods opportunities and nurture them till they come out of poverty and enjoy a decent quality of life.

National Rural Livelihood Mission

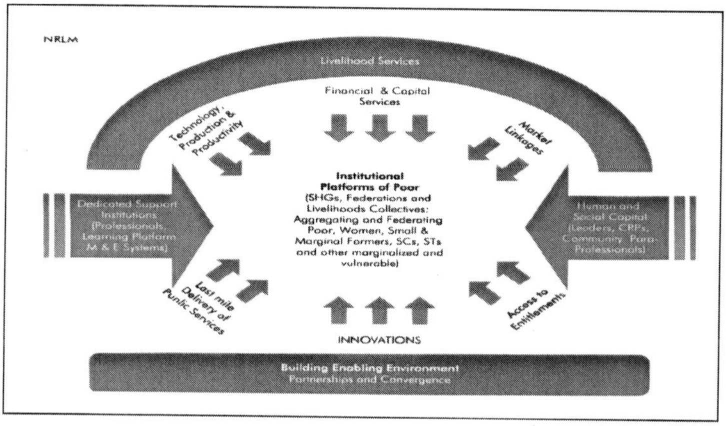

Government has approved restructuring the SGSY as the National Rural Livelihoods Mission (NRLM), to be implemented in a mission mode across the country. NRLM's mandate is to reach out to all the poor families, link them to sustainable livelihoods opportunities and nurture them till they come out of poverty and enjoy a decent quality of life.

The core belief of National Rural Livelihoods Mission (NRLM) is that the poor have a strong desire and innate capabilities to come out of poverty. They are entrepreneurial. The challenge is to unleash their innate capabilities to generate meaningful livelihoods, which enable them to move out of poverty. The first step in this process is motivating them to form their own institutions. Their true potential is realised when they are provided sufficient capacities to manage the external environment and easy access to finance, and are enabled to expand their skills and assets and convert them into meaningful livelihoods. This requires continuous handholding support by their institutions. An external dedicated, sensitive support structure, from the national level to the sub-district level, is required to induce such social mobilisation, institution building and livelihoods promotion.

NRLM Values

The core values which will guide all the activities under NRLM are as follows :

- Inclusion of the poorest, and meaningful role to the poorest in all the processes;
- Transparency and accountability of all processes and institutions;
- Ownership and key role of the poor and their institutions in all stages – planning, implementation, and monitoring; and
- Community self-reliance and self-dependence.

National Urban Livelihood Mission

National Skill Development Policy in 2009

In order to provide adequate training to the youth and develop necessary skills, the Government of India took steps to improve the skill training scenario in the country. In 2009,

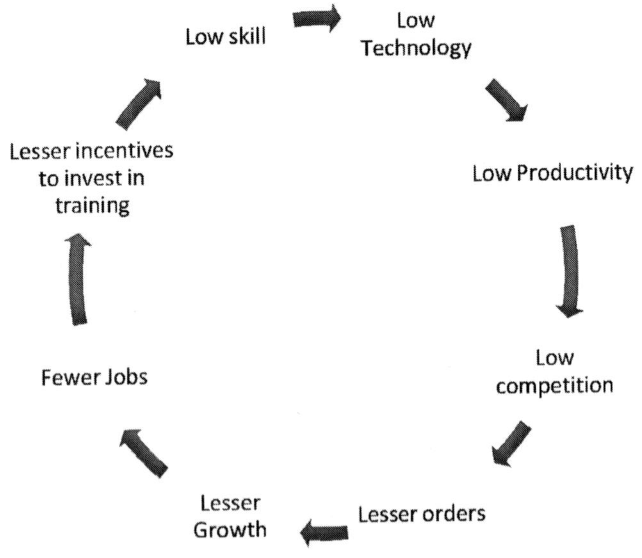

the government formulated the national skill development policy that laid the framework for skill development, ensuring that individuals get improved access to skills and knowledge.

Key features of the National Skill Development Policy

- Scope: The skill development policy includes:
- Institution-based skill development, including ITI's/ vocational schools/technical schools/ polytechnics/ professional colleges, etc.
- Learning initiatives of sectoral skill development organised by different ministries/ departments
- Formal and informal apprenticeships and other types of training by enterprises
- Training for self-employment/entrepreneurial development
- Adult learning, retraining of retired or retiring employees and lifelong learning
- Non-formal training, including training by civil society organisations
- E-learning, web-based learning and distance learning
- Institutional framework: The policy lays down the institutional framework comprising:
- Prime Minister's National Council on Skill Development
- National Skill Development Co-ordination Board
- National Skill Development Corporation (NSDC)
- National Council for Vocational Training (NCVT)

The policy states the roles and responsibilities of stakeholders, which include the government, industry, trade unions, local governments, civil society institutions and all skill providers.

- Promotes the expansion of outreach, equity and access under the skill development initiative: The skill development initiative requires that there is a considerable amount of capacity expansion, innovative delivery approaches and Public Private Participation. The policy provides for equal access of skill development for women, disadvantaged groups (SC, ST and OBCs), minorities, disabled persons and economically challenged people.

- Lays down standards for quality and relevance: The policy provides for quality standards to achieve global competitiveness. It lays downs standards for:
- Quality assurance (based on validation of qualifications for ensuring that qualifications reflect market needs, validation of training process, accreditation of training providers/institutions, research and information)
- Quality of infrastructure
- Quality of trainer
- National vocational qualification framework
- Labour market information systems and HR planning mechanisms
- Emphasises on skill development for the unorganised sector: The policy lays down special emphasis on skill development for the unorganised sector. The policy provides for having a separate institutional mechanism to plan, implement and monitor the skill development for the unorganised sector. It focuses on having target groups within the unorganised sector, literacy and soft skills, recognition of prior learning, and skill development for self-employment.

The Indian government recently developed 'The National Skill Development Policy' to provide skills to a huge population and make them employable. The core operating principles of the National Skill Development Policy are:

Government financial support must complement private investment: The Central Ministries must focus on areas where private investment in skilled development is unlikely to be available or forthcoming. The Government would aim at useful public-private partnerships.

States as key actors: The States being the key actors in Skill Development would set up overarching integrated framework for action for Skill Development through State level Skill Development Missions.

Deployment of funds: The funds would be deployed more for activities than for buildings and other hard assets. However, upgradation of machinery and equipment, teaching and learning aids will be a continuous process. Creation of infrastructure in latest technology, need-based new initiatives, creation of infrastructure in rural, remote and difficult areas will continue.

Focus of modular courses, open architecture and short term courses: With fast changing skills in the labour market, focus would be on short, relevant and effective courses that would get candidates into the workplace. They will be welded through National Vocational Educational Qualifications Framework to maintain dynamism and open to feedback.

Separate financing from delivery: Today Government funds are only available for government delivery. National Skill Development Corporation will support private skill development initiatives.

Following financing options will be explored:

(a) **Link financing to outcomes:** Today public and private training is financed largely on inputs viz. number of courses, number of students, faculty, etc. Efforts would be made to move towards Government financing linked to placement ratios and outcomes.

(b) **Focus funding on candidates:** The focus would be on funding the candidates rather than institutions to create choice. This could be structured as a scholarship, skill voucher, outcome based reimbursement, etc.

Create infrastructure for on-the-job-training and encourage apprenticeships: The enabling infrastructure for large number of formal apprentices needs to be built that includes modification to the Apprentices Act, 1961.

Publicise rating and outcome information on training institutions: A framework of accreditation and infrastructure for information dissemination around measurable criteria on institutions will be created. Ratings of public and private institutions would be put on public domain.

Effective assessment and credible certification: Quality assured learning, credible assessment and certification will be developed. This will allow employers to use the certificate as a proxy to fast track job applicants.

Restructure employment exchanges as career guidance centres: Employment Exchanges will be restructured as career guidance centres to channelise candidates into jobs, apprenticeships and training.

Expand formal employment: Formal employment is not only fiscally attractive but more amenable to financing innovations. This will require a review of existing State and Central legislations which encourage informal and unorganised employment.

ADAPTABILITY

- National Vocational Education Qualifications Framework (NVEQF)
- Introduction of NVEQF at Secondary and Higher Secondary Education (Classes IX–XII)
- Management Structure
- National Institute of Open Schooling (NIOS)
- On February 28th presenting The Union Budget for 2013-14 Finance Minister P. Chidambaram Stated-" The link between policy and welfare can be expressed in a few words: opportunities, education, skill, jobs and incomes".
- Joseph Stiglitz "There is a compelling case for equity but it is also necessary if there is to be sustained growth. A country's most important resource is its people."

ACCEPTABILITY

- Quality of infrastructure
- ICT, physical infrastructure
- Advanced curriculum framework
- Employable training and skill development

Financial Inclusion

Financial Inclusion is the process of ensuring access to appropriate financial products and services needed by all sections of the society in general and vulnerable groups such as weaker sections and low income groups in particular at an affordable cost in a fair and transparent manner by mainstream institutional players Financial Inclusion and Financial Literacy are twin pillars. While Financial Inclusion acts from supply side providing the financial market/services what people demand, Financial Literacy stimulates the demand side–making people aware of what they can demand.

Twin aspects of Financial Inclusion

Demand Side: Financial Literacy - Fair and Appropriateness

Supply Side: Financial Inclusion-Access

Developing Economies face the problem of low level of literacy, poor accessibility and low demand. Therefore, it is necessary for developing an Index for measuring both Access as well as the Level of Literacy.

Issues–Inclusion & Literacy

- There are several issues involved in Financial Inclusion and financial literacy such as Demographic Spread–How to provide banking services to villages with low population–Viability;
- Evolution of an Appropriate Business Model and an Efficient Delivery Mechanism;
- Financial Literacy–How to increase financial awareness mainly amongst the excluded masses;

- How to have a National Level Coordination of all stakeholders like Banks, Governments, Civil Societies, NGOs etc. required for achieving the objective of financial inclusion and literacy.

Financial Inclusion Initiatives

- Encouraged Electronic Benefit Transfer for routing social security payments through the banking channel.
- Separate program for Urban Financial Inclusion initiated.
- Roadmap for providing banking services – A structured way of covering villages. In the first phase villages with population above 2000 was targeted. The focus has now shifted to villages with population less than 2000.
- Financial Inclusion Plan for Banks-All domestic commercial banks-public and private sector have drawn a Board approved 3 year Financial Inclusion Plan (FIP) starting April 2010.
- Self-set targets - FIPs to be integrated with Business plan of the banks.
- Banks advised to finalise their next 3 year FIP for the period 2013-16.

FIPs–Performance Analysis–December 2012

- Banking connectivity has been extended to 2,11,234 villages up to December 31, 2012 from 67,694 villages in March 2010. 5694 rural branches have been opened.
- Numbers of Business Correspondents have increased from 34,532 to 1,52,328.
- 1714.27 lakh Basic Savings Bank Deposit Accounts, 317.33 lakh Kisan Credit Cards and 31.14 lakh General Credit Cards remain outstanding as on December 31, 2012.
- Share of ICT based accounts have increased substantially–Percentage of ICT accounts to BSBDAs has increased from 25 per cent to 45 per cent.

Financial Inclusion Plan Progress – December 2012

Sl. No.	*Particulars*	*Year ended Mar 10*	*Year ended Mar 11*	*Year ended Mar 12*	*Prog. Upto Dec 2012*
1.	Total No. of Branches	85457	91145	99242	103359
2.	No. of Rural Branches	33433	34811	37471	39127
3.	No. of branches in unbanked villages	0	0	3381	4323
4.	Total number of CSPs deployed	34532	60993	116548	152328
5.	Banking Outlets >2000 -Total	37791	66447	112130	118718
6.	Banking Outlets <2000- Total	29903	49761	69623	92516
7.	Banking Outlets - Branches	33378	34811	37471	39127
8.	Banking Outlets - BCs	34174	80802	141136	168380
9.	Banking Outlets - Other Modes	142	595	3146	3727
10.	Banking Outlets -TOTAL	67694	116208	181753	211234
11.	Urban Locations covered through BCs	447	3771	5891	17950
12.	BSBDA Total (No. in lakh)	734.53	1047.59	1385.04	1714.27
13.	BSBDA Total Amt. (Amt. in ' crores)	5501.71	7612.00	12040.62	17008.35
14.	OD facility availed in Basic Savings Bank Deposit A/c (No. in lakh)	1.83	6.06	27.05	32.82
15.	OD facility availed in Basic Savings Bank Deposit A/c (Amt. in ' crores)	9.98	26.48	108.41	135.17
16.	KCCs-Total-No. in Lakh	243.07	271.12	302.35	317.33
17.	KCCs-Total-Amt In ' Crores	124007.06	160005.04	206839.03	249139.78
18.	GCC-Total-No. in Lakh	13.87	16.99	21.08	31.14
19.	GCC-Total-Amt In ' Crores	3510.87	3507.06	4184.41	7660.35
20.	ICT A/Cs-BC-Total Transaction - No. in lakhs	265.15	841.64	1410.93	1837.55
21.	ICT A/Cs-BC-Total Transactions – Amt. in ' Crores	692.07	5800.42	9285.93	16533.34

Financial Inclusion through financial literacy

Financial Literacy stimulates the demand side – Financial Inclusion acts from supply side providing the financial market/ services what people demand. However, financial literacy in developing country like India faces the problem of a large population of alphabetically illiterate population requiring basic financial knowledge. A large section of financially excluded population need to be explained the benefits of financial inclusion and also to be provided, a large growing segment of educated middle class-requiring financial education, a large section of workers having no pension, a move from Defined Benefit Pension Schemes to Defined Contribution Pension Schemes. Hence, a large workforce need to be explained the risk of various investment portfolios.

To achieve the goal of financial literacy Institutions have been created like Financial Stability Development Council with Mandate to focus on Financial Inclusion and Financial Literacy, a technical group on Financial Inclusion and Financial Literacy under aegis of FSDC–Coordinating the efforts of all Financial Sector Regulators.

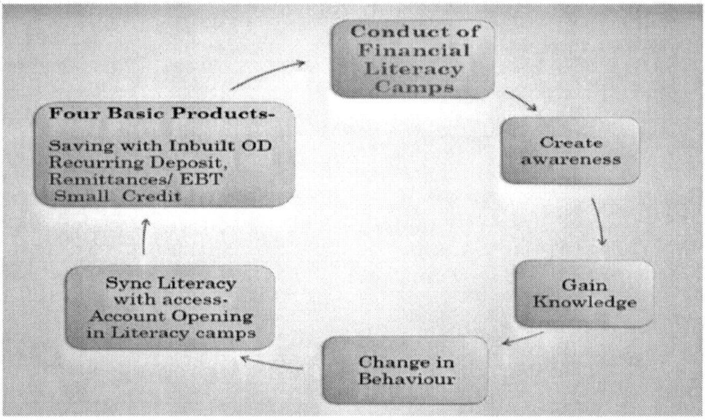

A national strategy on financial education was prepared with the plan of including Financial Literacy in School Curriculum at National Level. Till 2012, total 658 Financial Literacy Centers (FLCs) were functioning where 1.5 million people Were educated during the period April to December 2012.

RBI Reserve Bank of India has prepared financial literacy material targeting the unbanked audience. Messages are written in lucid manner in simple languages to be used as standard curriculum by banks during their financial literacy activities. We have issued guidelines on Conduct of Financial Literacy Camps–Mass Scale awareness–FLCs (650+)-At least once in a month–Quarterly Monitoring.

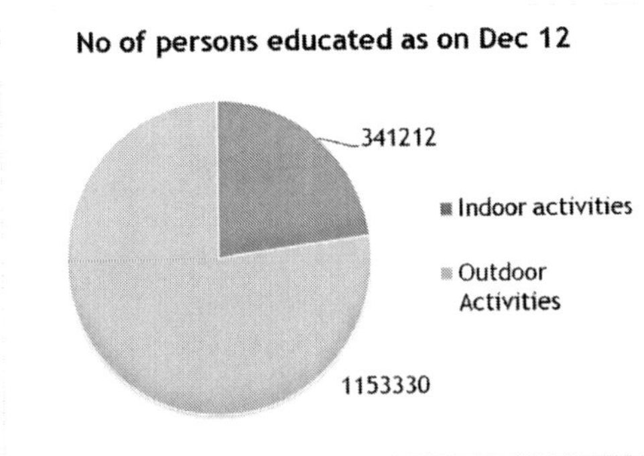

For Financial Access and Education Imperatives to succeed:

To make financial inclusion a reality we have to ensure an appropriate Business Delivery Model through the involvement of all stakeholders, access to financial services and Financial Education must happen simultaneously. It must be continuous and must target all sections of the population simultaneously.

References

1. Ernst & Young Report
2. Planning Commission Report 2008 & ILO
3. WWW.NIRD.COM
4. Ministry of Labour and Employment, Government of India
5. 12th Plan, Planning Commission of India, Government of India
6. Ministry of State for HRD and External Affairs, Government of India

4

Child and Youth Finance in India

There are 315 million young people aged 10-24 years in India representing 30 per cent of India's population. Median age for India about 27 years compared with over 40 years for most OECD economies. On a rough basis, about 10 million people would enter the job market every year for next 15 years. India grew at an average rate of 7.8 per cent during the years 2002-2007 and 7.9 per cent during the years 2007-2012. Despite being one of the fastest growing economies in the world, India as per Human Development Index was ranked at 136th place among 187 countries. The country has major challenges to address in terms of making the growth process more inclusive and socially sustainable. We are trying to promote the usage of bank accounts to inculcate the habits of saving among children and youth. RBI has taken the lead in creating a legal environment where minors can open Bank accounts. Banks are allowed to open basic, fixed and pure savings accounts in the name of minors with either parent as guardian.

Seizing the demographic dividend

On the one side is economic policy. On the other side is economic welfare. We are a developing country. The link between policy and welfare can be expressed in a few words: opportunities, education, skills, jobs and incomes. Every mother understands this. Every young man and woman understands this. The budget for 2013-14 before it one overarching goal: to create opportunities for our youth to acquire education and skills that will get them decent jobs or self-employment that will bring them adequate incomes that will enable them to live with their families in a safe and secure environment.

Financial Inclusion through Financial Education

The OECD defines Financial Literacy as the ability to grow, monitor and effectively use financial resources to enhance well being and economic security of oneself, one's family and one's business. Financial education plays an important role in making the demand side responsive to supply side initiatives. Financial literacy is an important element for promoting financial inclusion and financial stability. Investments in education both contribute to aggregate economic growth as well as enable citizen to broadly participate in the growth process through improved productivity, employment and wages and are therefore critical to our inclusive growth agenda.

Importance of Financial Literacy

Like knowledge of traffic rules and car technology does not create demand for cars but helps safer use of these. Financial Literacy helps you understand risk-return framework associated with financial products and services better. For the large unbanked population in India, basic banking products like savings accounts, deposits, small credits and remittances are relatively risk free. We have introduced a Basic Banking Deposits Accounts with nil mandatory balance. Thus, for us in India, Financial Literacy is a tool for promoting financial inclusion by weaning away the poor from the informal service providers and bringing them in the fold of mainstream financial institutions.

Strategy for financial education

There is a National Strategy for Financial Education (NSFE). With the adoption of National Strategy for Financial Education, India has joined select league of countries like the Netherlands, New Zealand, Spain, the UK and Czech Republic which have implemented NSFE.

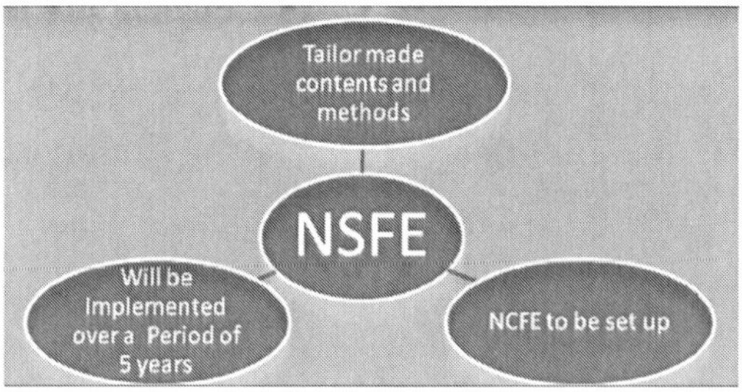

Financial Literacy Initiatives

We have adopted a Multi-Agency Approach to increase Financial Literacy - A large number of players are involved including all Financial Sector Regulators. Emphasis is to improve Financial Access through better Financial Literacy.

- Financial Literacy Centres (FLCs) opened in all 644 districts of the country.

- All FLCs to hold Financial Literacy Camps at least once a month. Quarterly monitoring being done. About 1.5 million people educated in 3 quarters.
- Rural bank branches (35000+) of commercial banks advised to conduct financial literacy camps at least once a month.
- Regular participation in local fairs and exhibitions to promote FL through distribution of comics, posters, banners and street plays on FL.
- Programmes in schools and colleges on FL through debates, quizzes, skits, essay competitions etc. by banks, corporates and RBI.
- Mass media campaigns, tie ups with educational institutes, financial awareness workshops/ help lines , books, pamphlets and publications on FL by NGOs, Financial market players etc.
- Standard curriculum for basic conceptual understanding - Financial Literacy Material prepared containing messages for financially illiterate people.

Institutional Mechanism for financial literacy

Government of India and Reserve Bank of India
Financial Stability & Development Council-Technical Group on Financial Inclusion & Financial literacy
Financial Inclusion Advisory Committee of RBI
17 offices of RBI spread across the country
46 Public and Private sector Banks, 67 RRBs, 35 SLBCs, 644 LDMs
Partnership with other stakeholders UIDAI, NABARD, State Governments

Child and Youth Finance–Indian Context

- India's demographic dividend presents the country with a great opportunity to enhance its growth and per capita income. Thirty per cent of India's population in the age group of 10-24 years. Children and youth have always been the integral part of all financial inclusion initiatives in India.

- The combined expenditure of central and state governments on education is just 3.3 per cent of GDP. In the face of various constraints, the expenditure by the central and state governments on education alone will not be sufficient to make a difference. The banks have a very crucial role in facilitating pursuit of education by resource constrained youth.

Data on Educational Loans

Year	*Public Sector Banks*		*Private Sector Banks*		*Foreign Banks*	
	A/cs	Amt	A/cs	Amt	A/cs	Amt
2003	239	28703	10	1164	2	662
2004	347	41795	11	1919	3	220
2005	470	63978	16	2760	3	205
2006	641	108038	21	3808	3	348
2007	1002	140120	24	3777	Negligible	13
2008	1298	198442	33	5093	—do—	10
2009	1580	269127	47	7967	—do—	1
2010	1912	352921	61	10676	—do—	1
2011	2213	413438	76	16524	—do—	Negligible
2012	2371	467405	110	16750	—do—	—do—

FACILITIES FOR VOCATIONAL COURSES

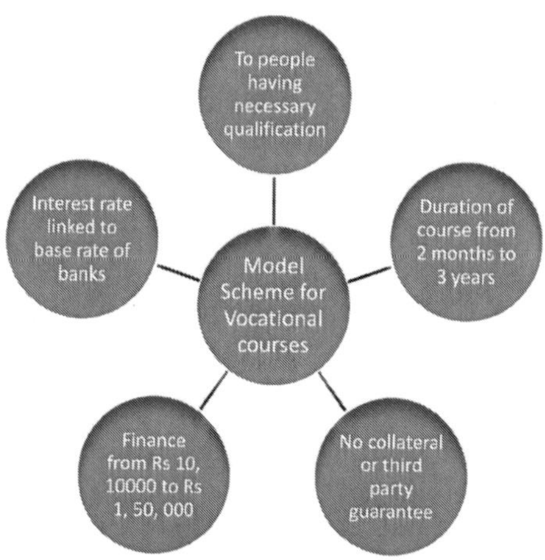

A Model Educational Loan Scheme for Vocational courses has been developed by the Indian Banks Association to support national initiatives for skill development. Features of the scheme are:

a. The scheme aims to provide financial support from the banking system to those who have the necessary qualification.
b. Vocational/ skill development courses are of duration from 2 months to 3 years.
c. Need based finance ranging from Rs 10, 000 to Rupees 1, 50, 000 is provided to the beneficiaries.
d. Interest rate to be charged is linked to the base rate of banks. The rate is reduced if interest subsidy is provided by the Central or State Government.
e. No collateral or third party guarantee is required. The repayment ranges from 2 to 7 years.

Main issues and challenges to achieve financial literacy are: Literacy level is very low mostly in rural/remote areas; Dependence is mainly on informal sources of credit from moneylenders on exploitative terms; Still perceived more as an obligation than a business opportunity by stake holders, Appropriate Business Model to be devised by banks for enhancing their presence through involvement of all stakeholders to make Financial Inclusion & Literacy a reality; Lack of Infrastructure necessary for scaling up: Physical and Technical Infrastructure; Extension from banking products to other financial products.

To make financial inclusion a reality we have to ensure an appropriate Business Delivery Model through the involvement of all stakeholders, access to financial services and Financial Education must happen simultaneously, it must be continuous and must target all sections of the population simultaneously.

Banking Ombudsman-Quick and Inexpensive forum of Alternate Dispute Resolution Mechanism

In India, there is a law for Consumer Protection though not specifically for the financial sector consumers. In regard to bank customers, there is a Banking Codes and Standards Board of India (BCSBI) which is the standards setting body for banking services. The self-regulatory organisation of the banking industry viz., Indian Banks Association has evolved a fair practices code to be adopted by its members. To ensure that consumers are protected even in case of plain simple products with to add on features products, the Reserve Bank of India has instituted the Banking Ombudsman, as an alternate dispute resolution mechanism and, we are examining the possibility of enacting comprehensive financial sector consumer protection legislation.

Financial Inclusion in India – A segmented approach

India is trying to leverage on its demographic dividend to attain higher growth rates. Financial inclusion is an imperative for inclusive growth. Financial Inclusion is the process of ensuring access to appropriate financial products and services needed by all sections of the society in general and vulnerable groups such as weaker sections and low income groups in particular at an affordable cost in a fair and transparent manner by mainstream institutional players. Child Finance is being encouraged by allowing minor child to open a bank account and other financial literacy initiatives. Youth Finance– Youth being provided educational loans. Finance to Young professionals–The limit for collateral free loans to the MSE increased from Rs 5 lakh to Rs.10 lakh. It has been made mandatory for banks. A Working Group has also recommended absorption of guarantee fees for the collateral free loans by CGTMSE. Financial Inclusion for other people is being provided through Financial Initiatives India is taking lead in south and south-east Asia in the area of promoting child and youth finance, financial education and financial literacy.

Trinity to make Financial Stability Possible

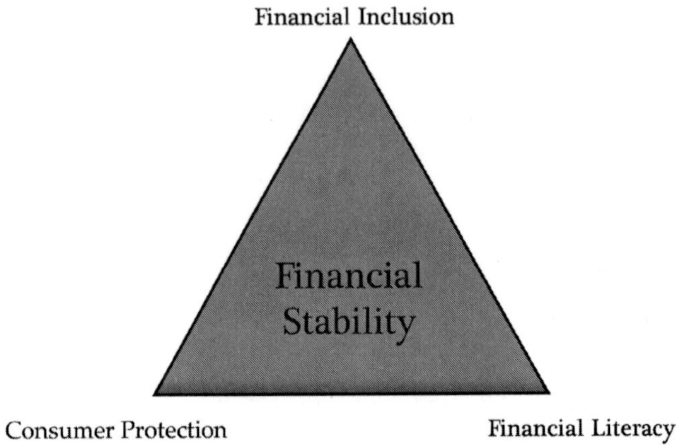

References

1. http://taxguru.in/rbi/trinity-financial-stability.html
2. *www.rbi.org.in* › Publication , Speech Delivered at OECD Conference.
3. Ministry of Labour and Employment, Government of India.
4. Planning Commission of India, Government of India.

5

Indian Rural Banking Sector: Big Challenges and the Road Ahead

The global financial crisis and the current Euro zone crisis have affected the banks in the advanced economies; the spillover is ricocheting on banks in emerging economies including India. Issues of financial stability, economic growth and managing inflation are the major challenges confronting regulators in advanced economies and are equally important for emerging economies like ours. Global economic growth has slowed from 3.9 per cent in 2011 to 3.2 per cent in 2012. We are not unaffected by what happens in the rest of the world our economy too has slowed after 2010-11. In the current year CSO has projected a growth estimation of 5 per cent while the RBI has put it at 5.5 per cent. "Whatever be the final estimate it will be below India's potential growth rate of 8 per cent, getting back to that growth rate will be the challenge that faces the country. This is clearly not feasible if large sections of society remain marginalised and people who lack access to financial services from Institutional service providers are not mainstreamed. The challenge of financial inclusion presents an inflexion point for Indian banking.

The biggest challenge for next decade or more for banks in the country is to capture the banking business of over 50 per cent population of this country of over 120 billion people. This chapter discusses contemporary challenges facing Indian Rural Banking, i.e., Priority Sector Lending, Regional Rural Banks, Financial Inclusion, Financial Literacy and Education.

Aptly Financial Inclusion is termed as the supply side of the equation and Financial Literacy the demand side.

(i) Priority Sector Lending

The definition of priority sectors has evolved over a period of time and at present, priority sectors are broadly defined as those sectors of the economy which (in the absence of inclusion in the priority sector categories) would not get timely and adequate finance. Typically, these are small loans to small and marginal farmers for agriculture and allied activities, loans to Micro and Small Enterprises, loans for small housing projects, education loans and other small loans to people with low income levels. Presently, the target for aggregate advances to the priority sector is 40 per cent of the Adjusted Net Bank Credit ANBC or the credit equivalent of Off Balance sheet Exposure (OBE), whichever is higher for domestic banks. Foreign banks with 20 or more branches in the country are being brought on par with domestic banks for assignment of priority sector targets in a phased manner over a five year period starting from April 1, 2013. For foreign banks with less than 20 branches the overall target of priority sector lending is fixed at 32 per cent.

The domestic banks, i.e, public and private sector, could not achieve the target of 40 percent for the year 2012 as can be evidenced from the following table below:

Priority Sector Lending by banks

(Amount in Rs Billion)

As on the Last Reporting Friday of March	*Public Sector Banks*	*Private Sector Banks*	*Foreign Banks*
2011	10,215	2,491	667
	(41.0)	(46.7)	(39.7)
2012	11,299	2,864	805
	(37.4)	(39.4)	(40.8)

Note: 1. Figures in parentheses are percentages to ANBC or credit equivalent of Off Balance Sheet Exposure (OBSE), whichever is higher, in the respective groups.

Source: RBI Annual Report 2012.

As per 59th NSS Survey, households with 2 hectare or lease land accounted for 84 per cent of all farmer households. The percentages of such small and marginal famers who have access to credit is only 46.3 per cent. A large section of farmers are still largely dependent on moneylenders for meeting their financial needs.

Shares in Total Debt of Cultivator Households

(Per cent)

Source of debt	1951	1961	1971	1981	1991	2002
Institutional	7.3	18.7	31.7	63.2	66.3	61.1
Non-Institutional	92.7	81.3	68.3	36.8	30.6	38.9
Moneylenders	69.7	49.2	36.1	16.1	17.5	26.8
Total	**100.0**	**100.0**	**100.0**	**100.0**	**100.0**	**100.0**

Source: All India Debt and Investment Survey, NSSO, GoI, various rounds.

The major challenge is to bring all farmers into the institutional credit framework. To boost flow of credit to agriculture sector, apart from a host of initiatives, the Kisan Credit Card (KCC) Scheme was introduced in the year 1998-99 to enable farmers to purchase agricultural inputs and draw cash for their production needs. In 2004, NABARD revised the Model KCC Scheme to provide adequate and timely finance for meeting the comprehensive credit requirements of farmers under a single window, with flexible and simplified procedure, adopting whole farm approach. The scheme now covers term the credit as also working capital for agriculture and allied activities and a reasonable component for consumption needs. During 2011-12, public sector banks have issued 68,03,051 KCCs with sanctioned limits aggregating to Rs 69,51,768.45 lakh. Since inception of the scheme, the number of KCCs issued by public sector banks stood at 5,47,49,373.00 till March 2012 with sanctioned limits aggregating to Rs 3,53,14,527.11 lakh. R.B.I. recently revised the guidelines on Kisan Credit Card scheme. Margin/Security norms are waived for loans up to Rs 1 lakh to enhance the flow and easy delivery of bank loans to small agricultural borrowers.

The revised priority sector guidelines lay emphasis on direct delivery of credit to the poor beneficiaries i.e. without the involvement of intermediaries, which will ensure better management of risks and also lead to reduction in transaction, delivery and administrative costs for these loans. These are essentially small ticket, low value high volume loans, do generate profits but these are assured flows translating to a stable low cost deposit stream for banks and to the fortune at the bottom of the pyramid.

To make priority sector lending viable for the banks, RBI has removed the interest rate ceiling on all types of loans including small loans by linking it to the Base Rate of the banks with effect from April 1, 2010. Thus, there is no preferential rate of interest for priority sector loans. Thus, priority sector lending is competitive and commercially viable.

Why did we removed caps on pricing? The cost of absence of bank lending to poor and vulnerable sections of the society is heavy, as the poor have no option but to borrow from the unorganised sector, the informal or alternative channels at usurious price. There is a need for reorienting the approach of banks to look at priority sector areas. The challenges in priority sector lending can be overcome only if banks consider priority sector lending as part of normal business operations of the banks and not as an obligation. Rural untapped markets offer a huge business opportunity to the banks. Banks need to innovate new products which cater to the needs of farmers, weaker sections and other vulnerable sections of the society, develop new delivery channels and embrace technological developments which will reduce the delivery costs. Priority sector must be treated as a viable business proposition.

(ii) Regional Rural Banks

Regional Rural Banks (RRBs) were established in the year 1976 as a low cost financial intermediation structures in the rural areas to ensure sufficient flow of institutional credit for agriculture and other rural sectors. RRBs were expected to possess the local feel and familiarity of the cooperative banks with the managerial expertise of the commercial banks. RRBs are jointly owned by GoI, the concerned State Government and Sponsor Banks. The issued capital of a RRB is shared by the owners in the proportion of 50 per cent, 15 per cent and 35 per cent respectively. In practice they borrowed the politicisation in lending rampant in cooperative Banks, with the worst form of unionism replicated from the commercial banks. The low cost structure was also washed away after the Obul Reddy report which brought parity of pay scales with Commercial Banks.

Several RRBs suffered humongous losses. Government of India and RBI initiated several measures to improve the financial health of RRBs. During a review carried out by GOI in the year 2009 it was found that the Capital Risk Weighted Assets Ratio (CRAR) of the RRBs were too low. Dr K.C. Chakrabarty committee suggested bringing the Capital to Risk Adjusted Ratio (CRAR) of RRBs to at least 9 per cent in a sustainable manner. The Committee *inter-alia* recommended recapitalisation support to the extent of Rs 2,200 crore, to 40 RRBs in 21 States, out of which Rs 1,100 crore was to be contributed by Central Government. The recapitalisation process which started in 2010-11 has been extended till 2013-14. Several Committees looked into issues of viability and finally amalgamation of RRBS on grounds of contiguity in a particular region was the policy adopted. Initially, there were 196 RRBs working in the country. After the second phase of amalgamation, which started w.e.f. October 1, 2012, 34 RRBs have been amalgamated to form 14 new RRBs. After a massive consolidation and merger exercise to strengthen the RRBs, the number of RRBs operating in the country today has come down to 62.

The number of sustainable viable RRBs (i.e. RRBs making net current profit and without accumulated losses) has increased to 60 as on March 31, 2012 as compared to 58 as on March 31, 2011.

(iii) Financial Inclusion

Turning to extension of banking penetration and branch building. A massive exercise in this regard has been taken up by RBI and this is being done through the lead bank scheme channel. RBI advised banks in November 2009 to draw up a roadmap to provide banking services through a banking outlet in every village with a population of more than 2000 and the target date was March 2012. Banks were advised that such banking services need not necessarily be extended through a brick and mortar branch but could be provided through any of the various forms of ICT-based models including through BCs. Under the roadmap for providing banking outlets in villages with population above 2000, banking outlets have been opened in hitherto 74199 unbanked villages comprising 2493 branches, 69374 Business Correspondents (BCs) and 2332 through other modes like ATMs, mobile van, etc.

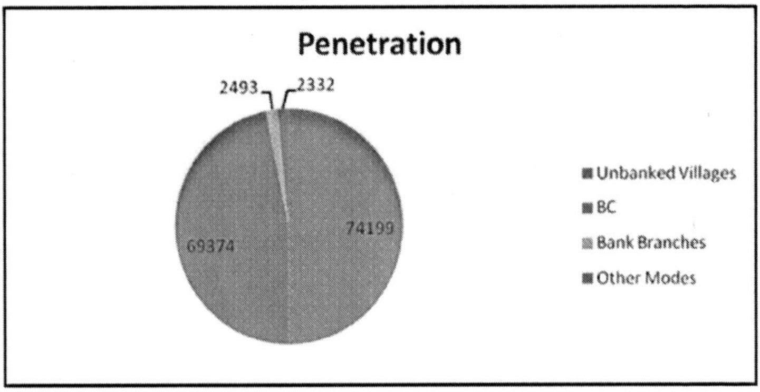

The challange is; How do we plan to provide banking services to villages having population less than 2000?

As per the announcement in the Annual Policy Statement 2012-13, State Level Bankers' Committees (SLBCs) were advised by RBI to prepare a roadmap covering all unbanked villages of population less than 2000 and notionally allot these villages to banks for providing banking services in a time bound manner, especially, to start with, Electronic Benefit

Transfer (EBT) services. The objective is to provide a bank account to every household/person throughout the country. To start with, banks have been advised to provide door step services to EBT beneficiaries to facilitate transfer of all State benefits including Mahatma Gandhi National Employment Guarantee Act (MGNREGA) for wages and various cash subsidies to beneficiaries by direct credit to the bank accounts, through regular visits of BCs to the allocated villages and over a period of time, provide all kinds of banking services viz. remittances, recurring deposit, entrepreneurial credit in the form of KCC and GCC, insurance (life and non-life) and other banking services to all the residents of the village through a mix of brick and mortar branch and BC network. There is an emphasizor planning for setting up sufficient number of brick and mortar branches so that there is a brick and mortar branch to provide support to a cluster of BC units, i.e., about 8-10 BC units at a reasonable distance of 3-4 kilometers. As per the Roadmap drawn about 4,84,000 villages with population less than 2000 have been allotted to various banks for provision of banking services in the next Three years.

Financial Inclusion Plan

Financial Inclusion (FI) is the process of ensuring access to appropriate financial products and services needed by all sections of the society, in general and vulnerable groups such as weaker sections and low income groups, in particular at an affordable cost in a fair and transparent manner by mainstream institutional players. Reserve Bank has adopted a bank-led model for financial inclusion which seeks to leverage on technology. In January 2006, the Reserve Bank permitted banks to utilise the services of non-governmental organisations (NGOs), micro-finance institutions (other than Non-Banking Financial Companies) and other civil society organisations as intermediaries for providing financial and banking services through the use of business facilitator and business correspondent (BC) models. The BC model allows banks to do 'cash in - cash out' transactions at a location much closer to the rural population, thus addressing the last mile problem.

Reserve Bank has been furthering financial inclusion in a mission mode through a combination of strategies ranging from relaxation of regulatory guidelines, provision of new products and other supportive measures to achieve sustainable and scalable Financial Inclusion. A structured and planned approach was followed under financial inclusion strategy where in all banks were advised in January 2010 to prepare Board approved Financial Inclusion Plans (FIPs) congruent with their business strategies and comparative advantage for a three year period extending up to 2013. The implementation of these plans was closely monitored by the Reserve Bank through quantitative and qualitative reporting formats and through review meetings held with CMDs/CEOs Chairman Managing Director/Chief Executive officer and other senior officials of banks.

The performance of banks under the first three year Financial Inclusion Plan period (2010-13)?

The Financial Inclusion Plan (2010-13), introduced in April 2010 has concluded in March 2013. The penetration of Banking services in the rural areas has increased to a great extent.

A snapshot of the progress made by banks, upto December 31 2012, under FIP for certain key parameters is given below:-

(i) Banking connectivity has been extended to 2,11,234 villages from 67,694 at the beginning of the plan period. 5694 rural branches have been opened during the period.

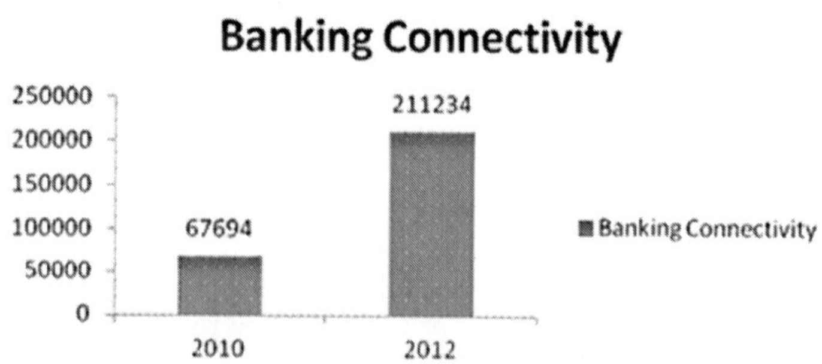

(ii) Numbers of Business Correspondents have increased from 34,532 to 1, 52,328.

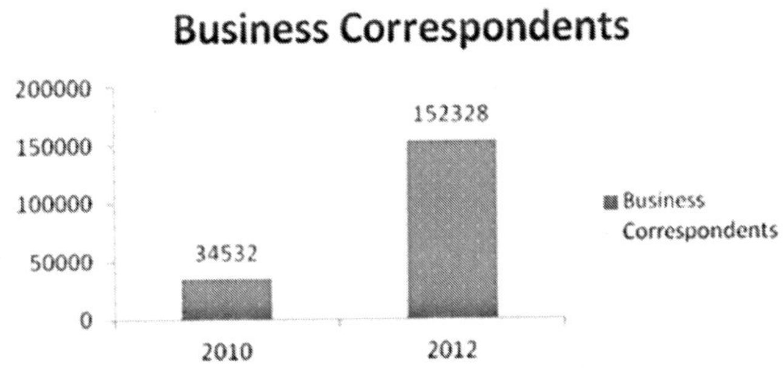

(iii) Total number of Basic Savings Bank Deposit Accounts (BSBDAs) have increased from 73.45 million in 2010 to 171.43 million up to December 31 2012, Number of Kissan Credit Cards outstanding have gone up from 24.31 million in 2010 to 31.73 million up to December 31 2012 and Number of General Credit Cards outstanding have gone up from 1.39 million in 2010 to 3.11 million up to December 31 2012.

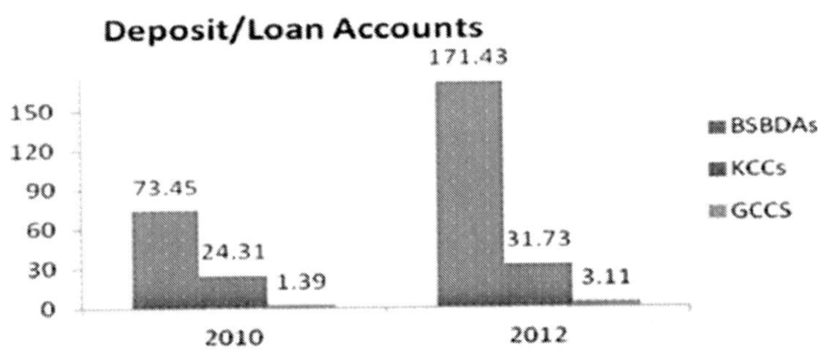

Source: BSR publication - Basic Statistical Returns of Scheduled Commercial Banks in India

(iv)

Share of ICT based accounts have increased substantially - Percentage of ICT accounts to BSBDAs has increased to nearly 42%.

A total of 4090.12 lakh BC based ICT transactions have been carried out during the period from April 2010 to December 2012.

(v) The number of ICT based BC transactions though encouraging is still very low as compared to the increase in the number of banking outlets. The focus on monitoring has, therefore, now shifted more towards the number and value of transactions in no-frills, credit and remittance accounts opened through BCs. In this direction, Banks have been advised to disaggregate the FIP upto the branch level and have involved the controlling offices of respective banks and also the Regional Offices of RBI in all the States are involved in the monitoring process.

What are some of the major issues being faced by banks in pursuing and achieving the Financial Inclusion Plan targets?

Efficient Business Model

Banks are yet to perceive FI as a profitable business model. Feedback received suggests that many banks are still pursuing FI as a regulatory requirement rather than treating it as a business model. Banks have to realise that the bankability of the poor holds a major opportunity for the banking sector in developing a stable retail deposit base and in curbing volatility in earnings with the help of a diversified asset portfolio. The recent crisis has underscored the need for reducing banks' reliance on wholesale deposits and borrowed funds and cultivating a retail portfolio of assets and liabilities for financial stability. Two basic issues that need to be understood by banks while implementing financial inclusion are that:-

- Financial Inclusion programmes should be implemented on commercial lines and not on a charity basis. It is important that banking with the poor is perceived and pursued as a sustainable and viable business model.
- While poor need not be subsidised, it is important to ensure that they are not exploited. The need is to ensure that poor people who deserve credit are provided access to timely and adequate credit in a non-exploitative manner.

BC Model-Viability Issues:

Business Correspondent model is still in the experimental stages and there are various challenges associated with the model. The viability of BC model has remained a critical issue. Surveys have revealed that branch officials do not visit BCs or customers and do not make any effort in introducing BCs to villagers. One primary reason cited by branch officials is the scarcity of staff provided to them for carrying out such visits to villages. Further, most of the accounts opened by BCs have remained non-operational. In order to ensure participation of all stake holders in the financial inclusion process, Banks are advised to disaggregate the FIPs upto the Controlling Office and branch level. This would ensure that bank officials at the ground level are aware of the banks objective under FI and of the specific targets given to each Zone/branch for achieving the objectives.

Technology Issues

Another bottleneck in achieving financial inclusion is the non-availability of physical and digital connectivity. For the success of the ICT based model, resolving technology related issues is the key.

(iv) Financial Literacy

Financial Inclusion and Financial Literacy are two sides of the equation. Financial Inclusion acts from supply side by providing financial market/services that people demand whereas Financial Literacy stimulates the demand side by making people aware of what they can ask for. Therefore, access to financial services and Financial Education must happen simultaneously. It must be continuous, an ongoing process and must target all sections of the population.

Financial awareness has to be spread amongst the excluded masses that are illiterate and poor. For this, evolving an appropriate Business Model and an Efficient Delivery Mechanism is the major challenge for banks. For disseminating financial literacy and awareness, a National Level Coordination of all stakeholders like Banks, Governments, Civil Societies, NGOs, etc. is required. In India, the need for financial literacy is even greater considering the low levels of literacy and the large section of the population still out of the formal financial system. To ensure effective coordination of the efforts made by all the financial regulators and other stakeholders, a Technical Group on Financial Inclusion and Financial Literacy has been constituted under the aegis of Financial Stability and Development Council.The technical group is headed by Deputy Governor, RBI, with members drawn from SEBI, PFRDA, IRDA, Government of India, State Governments, Central Education Board etc. The Group is in dialogue with NCERT/State Education Boards for inclusion of financial literacy in CBSE/State curriculum.

A national strategy on financial education has been prepared which would cater to all sections of the population in the country. Since the challenge is to link large number of financially excluded people to the formal financial system, the focus of the strategy at the base level will be to create awareness of basic financial products through dissemination of simple messages of financial prudence in vernacular language through large campaigns across the country.

The Reserve Bank of India had launched Project Financial Literacy in March 2007 with a view to create awareness, especially among the common persons, on matters relating to banking, finance and central banking. Under Project Financial Literacy, several initiatives have been taken to achieve financial awareness and literacy among various target groups, which included publication of comic books on banking and RBI; games on Financial Education; arranging school/college visits for creating financial awareness; participation in exhibitions/fairs/melas at the State & District levels; conducting essay competitions and quizzes in schools to create awareness about banking and RBI; outreach programmes undertaken by the Top Management and Regional Offices; RBI's Young Scholars Scheme, etc.

Banks have been advised to setup Financial Literacy Centres (FLCs) in the 630 plus offices of the Lead District Managers (LDMs). As at the end of December 2012, 658 FLCs were functioning and 1.5 million people were educated during the period April to December 2012. Further, 35,000 rural branches of SCBs including RRBs have been mandated to undertake outdoor financial literacy activities, at least once a month, with focus on financially excluded population. In order to link the financially excluded segment with the banking system, a 'Model' for conduct of Literacy Camps to be held by banks has been designed, detailing the operational modalities to culminate in effective financial access to the excluded people. Further, to ensure consistency in the financial literacy material reaching the target audience in a simple and lucid manner, RBI has prepared a comprehensive Financial Literacy Material consisting of a Financial Literacy Guide, Financial Diary and a set of 16 Financial Literacy Posters (few posters are have been displayed below).

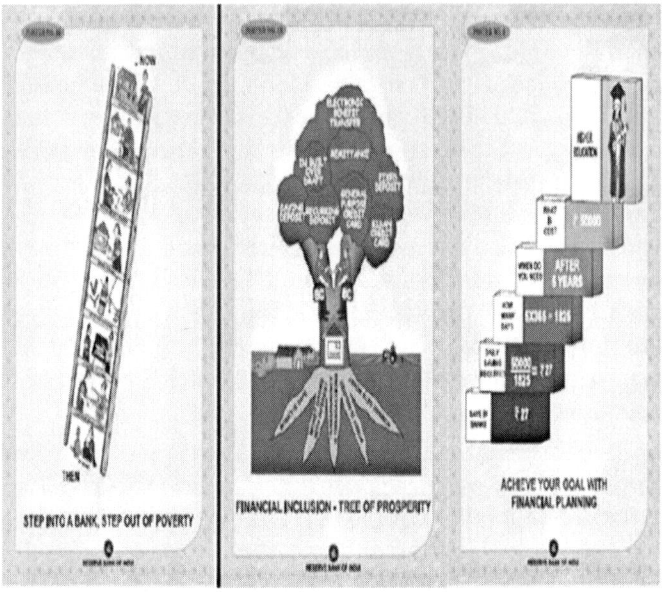

(v) Education

The efforts and outlay of the Government alone will not meet the requirements of outlay on education. The scope of education has widened both in India and abroad covering new courses in diversified areas. Realising the importance of education for economic development and raising overall living standards, RBI, has classified loans and advances granted to individuals for educational purposes, including vocational courses up to Rs. 10 lakh for studies in India and Rs.20 lakh for studies abroad, under 'priority sector'. With a view to enable banks, the Indian Banks' Association has brought out a model scheme for educational loan in the year 2001, which facilitated economically weaker sections of the society to avail educational loans from scheduled banks with modified easier norms. The Scheme was revised by IBA subsequently, the latest being in September 2012.

Loans for education should be seen as an investment for economic development and prosperity, since knowledge and information would be the principal driving force for economic growth in the coming years.

It is hoped that our recently revised priority sector norms, focusing on small loans directly to small and marginal farmers, micro and small enterprises low cost housing projects, student and people with low income; the banks will see priority sectors as a viable business opportunity to reach the financial excluded sections of the population. In the coming 10-15 years banks in India in particular would realign their position in the pecking order based on their ability to convert financial inclusion into a viable business opportunity. Banks which are able to craft appropriate business and delivery models to tap the large excluded sections of society would come on top. The triad of financial inclusion, financial literacy and financial stability would be extremely relevant in the foreseeable future. The depth and breadth of banking in the country would determine financial stability.

The Banking sector has played a crucial role in developing the rural economy by providing credit and creating financial awareness. However, as we are aware, despite all the efforts that we have made, a huge section of the rural population is still out of the banking net. Rural India has huge potential for development and as discussed earlier it provides tremendous business opportunity for the banks mentioned. The Bankers should put their heart and soul in making a rural India where each and every household has a bank account and is imbued with financial awareness. Where Bharat and India morph to one entity and growth with equity becomes a reality.

"Any economist will tell us what India can become as we are the tenth largest economy in the world. We can become the eighth or perhaps the seventh largest by 2017. By 2025 we could become a $5 trillion economy and among the top five in the world." What we will become depends on us and the choices that we make. As Swami Vivekananda, whose 150th birth anniversary we celebrated recently, said "Äll the strength and succor you want is within yourself, therefore make your own future" and this young friends is quite the best advice I can give to you along with my best wishes for a bright future.

Heights by great men
Reached and kept
We're not attained by sudden flight
They while their companions slept
We're struggling upward in the night

References

1. RBI annual report
2. Report on Trend and Progress of Banking in India
3. *www.rbi.org.in/financialeducation/home.aspx*

6

Consumer Protection–Agenda for Inclusive Growth

Consumer empowerment is a central goal. Education of consumers through information disclosure or through consumer literacy is utilised as a mean to even out asymmetries of bargaining power between consumers and financial services providers. In the area of consumer credit and financial literacy, investment empowerment relies on the consumers' ability to understand complex financial products and their knowledge and experience of using such products and services.

All financial products contain risks and also offer rewards. Financially literate consumers are individuals who are equipped to assess risks and to make informed decisions about the suitability of financial products to their situation.

There are differences between individual consumers. This granularity arises due to the differences in incomes of consumers. The largest issue to be tackled is an asymmetry of bargaining power between the financial services provider and the consumer of services. The consumers are always the weaker parties in need of protection. Consumers need to be enabled to navigate the financial markets to make choices beneficial to their needs. They should be able to understand complex financial products and should be equipped with the knowledge and skills to assess risks and make informed decisions about the suitability of financial products to their situation.

A well-functioning consumer protection regime provides effective safeguards for retail financial services consumers while empowering consumers to exercise their legal rights and fulfill their legal obligations.

The Banking Ombudsman Scheme provides clear consumer protection rules with regard to banking products and services. The necessary institutional arrangement for grievance redress is in place. However, these rules need objective, timely and fair implementation. All these three aspects are important. Banking Codes Standards Board of India has also developed codes of conduct and these codes are widely publicised and expected to be adhered to.

Dispute resolution mechanisms to be effectively utilised require financial literacy of consumers and this is the process of consumer empowerment which alone can ensure financial inclusion.

Financial Inclusion and Inclusive Growth

Financial exclusion is a barrier to attaining a high growth rate it should be the unremitting endeavour to draw the excluded into the pale of mainstream financial institutions. A developed financial system broadens access to funds and banking facilities conversely in an underdeveloped financial system high cost informal sources as moneylenders proliferate. Lower the availability of funds and higher their cost fewer are the economic activities that can be financed and hence lower the resulting economic growth. Today we are painfully aware that there are a vast number of unreached people excluded from formal financial services. Potential entrepreneurs small enterprises fail to grow and prosper due to capital constraints. Financial deepening is thus necessary for economic growth. The goal of the development process is to include every last member of our society especially those at the margins. This not only broadens the support base for development, it also strengthens the ability to perform the core developmental goal.

Extent of Financial Exclusion in India

Let us be clear as to the enormity of the challenge as half of the country is still unbanked. Even after thirty four years of bank nationalisation and extensive bank branch building in 6 lakh villages in India rural branches of SCBs including RRBs number 33,495.

Post Nationalisation, number of bank branches of Scheduled Commercial Banks increased Starting. From 1990s the focus shifted to strengthening financial institutions as part of financial sector reforms. Number of rural branches actually came down in the decade of the nineties leading in the middle of the next decade to critical concerns on inclusion.

Population Group-Wise Number of Branches of Scheduled Commercial Bank

Year	*Rural*	*Semi*	*Urban-urban*	*Metropolitan*	*Total*
1969	1833	3342	1584	1503	8262
1990	34791	11324	8042	5595	59752
2005	32082	15403	11500	9370	68355
2012	35850	25439	18625	17197	97111

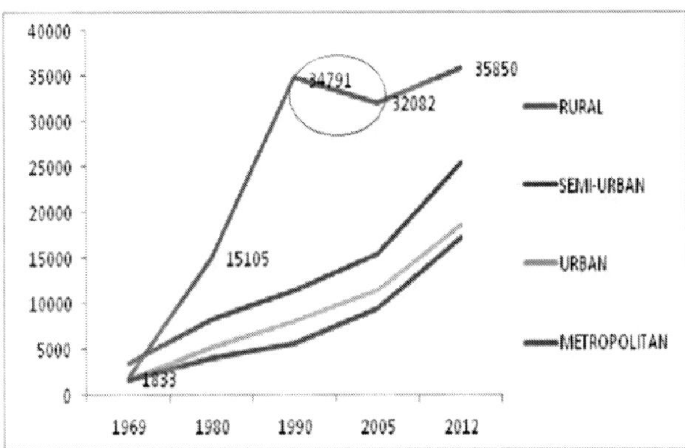

Source: BSR publication - Basic Statistical Returns of Scheduled Commercial Banks in India 2013.

Trinity to make Financial Stability Possible

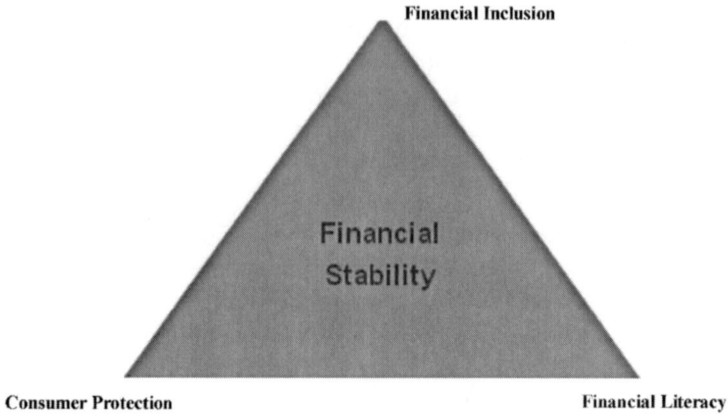

Financial Inclusion and Inclusive Growth

Inclusive growth allows people to 'contribute to and benefit from economic growth'.

Bank led Model

Keeping in view the existing infrastructure of bank branches in India, we have adopted a bank-led model for financial inclusion which leverages technology for optimisation of results. The FI initiatives which are ICT enabled and ride on new delivery models be customised by market participants to best suit their requirements. The development of the habit of banking would lead to an increase in savings and investment improve the efficiency of allocation of capital and increase the ability of monetary authorities to stabilise the economy in times of crisis.

Our experience shows that the goal of financial inclusion is better served through mainstream banking institutions as only they have the ability to offer the suite of products required to bring in effective/meaningful financial inclusion. A well functioning financial system creates necessary conditions for more rapid economic growth so that there is a positive correlation between economic growth and the financial system.

Limitations of Self Help Groups—They only smoothen comsumption by offering credit and function as rotating savings and credit association while micro finance institutions limitation is that they are mono product and offer only Credit.

Minimum bouquet of products and services

To meet the criterion of availability of banking services, a minimum of four basic products must be offered to customers:

- A savings cum overdraft account
- A pure savings account, ideally a recurring or variable recurring deposit
- A remittance product to facilitate EBT and other remittances, and
- Entrepreneurial credit products like a General Purpose Credit Card(GCC) or a Kisan Credit Card (KCC)

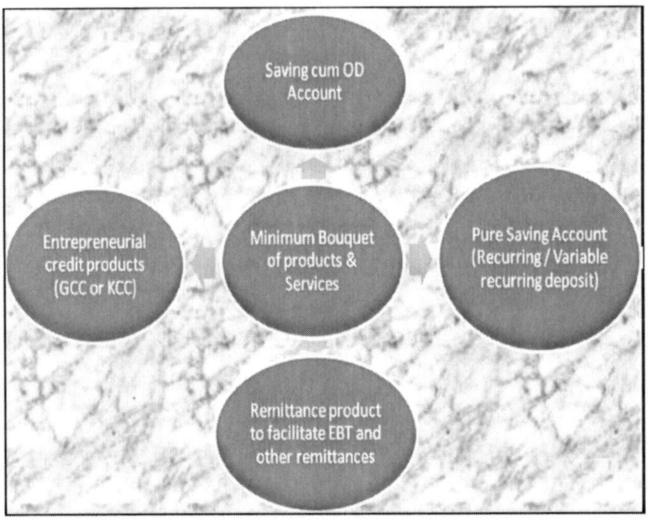

Since size of population and the distribution foot print of bank branches are not enough to cater to each and every person in the country; to increase number of bank branches through FIP following initiatives were taken:

Relaxed Regulatory Requirements

i. Relaxed regulatory dispensation on KYC norms: Know Your Customer (KYC) requirements for opening bank accounts have been relaxed and simplified, especially for small accounts with balances not exceeding Rs 50,000 and aggregate credits in the accounts not exceeding Rs one lakh a year. In modification to the earlier guidelines on KYC norms, RBI has now advised banks not to insist on introduction for opening bank accounts of customers. In addition to this RBI has now allowed banks to use Aadhaar Card as a proof of both identity and address and the MNREGA Job Card as an officially valid document for opening of bank accounts.

ii. Mandatory requirement for opening branches in unbanked villages: To further step up the opening of branches in rural areas so as to improve banking penetration and financial inclusion rapidly, the need for opening of more brick and mortar branches, besides the use of BCs, was felt. Accordingly, domestic SCBs have been mandated in the Monetary Policy Statement–April 2011 to allocate at least 25 per cent of the total number of branches to be opened during a year in unbanked rural (Tier 5 and Tier 6) centres.There are very few studies on the impact of bank branches and development. In 2003 Burgess and Pande examined the branch expansion policy of commercial banks implemented post nationalisation. From 1990 to 1997 the RBI branch authorisation policies specified that banks could establish a new bank branch in a location with one or more bank branches only if they set up four branches in a location with no new bank branches. This regulatory prescription ensured that banks opened rural branches in states where financial development was lower to address the regional inequities in development. Their results to evaluate the impact of a new rural branch on poverty suggested that a one percent increase in the number of banks in rural locations reduced rural poverty by 0.36 per cent and increased total output by 0.55 per cent. Rural branch expansion also increased non primary sector output and non agricultural employment. These favourable effects show the positive influence of bank branches on economic development. Banks in the 1990s disbursed a greater share of credit to the less developed states, but this trend reversed after the 1990s.

iii. In the Annual Policy Statement for 2013-14, banks have been advised to consider frontloading (prioritising) the opening of branches in unbanked rural centres over a three year cycle co-terminus with their FIPs. This is expected to facilitate faster branch expansion in unbanked rural centres.

"Step Into A Bank Step Out of Poverty is Our Central Message"

iv. Business Correspondent/Business Facilitator Model: In January 2006, the Reserve Bank permitted banks to utilise the services of non-governmental organisations (NGOs), micro-finance institutions (other than Non-Banking Financial Companies) and other civil society organisations as intermediaries for providing financial and banking services through the use of business facilitator and business correspondent (BC) models. The BC model allows banks to do 'cash in - cash out' transactions at a location much closer to the rural population, thus addressing the last mile problem. As on March 31 2013, banks have reported deploying 1,95,380 BCs which covered 2,21,341 villages.

Introducing Technology : To ensure sustainability and scalability of business models, technology was adopted. It leads to higher costs at initial stage however; it brings better opportunities and optimisation of results. The Aadhar Card offered by the Unique Identification Development Authority of India The Aadhar Card offered by the UIDAI Unique Identification Development Authority of India is also a good instrument for connecting to all the people once it gets effectively operational.

The Direct Benefit Transfer scheme : the Aadhar number are going to be very significant in the years to come the RBI has accepted Aadhaar as a proof of identity and as fulfilling KYC requirements from the 1st of January, 2013. Nearly 11 lakh beneficiaries have received the direct benefits directly into their bank accounts.

Financial Inclusion Plans of banks for 3 years

RBI in January 2010 had advised all public and private sector banks to submit a Board approved three-year Financial Inclusion Plan (FIP) starting April 2010. Banks were advised to devise FIPs congruent with their business strategy and comparative advantage to make it an integral part of their corporate plans. These plans broadly included self-set targets in respect of rural brick and mortar branches opened, BCs employed, coverage of unbanked villages with population above 2000 as also other unbanked villages with population below 2000 through branches/BCs/other modes, no-frills accounts opened including through BC-ICT, Kisan Credit Cards (KCC) and General Credit Cards (GCC) issued, and other specific products designed by them to cater to the financially excluded segments. Banks were advised to integrate Board-approved FIPs with their business plans and to include the criteria on financial inclusion as a parameter in the performance evaluation of their staff. The implementation of these plans was closely monitored by the Reserve Bank on a monthly basis through a quantitative reporting format. Qualitative aspects under FIP was monitored through a qualitative report submitted by banks on a quarterly basis.

A snapshot of the progress made by banks under the 3 year Financial Inclusion Plan (April 10-March 13) for key parameters during the three year period is given below:-

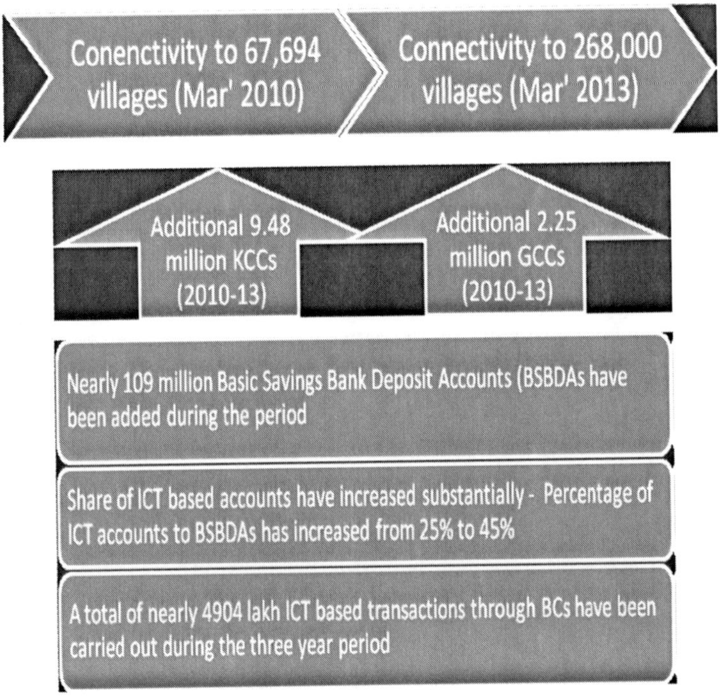

Challenges in Financial Inclusion

- Business Model: The business models are yet to emerge hence upscaling is not taking place. Banks need to evolve Appropriate Business Model. Credit linkage is vital Electronical Benefit Transfers are useful but to be users of financial products the SCRIPT—Savings Credit Remittance Insurance Pension and Transfers must be available both sides of the equation Access and Usage must be equally strong.
- BC model was envisaged as cheaper model of doorstep delivery as opposed to bank branches however the ease

and comfort of transaction for the customer is higher at bank branch level.

- Limitations and Lack of infrastructure for scaling up; physical and technical infrastructure roads and in several cases digital connectivity also hampers the process.
- The biggest challenge remains the need for attitudinal change and of empathy with the customer the need for a Buy In and of passionate belief and commitment to the idea of financial inclusion.

New banks

New banks are expected to bring sustainable business models, bring innovation in banking products and services and improve penetration of banking activities. We need new banks to bring new business models and for basic products and good banking. At mezzanine finance level, Banks also need sensitivity to default rates. They require an estimation of extent of losses, loss given default our message is that Financial Inclusion should be viewed neither from the prophet or the profit motive but as a pragmatic business opportunity by the

1. Progress in Modes of FI delivery

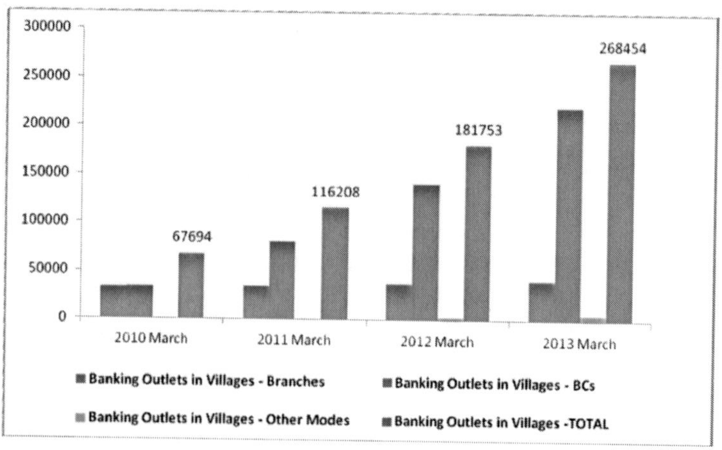

Source: FIP monthly return

Banks. I would do well to sum up with Dr P Chidambarams enunciation Dr Chidambarams enunciation state that the reforms since 1991 have changed the face of the Indian economy India is slowly but surely being recognised. Economic reforms have led to a sharp decline in people below the poverty line Sustainability of the reform process demands that all sections of society stand to gain from it only if the poorer sections of society also perceive a visible change in quality of their life while the reform process continue in our vibrant democracy.

2. Progress in KCCs and GCCs

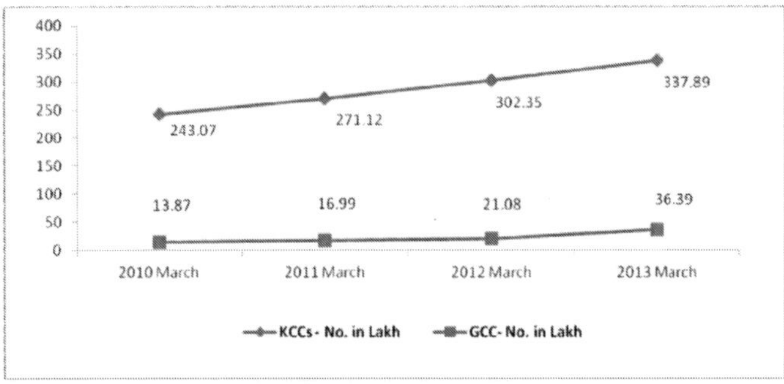

Source: FIP monthly return

3. Progress in number of Accounts

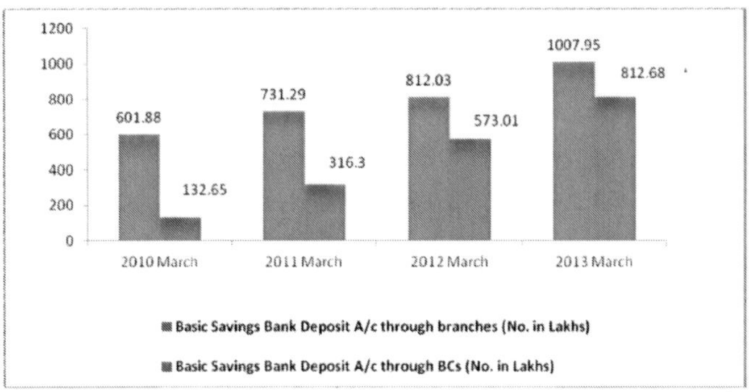

Source: FIP monthly return

4. Progress in O/D facility availed

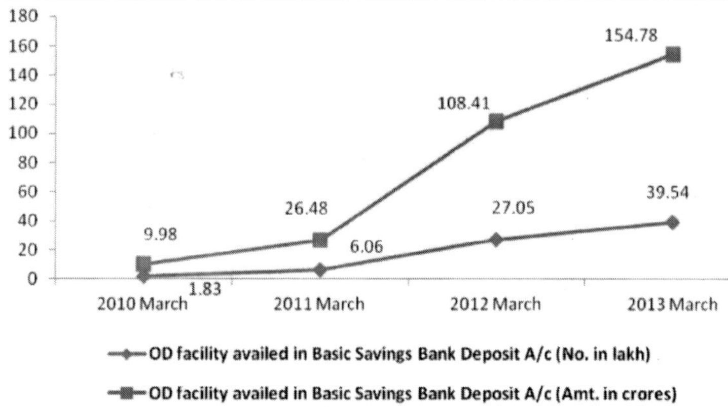

Source: FIP monthly return

References

1. RBI annual report
2. Report on **Trend and Progress** of Banking in India
3. *www.rbi.org.in/financialeducation/home.aspx*
4. http://rbidocs.rbi.org.in/rdocs/Speeches/PDFs/DGWB240212KC.pdf

7

Enabling Urban Microfinance

'Enabling Urban Microfinance' which is truly appropriate as it chooses to bring to centre stage issues of urban poverty. The scale of urban poverty in India is staggering. Current estimates suggest that 100 million poor people live in urban settlements comprising 40 per cent of the urban poor. These numbers are expected to rise. The prediction is that the total urban population of India will increase from 26 per cent of total population to over 36 per cent 50 per cent over the next twenty-five years. The number of urban poor would increase to 200-300 million. Until and unless cities are able to meet the growing needs of the expanding population, any advantages that economic opportunities might present the urban poor are likely to be outweighed by these factors for policy makers. Therefore, it means that the characteristics of urban development must be understood and included in initiatives to reduce overall poverty in India. The general consensus is that poverty can be most effectively addressed through economic development for which rapid urban development is a key driver. The National Institute of Urban Affairs estimates that urban India currently contributes more than 50 per cent of the country's GDP whilst accommodating less than a third of its population and this contribution is likely to increase to 60 per cent. The manufacturing and services sectors that are the most dynamic constituents of the Indian economy are predominantly urban. In addition, with agriculture exempt from Income Tax, the fiscal base of the economy is also disproportionately reliant on the urban economy as the proportion of people thronging urban areas continues to rise. The opportunities for poorer people to tap this growing economic base are enormous. In the wake of the often unplanned and unregulated urbanisation, the urban poor face physical, environmental, social and psychological problems. These impose a heavy burden of disease and inequity on the urban poor. They are compelled to live in squalid and untenable settlements and suffer the consequence of environmental degradation, resulting in ill-health, disability and loss of earnings. As cities grow, the pressure on existing services and associated infrastructure increases with resultant increase in the number of people without access to these services. The poor and therefore the most vulnerable are excluded and end up paying higher prices for lower quality products via the informal sector. Ironically, it is the poor who provide the essential services which keep cities functioning. The problem of service provision for the poor is compounded by the fact that decision makers do not necessarily know their needs or recognise their civic rights. Employment opportunities are severely restricted in urban areas. The main asset of the poor is the capacity to sell their labour. They have few other assets to build on. Their home may be rented or unfit for habitation, they may not own land or capital or cattle in towns and the social networks built by households over generations in the village are less strong in a dynamic urban context where people come and go. There is always lack of employment opportunities; the poor are not necessarily equipped with the skills and training to take advantage of newer opportunities in modern industry and in the nascent services sector. The formal wage sector has been unable to absorb the expanding labour force. As a result, there has been a massive growth in the informal sector and in the casualisation of employment, wages are forced downward, working conditions are not protected and unregulated access to opportunities is mediated by the capacity of individuals. A way of strengthening the bargaining power of the poor in urban contexts is through the formation of neighbourhood groups federated as Community Development Societies at the state level in addition to engaging in self-help schemes, as micro planning credit extension or directly operating and maintaining infrastructure. The CDS can create the infrastructure for receiving benefits of Government programs like the SJSRY. Access to financial services is a critical aspect of both, social development and social protection measures for the poor. These services create an opportunity for access to low interest credit which can be used for skill enhancement or micro enterprise growth. This also creates an opportunity to use savings and loans as a buffer against crisis. The poorer the household, the greater the desire to save financial services provide a critical safety net as well as a spring-board to advancement.

We need financial inclusion for the urban areas to link people to mainstream financial service providers so that they can access the entire suite of financial products and services from the mainstream financial institutions. Till this happens, we see an important role for microfinance. Conventional wisdom has it that access to microfinance services can enable the poor to smoothen their consumption, manage their risks better, build their assets, develop their microenterprises, enhance their income-earning capacity and enjoy an improved quality of life. The primary clientele of MFIs consists, almost by definition, of those who face severe barriers to access financial products from conventional financial institutions. These barriers comprise mainly high operational costs and risk factors. MFI clientele in urban areas may possess few negotiable assets and live in hostile environments where enforcement of property rights and other contracts is expensive and uncertain. MFIs can help in providing handholding support and markets typically for encouraging small service enterprises and cottage and small industries. Cottage industries have traditionally played an important role in the Indian economy. The bustling urban enclave of Dharavi is a case in point. It generates large volume employment and provides subsidiary services. The cottage and small industry's need for capital is not very large and they help in ensuring equitable income distribution. There are several artisan based clusters in India, these are skill-based and use simple manufacturing processes and technology. These clusters consist of unorganised sector, tiny units, with little access to market information. If credit and the entire range of banking products and services from mainstream financial institutions is made available, it will enable the small units to scale up and grow. The problems of urban poverty can only be addressed by encouraging the small scale service/ manufacturing enterprises which generate employment. Much has been written about the benefits and positive externalities of agglomeration. The cluster based approach to lending is intended to provide a full-service approach to cater to the diverse needs of the MSE sector. This can easily be achieved through extending banking services to recognised MSE clusters. A cluster based approach is beneficial: (a) in dealing with well-defined and recognised groups; (b) in ensuring the availability of appropriate information for risk assessment; (c) in monitoring by the lending institutions and (d) achieving reduction in costs.

United Nations Industrial Development Organisation (UNIDO) has identified 388 clusters spread over 21 states across various parts of the country. The Ministry of Micro, Small and Medium Enterprises has also approved a list of clusters under the Scheme of Fund for Regeneration of Traditional Industries (SFURTI) and the Micro and Small Enterprises Cluster Development Program (MSE-CDP) located in 121 Minority Concentration Districts. Accordingly, banks have been advised to take appropriate measures to improve the credit flow to the identified clusters of micro and small entrepreneurs from the minority communities residing in the minority concentrated districts of the country.

The RBI has advised banks to open more MSE focused branch offices at different MSE clusters which can also act as counselling centres for MSEs. Each lead bank of the district may adopt at least one cluster.

A Microfinance model which has been relatively successful is the SHG Bank linkage model which leverages the penetrative reach of the NGOs and civil society organisations and the financial strength and managerial expertise of the commercial banks. Starting from a modest scale as a pilot in the year 1992, the SHG-Bank linkage program linked 79.60 lakh savings-linked Self Help Groups (SHGs) covering over 10.3 crore poor households as on 31 March 2012. As per the NABARD Annual Report, however, the concentration of the SHG Bank linkage model continues to be to the southern states and is not evenly spread over the BIMARU (Bihar, Madhya Pradesh, Rajasthan and Uttar Pradesh) states. The second model is that of the registered NBFCs. These work as profit companies and extend loans to the entrepreneurial poor at the middle of the pyramid. This is an important distinction which needs to be emphasised as this brings into salience the continuing need and relevance of this model. There is an important role which both models of microfinance fulfill in the critical areas of training and capacity building of the poor. This enables them to graduate to larger loans and to setting up sustainable, scalable, self-sustaining enterprises and income-generating projects which pay for themselves.

The most serious limitation of microfinance is that it does not address all needs holistically. There is a problem of scaling up, and in this lies the promise of inclusive finance which links the poor to the formal financial system. There is a clear comparative competitive advantage which commercial banks enjoy in extending microfinance. As financial inclusion and basic bank deposit accounts are in place, banks should now move to the next step of crafting products and services for the poor. The advantages of banks over MFIs stem from their being regulated institutions fulfilling the necessary preconditions of ownership, financial disclosure and capital adequacy that help ensure prudent management. They have the physical infrastructure, large networked branches on Core Banking Solution from which to expand access and reach out to a substantial number of poorer clients. They have well established internal controls and administrative and accounting systems to keep track of a large number of high volume, small value transactions. As they are well capitalised, they are not dependent on scarce and volatile donor resources unlike NGOs and MFIs. Banks offer savings, remittance, loans and other financial products that are prima facie attractive to the hitherto unserved micro finance clients. On the downside, however, banks lack key ingredients, most of all, the financial methodologies to reach the low income population. There are several issues trammeling banks. The issue of commitment is fairly significant. The commitment of commercial banks (particularly the larger banks) to micro enterprise lending is often fragile and generally vests on the direction provided by one or two Board Members rather than it being rooted in their institutional mandate. Secondly, they are hampered by their organisational structures. Programs for the poor or microfinance programs need to be inserted into the larger bank structure while retaining flexibility, operational independence and autonomy. Banks need an appropriate financial methodology to work with efficiency. For gains in the penny economy, they need suitable financial methodology to service the micro enterprise sector and financial innovations that enable cost effective analysis of credit worthiness, the monitoring of relatively poor clients and acceptance of effective collateral substitutes. Human Resources also need attention given that microfinance programs differ so radically from traditional banking.

Banks need to recruit and retain specialised staff to manage these programs. Issues of recruitment, training and performance linked incentives for bank personnel need special consideration. Cost effectiveness is a critical issue. Microfinance programs are costly to administer given the overheads of banks. Despite these apparent disabilities, if banks work on this, they are ideally suited to microfinance provision. The targeted interventions of the Swarn Jayanti Shahri Rozgar Yojana and the District Industries centres which are designed to impart vocational training to the target group of this program as also the Prime Minister Rozgar Yojana have enjoyed only limited success ratios attributable not so much to infirmities in policy design issues; as to faulty implementation and poor targeting, lack of pre-disbursement credit assessment, coupled with poor post-disbursement credit supervision and no space for capacity building and handholding in between. The clear winner is financial inclusion. Savings credit extended to the urban poor by the banks can help grow the micro enterprises and power economic growth. Let us a take simple example. Micro enterprises like the ubiquitous street-corner *paan wallah* who runs a small self-sustaining enterprise, if extended credit by banks, can expand his business, can employ two other helpers. Such micro enterprises have tremendous potential to create employment and put in place virtuous cycles of economic growth. How do we enable micro finance in the urban areas well to be facile? It is not an easy task. First, we need to build a suitable framework. The framework will need to be localised, customised and contextualised to suit the differing needs of different localities, and addressing issues such as the development of an overarching macro policy environment, long-term financial sustainability of microfinance institutions, increasing outreach by capacity building and effective governance, and broad-based research and monitoring/evaluation. Its linkage to other developmental priorities, particularly those related to environmental issues at the local level will be an important justification in its adoption. There is need to recognise the importance of bringing people from the margins to the mainstream of economic activity as producers of goods and services. The challenge of financial exclusion is widespread in metropolitan areas, especially among the disadvantaged and low-income groups. To facilitate doorstep banking to the excluded segment of the urban poor and provide an institutional mechanism for co-ordination between the government and banks, lead bank responsibility has been assigned to 16 districts in metropolitan areas, thus bringing the entire country under the fold of the lead bank scheme and covering a total of 659 districts under the lead bank scheme.

The Peruvian economist Hernando de Soto showcased the unreported, unrecorded activity of a vibrant informal sector whose participants remained at the margins. It successfully created many small entrepreneurs but could not secure credit from mainstream financial institutions as they lacked legal ownership of their property, making it difficult for them not only to obtain credit, but sell the business, or expand. They cannot seek legal remedies to business conflicts in court, since they do not have legal ownership. Lack of information on income prevents governments from collecting taxes and acting for the public welfare. "The existence of such massive exclusion generates two parallel economies, legal and extra-legal. An elite minority enjoys the economic benefits of the mainstream financial institutions, law and globalisation, while the majority of entrepreneurs are stuck in poverty." He terms them extra-legal. To survive, to protect their assets, and to do as much business as possible, the extra-legal create their own rules. But because these local arrangements are full of shortcomings and are not easily enforceable, the extra-legal also create their own social, political and economic problems that affect the society at large. It is essential that these issues are given due attention of policy makers to encourage and promote the growth of micro enterprises.

The Prime Minister's task force (TKA Nair 2010) laid emphasis on the micro enterprise sector which generates opportunities for self-employment and stipulated that 60 per cent of MSE advances should go to the micro enterprises. MSMEs make a significant contribution in the country's GDP, manufacturing output, exports and employment generation. MSMEs contribute 8 per cent of the country's GDP, 45 per cent of the manufactured output and 40 per cent of our exports. The labour and capital ratio in MSMEs and the overall growth in the MSMEs is much higher than in the larger industries. MSMEs are better dispersed. In view of these factors, MSMEs are important for achieving national objectives of growth with equity and inclusion. As per the quick estimates of 4th All-India Census of MSMEs, the number of enterprises is estimated to be about 26 million and these provide employment to an estimated 60 million persons. Of the 26 million MSMEs, only 1.5 million are in the registered segment while the remaining 24.5 million (94 per cent) are in the unregistered segment. The state-wise distribution of MSMEs shows that more than 55 per cent of these enterprises are in 6 states, namely, Uttar Pradesh, Maharashtra, Tamil Nadu, West Bengal, Andhra Pradesh and Karnataka. Fewer MSMEs are owned by women, the unorganised sector, in which enterprises are typically established through own funds or funds obtained through non-institutional sources, they lack managerial bandwidth, do not have established channels for marketing and are centred around a single traditional technology. More than 94 per cent of MSMEs are unregistered, with a large number established in the informal or unorganised sector.

The National Commission for Enterprises in the Unorganised Sector (NCEUS) defines unorganised sector as enterprise employing less than 10 workers. It has estimated such enterprises at 58 million with employment generated of 104 million persons. Shortage of capital, particularly working capital, is the major problem faced by the enterprises in the unorganised sector. Further, the field studies undertaken by National Commission for Enterprises in the Unorganised Sector indicate that seasonality of markets is another hassle. In addition to the growth potential of the sector and its critical role in the manufacturing and value chains, the heterogeneity and the unorganized nature of the Indian MSMEs are important aspects that need to be factored into policy making and program implementation. The policies and programs for the micro and small enterprises in the unorganized sector would need to address their survival strategies and should be in the direction of providing livelihood alternatives such as social security, skill formation and credit. On the other hand, policies/ programs for the larger sized MSMEs need to address issues relating to growth marketing, access to raw material, credit, skill development and technology upgradation.

Credit to MSMEs by SCBS

Credit to Micro and Small Enterprises by SCBs

As on last Friday of March	*Outstanding Cred it to MSE sector*		*MSE creditas percent of ANBC*
	Number of accounts (in million)	*Amount outstanding ('billion)*	
1	2	3	4
2012	9.86 (6.0)	5,276.85 (10.3)	16.5
2013*	11.23 (13.9)	6,847.97 (29.8)	14.7

*:As on March 31, 2013.

Note: 1. Data for 2013 are provisional.

2. Figures in parentheses indicate y-o-y change in per cent.

The millenium development goal is halving poverty by 2015. If this is to be attained, it is central to address the concerns around urban poverty through strategies of increasing income to make basic needs more affordable. If our cities are not to become centres of squalor and crime, these issues will require urgent redress.

References

1. RBI Annual Report
2. Report on Trend and Progress of Banking in India
3. *www.rbi.org.in/financialeducation/home.aspx*
4. http://rbidocs.rbi.org.in/rdocs/Speeches/PDFs/DGWB240212KC.pdf
5. Ministry of Labour and Employment, Government of India.

8

Technology as an Enabler of Financial Inclusion

Financial Inclusion is not a new dispensation. Bank Nationalisation in 1969 and the tremendous push for branch building which followed in its wake were attempts at including the excluded. Despite geographical and functional reach of the Commercial Banks, large numbers of people remain excluded. Small and Marginal farmers, women, unorganised sector workers, artisans, self-employed, unemployed, pensioners, etc. remain excluded from the opportunities and services provided by the formal financial sector.

If this is something we have been working on since 1969 what is the difference now? Critically its technology which enables undreamt of outreach. For Financial Inclusion to succeed and an effective Business and Delivery model to be in place it is essential that servicing costs are brought down and large numbers covered rapidly. This exponential growth is a possible dream with the use of technology.

Banks including RRBs, have migrated to Core Banking System (CBS), have developed in built capability to provide remittances using electronic payment systems such as the Real Time Gross Settlement System (RTGS), National Electronic Funds Transfer (NEFT), National Electronic Clearing Service

(NECS), Immediate Payments Service (IMPS), Aadhaar Enabled Payment Systems (AEPS) etc. Banks are increasingly using alternate channels of delivery; the number of ATMs are even more than the number of branches. All the rural branches are expected to have an e-ATM in place in the near future.

Access to finance for those who are getting crowded out of the credit markets is an equally important element. Therefore, the Reserve Bank has reinforced its efforts to improve financial access, especially for small businesses and individual households. The RBI has set up a Committee on Comprehensive Financial Services for Small Businesses and Low Income Households under the Chairmanship of Dr. Nachiket Mor a Director on the RBI Central Board of Directors. The mandate of the Mor Committee is to frame a clear and detailed vision of financial Inclusion and Financial Deepening in India and to lay down a set of design principles that will guide the development of institutional frameworks and regulation for ensuring these outcomes.

Financial Inclusion is defined by the RBI "as the process of ensuring access to financial services and timely and adequate credit where needed by vulnerable groups such as the weaker sections and low income groups at an affordable cost from Mainstream financial institutions".

In January 2010, the Reserve Bank advised all public and private sector banks to submit a Board-approved three-year Financial Inclusion Plan (FIP) starting in April 2010. They were advised to devise FIPs congruent with their business strategy and comparative advantage and to make FIPs an integral part of their corporate plans. These plans include: self-set targets for rural brick and mortar branches opened; BCs deployed; coverage of unbanked villages with population above and below 2,000 through branches/ BCs/ other modes; no-frills accounts opened, including through BC-ICT; Kisan Credit Cards (KCC) and General Credit Cards (GCC) issued; and other products designed for financially excluded segments. Banks were advised to integrate the Board-approved FIPs with their business plans and to include the criteria on financial inclusion as a parameter in the performance evaluation of their staff.

We have adopted a planned and structured approach to achieve Financial Inclusion through the financial inclusion Plans, as a self set targeted intervention with measurable and monitorable outcomes. The implementation of these plans is closely monitored by the Reserve Bank on a monthly basis through a quantitative reporting format. The qualitative aspects of the FIPs are monitored through a qualitative report submitted by banks every quarter.

Periodic monitoring of progress – Quantitative and Qualitative parameters. These Board approved plans are the subject of an annual comprehensive review – Deputy Governor holds one to one meetings with CMDs of major banks to discuss the progress made by them against their own self set goals, the barriers to progress, the initiatives of their Banks and the way forward. RRBs, having migrated to CBS in the end of 2011, have also formulated similar comprehensive FIPs.

PROGRESS

A snapshot of the progress made by banks under the 3-year FIP (April 2010 – March 2013) on key parameters itself speaks of the journey travelled so far:—

i. Banking outlets in villages have increased to nearly 2,68,000 from 67,694 outlets in March 2010.

ii. About 7,400 rural branches have been opened during this 3-year period compared with a reduction of about 1300 rural branches during the last two decades.

iii. Nearly 109 million Basic Savings Bank Deposit Accounts (BSBDAs) have been added, taking the total number of BSBDA to 182 million. The share of ICT-based accounts has increased substantially. The percentage of ICT accounts to total BSBDAs increased from 25 per cent in March 2010 to 45 per cent in March 2013.

iv. With the addition of nearly 9.48 million farm sector households during this period, 33.8 million households have been provided with small entrepreneurial credit as at the end of March 2013.

v. With the addition of nearly 2.24 million non-farm sector households during this period, 3.6 million households have been provided with small entrepreneurial credit as at the end of March 2013.

About 490 million transactions have been carried out in ICT-based accounts through BCs during the three-year period. The number of transactions through ICT-based BC outlets, though increasing, is still very low when compared with the manifold increase in the number of banking outlets and the number of accounts. The focus on monitoring is now more on the usage of these accounts, which is to be monitored through the number and value of transactions in BSBDAs and on the credit disbursed through ICT-based BC outlets.

Financial Inclusion Plan 2013—16

The first three-year Financial Inclusion Plans of banks for the period 2010—2013 has ended. Although there has been reasonable progress in the penetration of banking services and opening of basic bank accounts, the number of transactions through ICT-based BC outlets is still low. To continue the process of ensuring access to banking services to the excluded, banks are to draw up a 3-year FIP for the period 2013–16. Banks have now been advised that their FIPs should be disaggregated to the branch level. The disaggregation of the plans is being done to ensure the involvement of all stakeholders in the financial inclusion efforts.

Direct Benefit Transfer

The Reserve Bank has played a proactive role in the rollout of the Direct Benefit Transfer (DBT) scheme. State-Level Bankers' Committee (SLBC) Convenor Banks were advised to co-ordinate with the government functionaries for implementation of Aadhaar-enabled payments. Banks have to expedite the process of opening bank accounts in camp mode and seeding of accounts with Aadhaar numbers. The status of the rollout of Aadhaar-enabled payments is a regular agenda item for discussion in SLBC meetings as part of Financial Inclusion/Electronic Benefit Transfer (EBT) implementation. The DBT was rolled out in 43 districts in the first phase from January 1, 2013, and has been extended to 78 districts from July 1, 2013. Eventually, all districts in the country will be covered.

11. High-Level Financial Inclusion Advisory Committee: Moving towards universal financial inclusion has been a national commitment as well as a policy priority for the Reserve Bank. In order to spearhead efforts towards greater financial inclusion, the Reserve Bank has constituted a Financial Inclusion Advisory Committee (FIAC) chaired by a Deputy Governor. The FIAC has a few Directors from the Central Board of the Reserve Bank, experts drawn from NGOs and civil society representatives as members. The expertise and experience of the members will be leveraged: to develop viable and sustainable banking service delivery models that provide accessible and affordable financial services; to develop products and processes for rural as well as urban consumers who are currently outside the banking network; and to create an appropriate regulatory framework to ensure that financial inclusion and financial stability move together.

Financial Literacy:

Building financial capability through financial literacy is a key component of financial inclusion. It means providing financial education so that individuals can identify and use appropriate financial products and services in order to build and preserve their assets over time. It should make people better informed, better educated and more confident, able to take greater responsibility for their financial affairs and able to play a more active role in the market for financial services.

718 FLCs have been set up as at the end of March 2013. A total of 2.2 million people have been educated through indoor education to walk-in persons and through outdoor activities such as awareness camps/choupals, goshtis, seminars and lectures in a one-year period, from April 2012 to March 2013. It has advised all FLCs and rural branches of Scheduled Commercial Banks to conduct a minimum of one outdoor financial literacy camp every month.

National Strategy for Financial Education (NSFE):

The NSFE has been prepared under the aegis of a Technical Group of the Financial Stability Development Council (FSDC). The NSFE will be implemented in a timeframe of five years and aims to establish initial contact with 500 million adults and educate them on key savings, protection and investment-related products so that they are empowered to take prudent financial decisions. It also seeks to create awareness about consumer protection and the grievance redressal mechanisms available in the country. Under the NSFE, a National Centre for Financial Education (NCFE) is proposed to be set up as an institutional mechanism to co-ordinate the efforts of all financial sector regulators. The NCFE will launch a common website on financial education for the country.

Now to flag some issues:

The World Bank (2012) Findex Survey on,"Measuring Financial Inclusion Indicators" World Bank Policy Research Working Paper #6025 states that in India only 35 per cent of adults had access to a formal Bank account, only 2 per cent of adults use a formal account to receive remittances from relatives and 4 per cent use an account to receive government payments. These are 2011 figures and further ground has been covered but the challenges still remain.

Financial Inclusion Plan – Summary progress of all banks including RRBs

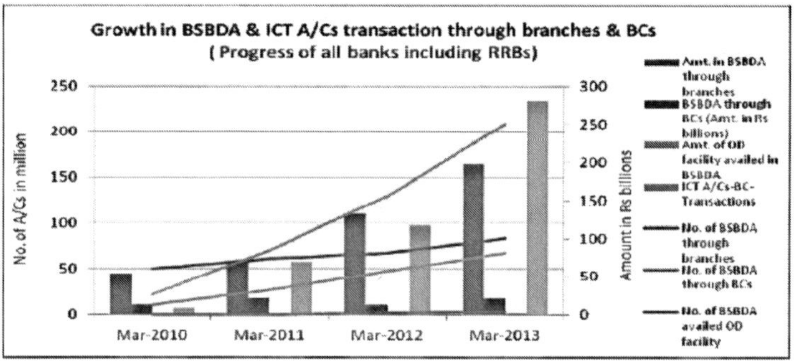

Source: FIP monthly return

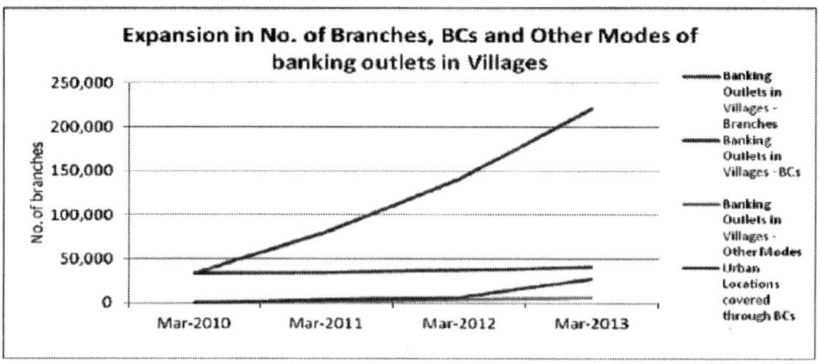

Source: FIP monthly return

17. The first of many questions is why this specification of Mainstream Financial Institutions, why a bank led model? For three reasons inter alia, firstly Bank deposits are guaranteed by the Deposit Insurance Guarantee Corporation and the depositor's money remains safe and secure. Secondly, Banks are Regulated and well capitalised institutions subjects to RBIs direct control exercised through the processes of onsite and offsite inspections and supervision. Regulation is aimed at protecting depositors' interests, orderly development and conduct of banking operations and fostering the overall health of the banking system. Thirdly, we have a robust widespread banking system unlike several other countries. For these countries where the Banking brick and mortar network is not

present the only way forward is to leverage technology. It is simpler to build digital gateways across Africa while for us let me say we use the Banking System because it is there as we have penetrative outreach through Commercial Banks, with vast network of branches we have followed a multi pronged approach to financial inclusion and this has enabled real gains.

Thirdly, why the close supervision of the BC Model and restriction of the area within which the BC must operate. Firstly, because it is operationally feasible for the BC to provide intensive services within a defined radius and secondly, because Cash management is a major issue. Cash collected by the BC is ultimately the Banks cash and it is the credibility of the Bank which is at stake. Thirdly, the customer is not a customer of the BC but of the Bank. The BC is envisaged merely as a pass through agent who enables extension in the penetrative reach of the Bank and through the ICT model and by using a hand-held technology device enables banking services and other services such as the electronic benefit transfer services at the doorstep of the borrower.

Combination of Branch and Branchless Banking

As a prerequisite to the implementation of the Direct Benefit Transfers (DBTs), every eligible individual should have a bank account. Further, to make disbursements at the doorstep through the ICT-based BC model, banking outlets, either through brick and mortar branches or the branchless mode, are required in all villages across the country. For this to succeed, it is important that quality services are provided through the new ICT-based BC outlets. Therefore, an intermediary low-cost brick-and-mortar structure is required between the base branches and BC locations. This will provide timely support to BC outlets, ensure close supervision of BC operations and give them credibility and increase people's confidence in BC services. Hence, banks have been advised to plan for an increase in the proportion of branches that cover unbanked areas. Banks have also been advised to consider setting up Financial Inclusion Centres, which would act as centres exclusively focussing on customers serviced through BC's.

To step up the opening of branches in rural areas, RBI has mandated banks to open at least 25 per cent of the branches in unbanked rural centres. To help facilitate in achieving this mandate, banks have been advised to open small intermediary brick and mortar structures between the base branch and the unbanked villages. The idea is to create an eco-system for ensuring efficient delivery of services, efficiency in cash management, redressal of customer grievances and closer supervision of BC operations. To further encourage the banks in pursuing this mandate, banks have been advised to consider frontloading (prioritising) the opening of branches in unbanked rural centres over a three year cycle co-terminus with their FIPs. This is expected to facilitate quicker branch expansion in unbanked rural centres.

Along with increasing brick and mortar presence through branch expansion, RBI has also encouraged banks to adopt other branchless modes such as BC outlets, other modes such as Kiosks, off-site Rural ATMs, mobile vans, etc. so as to resolve the last mile connectivity issues.

Enlarging the Universe of BC's

The universe of BCs has been enlarged as we go along and we have been enabled the entry of For Profit companies in 2010. We have done this as we want to leverage their well established distribution networks especially in the rural heart land for the extension of Financial Inclusion to reach the unreached.

Tapping Technology Platforms

To enable successful financial inclusion, innovation of products for the specific needs of the poor is not only necessary but also an essential condition. Today, banks can provide a bouquet of financial services through the various networks of agents and branches by leveraging and fine tuning technology platforms. Technology holds the key to providing models for efficient delivery of small value transactions in large volumes while reaping economies of scale. The implementation of such effective, scalable and platform-independent technology will help drive down the cost of providing banking services to the poor.

The Immediate Payments Service (IMPS), an instantaneous 24x7 electronic funds transfer system has been developed by the National Payment Corporation of India (NPCI). IMPS facilitate customers to use mobile instruments as a channel for accessing their bank accounts and put high interbank fund transfers in a secured manner with immediate confirmation features.

Aadhaar Enabled Payment Systems (AEPS)

The AEPS architecture designed by Unique Identification Authority of India (UIDAI) in collaboration with the NPCI is a platform which banks can leverage upon for expanding their financial inclusion initiatives. The basic premise of AEPS is that one BC Customer Service Point (CSP) will have the ability to service customers of many banks based on the unique bio-metric identification data stored in the Aadhaar database. The AEPS platform is expected to empower a bank customer to use Aadhaar as his/her identity to access the respective Aadhaar enabled bank account and perform basic banking transactions like balance enquiry, cash withdrawal and deposit through the BC.

Conclusion

RBI has adopted a Bank led model but one which is essentially Model Neutral. We have tried to create an enabling environment that facilitates competition and fosters innovation.

Once the financial Inclusion plans are implemented customers will be able to transact electronically with each other as well as with individuals and firms outside the village. This will in days to come reduce dependence on Cash and High volumes will lower the costs of transactions.

International experience reflects that digitising social transfers is an effective way of bringing the excluded within the financial system the Business Case for Banks in this segment, as of now, depends on government payments. Going forward we hope that Banks will introduce new products and services crafted to the needs and income streams of poor borrowers which will enable self sustaining financial inclusion.

As Banking is a public good this is essential in the interests of Public Policy.

References

1. *www.rbi.org.in* › Publication ,
2. uidai.gov.in/authentication-2/payments.htm
3. *Report on Trend and Progress* of Banking in India
4. *Annual Report - Reserve Bank of India*

9

Financial Inclusion Journey so far and Road Ahead

The need for broad based diversified growth leading to rapid reduction in poverty has been clearly understood. Reserve Bank's developmental initiatives over the next few quarters will rest on five pillars, one important pillar is Financial Inclusion i.e. Expanding access to finance to small and medium enterprises, the unorganised sector, the poor, and remote and underserved areas of the country through technology, new business practices, and new organisational structures; that is, we need financial inclusion.

The expectations of poor people from the financial system are principally ease of access, security and safety of deposits, low transaction costs, convenient operating time, minimum paper work, ability to transact easily effect frequent deposits, avail quick and easy access to credit and other products including remittances suitable to their income streams and consumption patterns. The provision of uncomplicated, small, affordable products can help bring low income families into the formal financial sector. Low-income households in the informal or subsistence economy often have to borrow from friends, family or usurious moneylenders. They have little awareness and practically no access to financial services that could protect their financial resources in exigent circumstances such as illness, property damage or death of the primary breadwinner. Taking into account their seasonal inflow of income from agricultural operations, migration from one place to another seasonal and irregular work availability and income, the existing financial system needs to be designed to suit their requirements and to be more responsive to their needs. The mainstream financial institutions like banks have an important role to play in this effort not as a social obligation but as a pure business proposition. The push for financial Inclusion has come from the financial regulator/Government at the level of macro policy the Banks have to translate this to concrete outcomes at ground level to spur financial deepening.

Having said this let us discuss through financial inclusion journey so far and the way forward. "Financial Inclusion" was formally articulated by the Governor RBI in the Annual Policy Statement of 2005-06, while recognising the concerns in regard to the banking practices that tend to exclude rather than attract vast sections of population, urged banks to review their existing practices to align them with the objective of financial inclusion. The main features of the approach involve 'connecting' people with the banking system and not just credit. "Financial exclusion is mainly in two ways one is exclusion from the payments system i.e. not having access to a bank account and the second type of exclusion is from formal credit markets requiring the excluded to approach informal and exploitive markets". Taking a clue from the Committee on Financial Institution which first studied the issue of Financial Inclusion in depth we have defined Financial Inclusion as the process of ensuring access to financial services and timely and adequate credit where needed by vulnerable groups such as weaker sections at an affordable cost from Mainstream Financial Institution. Financial institutions have the capacity to provide full services and meet the SCRIPT by extending complete breadth of services: Savings, Credit, Remittance, Insurance, Pension, Payments transactions. Mainstream Institution i.e. banks must fulfill their core function of intermediating and transferring resources from surplus to deficit units but both deficit and surplus units are those with low incomes consequently the RBI moved swiftly to enforce multiple policy level changes ranging from provision of new products, relaxation of regulatory guidelines and other supportive measures to achieve sustainable and scalable financial inclusion. To ensure that customers who are linked to the banking system are provided with all the basic financial products that are required to enhance their income generation capacity thus helping them to work their own way out of poverty.

Milestones of our journey so far

I. Opening of No-Frills accounts: In November 2005, a new concept of basic banking 'no-frills' account with 'nil' or very low minimum balance was introduced to make such accounts accessible to vast sections of the population. In 2012 the nomenclature was changed to Basic Savings Bank Deposit Accounts (BSBDAs) for all individuals with zero minimum balance and facility of ATM card/ Debit card, there is no charge in deposits and upto four withdrawals in a month are allowed. To summarise, every person has the right to open a basic account. Banks have been advised to provide small overdrafts in such accounts to meet emergency credit requirement in hassle free manner.

II. Engaging Business Correspondents: In January 2006, the Reserve Bank permitted banks to engage Business Facilitators (BFs) and Business Correspondents (BCs) as intermediaries for providing financial and banking services. The BC Model allows banks to provide door step delivery of services especially to do 'cash in - cash out' transactions, thus addressing the 'last mile' problem. The list of eligible individuals/entities who can be engaged as BCs is being widened from time to time we have adopted a test and learn approach to this process. In September 2010, RBI has allowed for profit organisations excluding NBFCs to operate as BCs. Banks can now leverage on the penetrative network of mobile companies. Mobile network companies have joined hands with banks to make available banking services to India's unbanked population. The agents of mobile companies work as BC thus expunding the outreach of banks. Customer Service Providers (CSPs) and provide BC services, thus expanding the outreach of banks.

III. Use of Technology : Recognising that technology has the potential to address the issues of outreach and credit delivery in rural and remote areas, in a viable manner, commercial banks were advised to implement CBS so as to enable them to make effective use of ICT, to provide door step banking services through Business Correspondents Model wherein the accounts can be operated by even illiterate customers by using biometrics, thus, ensuring the security of transactions and enhancing confidence in the banking system. RRBs, due to their proximity to rural areas, have the strength to scale financial inclusion, they roped in by bringing them on the CBS platform. A robust payment system is an essential adjunct of Financial Inclusion this is an extremely important area.

IV. Relaxation of KYC norms: The strict KYC norms inhibited linkage of common people with the Banking System. Know Your Customer (KYC) requirements for opening bank accounts were relaxed for small accounts in August 2005, thereby simplifying procedure. To facilitate easy opening of accounts especially for small customers, Know Your Customer (KYC) guidelines have been simplified to such an extent that small accounts can be opened without any documentation by just giving a self certification in the presence of bank officials. Further, in order to leverage on the initiative of UIDAI, we have allowed 'Aadhaar', the unique identification number being issued to all citizens of India, to be used as one of the eligible document for meeting the KYC requirement for opening a bank account. Recently in September 2013, we have allowed banks to provide e-KYC services based on Aadhaar, thus paving the way for account opening of all the people.

V. Simplified branch authorisation: To address the issue of uneven spread of bank branches, in December 2009, domestic scheduled commercial banks were permitted to freely open branches in Tier 3 to Tier 6 centres with population of less than

50,000 under general permission, subject to reporting. In the second quarter review of Monetary Policy Branch authorisation has been relaxed to the extent that banks do not require prior permission to open branches even in tier/centres, subject to reporting.

VI. Opening of branches in unbanked rural centres: To further step up the opening of branches in rural areas, banks have been mandated to open at least 25 per cent of the branches in unbanked rural centres. To help facilitate achieving this mandate, banks have been advised to open small intermediary brick and mortar structures between the base branch and the unbanked villages. The idea is to create an eco-system for ensuring efficient delivery of services, efficiency in cash management, redressal of customer grievances and closer supervision of BC operations. To further encourage the banks to pursue this mandate, banks have been advised to consider front-loading (prioritising) the opening of branches in unbanked rural centres over a three year cycle coterminus with their FIPs. This is expected to facilitate quicker branch expansion in unbanked rural centres.

VII. Roadmap for providing Banking Services in unbanked villages with population more than 2000: With financial inclusion gaining increasing recognition as a business opportunity and with all banks geared to increase presence, we adopted a phase-wise approach to provide banking services in all unbanked villages in the country. On completion of the first phase where nearly 74000 villages with population more than 2000 were provided with a banking outlet, we are now in the second phase where the remaining unbanked villages, numbering close to 4,90,000, are identified in villages with less than 2000 population and allocated to banks, for opening of banking outlets by March 2016.

VIII. Direct Benefit Transfer: The introduction of Direct Benefit Transfer validating identity through Aadhaar will facilitate delivery of social welfare benefits by direct credit to the bank accounts of beneficiaries. Government proposes to route all social security payments through the banking network using the Aadhaar based platform. In order to ensure smooth roll out of the Government's Direct Benefit Transfer (DBT) initiative, banks have been advised to open accounts of all eligible individuals in camp mode with the support of local government authorities, seed the existing and new accounts with Aadhaar numbers and put in place an effective mechanism to monitor and review the progress in implementation of DBT.

IX. Financial Literacy: Financial Literacy is an important adjunct for promoting financial inclusion; We have adopted an integrated approach, wherein our efforts towards Financial Inclusion and Financial Literacy go hand in hand. Through Financial literacy and education, we disseminate information on the general banking concepts to diverse target groups, including school and college students, women, rural and urban poor, pensioners and senior citizens to enable them to make informed financial decisions. To ensure that the initiatives on the supply side are supported by initiatives on the demand side, there are nearly 800 financial literacy centres set up by banks. In addition to this we are leveraging the infrastructure created at the state level, comprising of State Level Bankers Committee (SLBC) at the Apex which is ably supported by the Lead District Managers (LDMs) at the District level. A mass scale Financial Literacy Program has been designed with an objective to integrate the financially excluded population with low level of income and low literacy level with the formal financial system. Financial Literacy Centres organise Outdoor Literacy camps which are spread over a period of three months and delivered in three phases wherein along with creating awareness, accounts are also opened in the Literacy camps The program has been received well on the ground as an integrated approach of financial inclusion through creating awareness and providing access simultaneously.

X. Financial Inclusion Plan of banks: We have encouraged banks to adopt a structured and planned approach to financial inclusion with commitment at the highest levels, through preparation of Board approved Financial Inclusion Plans (FIPs). The first phase of FIPs was implemented over the period 2010–2013. The Reserve Bank has used the FIPs to gauge the performance of banks under their FI initiatives. In this direction we have put in place a structured and comprehensive monitoring mechanism for evaluating banks' performance vis-a-vis their targets. To ensure support of the Top Management of the Bank to the Financial Inclusion process and to ensure accountability of the senior functionaries of the bank, one on one annual review meetings, chaired by Deputy Governor, held with CMDs/CEOs of banks.

A snapshot of the progress made by banks under the 3 years Financial Inclusion Plan (April 10 – March 13) for key parameters during the three year period indicates that banking outlets increased to nearly 2,68,000 banking as on March 13 as against 67,694 banking outlets in villages in March 2010. 7400 rural branches have been opened during this period of 3 years. Nearly 109 million Basic Savings Bank Deposit Accounts (BSBDAs) have been added taking the total no of BSBDA to 182 million. Share of ICT based accounts have increased substantially–BSBDAs has increased from 25 per cent in March 10 to 45 per cent in March 13. About 4904 lakh transactions have been carried out in ICT based accounts through BCs during the three years period.

After completion of the first plan period, we realised that there is a access usage conundrum. A large banking network has been created along with the opening of large number of bank accounts. However, it is clear that simply creating the banking infrastructure and opening bank accounts will not fulfill the objectives of achieving total Financial Inclusion. To take the process, forward banks have been advised to draw up fresh three year Financial Inclusion Plans for the period 2013–16. To ensure involvement of all the stake holders in the FI efforts and to ensure uniformity in the reporting structure under the Financial Inclusion Plan, banks have to ensure that the FIPs prepared by them are disaggregated and percolate down to the branch level. The focus under the new plan is to ensure that the large bankings network created is utilised for extending other products viz. credit products, which will help make the business more viable for banks. This would also ensure that the large numbers of accounts opened see an equally large volume of transactions taking place and people reap the benefits of getting linked to the formal financial institutions.

XI. Robust Institutional Mechanism – Over the years one of major achievements and strength has been the creation of a robust institutional mechanism which supports the roll out of banking services across the country. The Financial Stability and Development Council (FSDC) has been set up which is headed by the Finance Minister. There is a Sub-Group of the FSDC headed by the Governor, RBI and within that a Technical Group, headed by Deputy Governor, exclusively mandated to address issues related to financial inclusion and financial literacy. In order to gauge the performance of banks and to continuously review the various models adopted under Financial Inclusion. RBI has constituted a Financial Inclusion Advisory Committee (FIAC), headed by a Deputy Governor.

XII. Road Ahead – Extending the frontiers of the formal financial system : For growth to be truly inclusive it requires broadening and deepening the reach of banking. A wider distribution and access of financial services helps both consumers and producers increase welfare and productivity. Such access is especially powerful for the poor as it provides them opportunities to build savings, make investments, avail credit and more important, insure themselves against income shocks and emergencies. As the real economy is dynamic, it is imperative that the banking system is flexible and competitive to cope with multiple objectives and demands made on it by various constituents of the economy. To address the issues of urban poverty The Bandhan IDFC have been brought the metropolitan urban areas like Mumbai New Payment Banks under the planning and review mechanism of the lead bank scheme.

New Bank Licenses: To ensure that the banking system grows in size and sophistication to meet the needs of a modern economy and for improving access to banking services, we are in the process of evaluation of new bank license applications. They are expected to go beyond simply beefing New small financial banks which are proposed to be setup new payment Banks infrastructure like handheld devices, smart cards, better vendors and service providers, etc. necessary to scale up the FI activities. These new banks are expected to bring new technology innovative models, bring in new business and delivery models which would speed up the roll out of financial services to remote areas. Financial Inclusion will work on the ACTA model Accounts, Cash in Cash out, Transactions and Adjacencies which will help to build a revenue stream.

Business and Delivery Model: We face several challenges in implementation of financial inclusion policies. Of 2,68,000 banking outlets nearly 2,21,000 are BC's i.e., nearly 82 per cent. Sustainability and scalability of the BC model is essential. More and more innovative products will have to be introduced which would benefit both banks as well as the rural people and at the same time make the BC model more viable. A review of the cash management practices for delivery of banking services through the branchless modes also needs to be implemented for ensuring scaling up of the various models.

Usage of banking services: Using the first phase of our FI initiative, we have successfully opened 74,000 outlets in the rural areas. Going forward idea is to enable more and larger transactions in these accounts by providing more credit products, which will not only help rural people to avail of credit at comparatively lower rates of interest but at the same time also make the BC model viable for banks. Skills and capacity building of BC is as important as ensuring an adequate revenue stream. An ATM network is also in place.

Financial Education has been adopted: An integrated approach for financial inclusions wherein the supply side initiatives are supported by initiatives on the demand side. In this direction banks have to support financial literacy and awareness drives to make people understand the benefits of linking with the banking system. Inclusion of Financial Education in the school curriculum educate children about the benefits of banks and banking services. This will go a long way in inculcating responsible banking habits at a young age. The Technical Group of the FSDC has designed a National Strategy on Financial Education.

Collaborative efforts: Finally, financial inclusion cannot be achieved without the active involvement of all stakeholders like RBI, other financial regulators, banks, governments, NGOs, civil societies, etc. The current policy objective of inclusive growth with financial stability cannot be achieved without ensuring universal financial inclusion. Banks cannot achieve this on their own, an entire support system has to partner with them in this mission. All the stakeholders need to join hands and make it possible. The support of policymakers, regulators, governments, IT solution providers and public at large would bring a decisive transformational change in Indian banking.

We have to reach everyone, however remote or small, with financial services. Financial inclusion does not just mean credit for productive purposes; it means credit for healthcare emergencies or to pay lumpy school or college fees. It means a safe means of remunerated savings, and an easy way to make payments and remittances. It means insurance and pensions. It means financial literacy and consumer protection. The need for large banks like the ones represented in this room to move beyond simply opening bank accounts to ensuring that poor customers are confident and comfortable enough to use them. Innovation in reaching out to the underserved customer, rather than simply posting higher numbers in branches or bank accounts opened, has to be part of our efforts. We need a frugal, trustworthy, and effective Indian model for financial inclusion. Our measure of success should be the jobs that are created, not by giving government subsidies or protections to labour-intensive industries or sectors but by developing a facilitating, though competitive, environment that will result in the emergence of the best solutions. This is the suggested way forward for meeting our dream of Financial Inclusion. Some of the measures are already in the pipeline. The committee on technology will also guide us on how to expand mobile banking in India through encrypted SMS based funds transfer which can be used on any type of handset. So in sum while several challenges do present themselves they carry within them the core of opportunities which will spur development impulses and lead to growth with equity.

Graph 1:

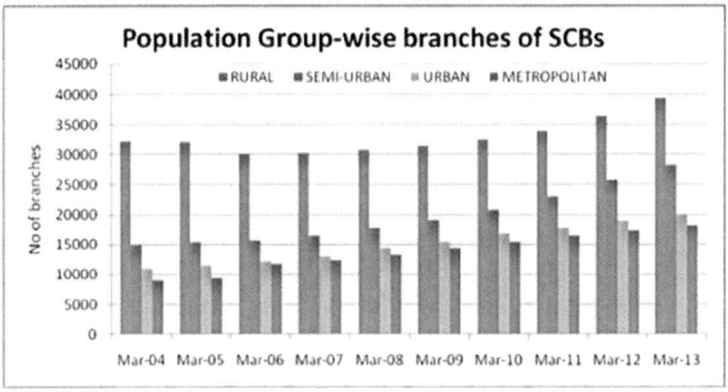

Source: Basic Statistical Returns of Scheduled Commercial Banks in India.

Graph 2:

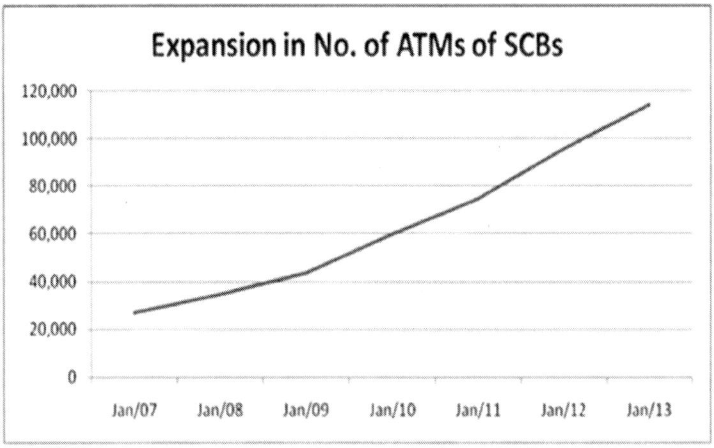

Source: Payment system indicator table in Monthly Bulletin.

SR	Particulars	Year ended Mar 10	Year ended Mar 11	Year ended Mar 12	Year ended March 13
1	Banking Outlets in Villages - Branches	33378	34811	37471	40837
2	Banking Outlets in Villages - BCs	34174	80802	141136	221341
3	Banking Outlets in Villages - Other Modes	142	595	3146	6276
4	Banking Outlets in Villages -TOTAL	67694	116208	181753	268454
5	Urban Locations covered through BCs	447	3771	5891	27143
6	Basic Savings Bank Deposit A/c -branches (No. In millions)	60.19	73.13	81.20	100.80
7	Basic Savings Bank Deposit A/c - branches (Amt. In billions)	44.33	57.89	109.87	164.69
8	Basic Savings Bank Deposit A/c - BCs (No. in millions)	13.27	31.63	57.30	81.27
9	Basic Savings Bank Deposit A/c - BCs (Amt. in billions)	10.69	18.23	10.54	18.22
10	OD facility availed in BSBDA's (No. In millions)	0.18	0.61	2.71	3.95
11	OD facility availed in BSBDA's (Amt. in billions)	0.10	0.26	1.08	1.55
12	KCCs - (No. in millions)	24.31	27.11	30.24	33.79
13	KCCs - (Amt In billions)	1240.07	1600.05	2068.39	2622.98
14	GCCs - (No. in millions)	1.39	1.70	2.11	3.63
15	GCCs - (Amt In billions)	35.11	35.07	41.84	76.34
16	ICT A/Cs-BC- Transaction -No. in millions	26.52	84.16	155.87	250.46
17	ICT A/Cs-BC- Transactions -Amt in billions	6.92	58.00	97.09	233.88

References

1. www.rbi.org.in › Publication,
2. Report on Trend and Progress of Banking in India
3. Annual Report-Reserve Bank of India

10

Strategy Adopted for Financial Inclusion

One of the major challenges for the next decade or more for banks in the country is to capture the banking business of over 50 per cent population of this country of over 1.2 billion people. Poor people need to be provided with access to financial products at low transaction cost. They need to be provided assistance on the demand side (in terms of financial awareness and literacy) as well as on the supply side (in the form of availability of customised financial products). Taking into account their seasonal inflow of income from agricultural operations, migration from one place to another seasonal and irregular work availability and income, the existing financial system needs to be designed to suit their requirements and to be more responsive to their needs. No doubt banks and regulators play a major role in this, but we also need to think beyond traditional ways and delivery channels to speed up the efforts.

Dr Raghuram Rajan, Hon'ble Governor, RBI has powerfully enunciated the need for broad based diversified growth leading to rapid reduction in poverty. Governor has also laid down RBI's developmental measures for the near future on five pillars and one of the most important pillar amongst them is Financial Inclusion where the objective is to expand access of finance to small and medium enterprises, the unorganised sector, the poor, and remote and underserved areas of the country.

The approach adopted for achieving the objectives under Financial Inclusion

RBI's perspective on Financial Inclusion aims at giving a specific direction to the collaborative efforts to gain synergic benefits. Therefore, we have defined Financial Inclusion as "the process of ensuring access to appropriate financial products and services needed by all sections of the society in general and vulnerable groups such as weaker sections and low income groups in particular at an affordable cost in a fair and transparent manner by mainstream institutional players".

Reserve Bank of India has made sustained efforts to increase the penetration of formal financial services in unbanked areas, while continuing with its policy of ensuring adequate but viable flow of credit to priority sectors of the economy. A structured, planned and integrated approach towards FI is focusing on improving access to financial services and also encouraging demand for financial services through financial literacy initiatives. Some of the defining features of our approach to FI are:

Institutional Mechanism

Under the institutional mechanism put in place for financial inclusion, There is the Financial Stability and Development Council (FSDC), which has an exclusive mandate for financial inclusion and financial literacy. A separate Technical Group on financial inclusion and financial literacy, under the Chairmanship of a Deputy Governor, has been set up under the aegis of FSDC. The Group has representatives from all the financial sector regulators. In order to spearhead efforts towards greater financial inclusion, RBI has constituted a Financial Inclusion Advisory Committee (FIAC) under the Chairmanship of Deputy Governor. The FIAC has few Directors from the Central Board of RBI and experts drawn from NGO sector/other civil society representatives, etc. as members. At the State level, there are State Level Bankers Committee (SLBC) further supported by Lead District Managers (671 Districts) at the district level.

Bank–led Model

In India, we have adopted a bank-led model for financial inclusion, which seeks to leverage on technology. The FI initiatives would have to be ICT based and would ride on new delivery models that would need to be developed by the market participants to best suit their requirements.

Our experience has shown that the goal of financial inclusion is better served through mainstream banking institutions as they have the ability to offer the suite of products required to bring in effective/meaningful financial inclusion. Other players such as mobile companies have been allowed to partner with banks in offering services collaboratively.

Integrated approach – Financial Inclusion & Financial Literacy

Considering that financial Literacy is an important adjunct for promoting financial inclusion, consumer protection and ultimately financial stability, RBI has adopted an integrated approach wherein efforts towards Financial Inclusion and Financial Literacy would go hand in hand.

Bouquet of Financial Products

In the absence of banks a large number of informal intermediaries had mushroomed, mostly in the rural areas, which were acting as proxy for the banks. Such unregulated entities were in the business of extending only credit products that too at exorbitant rates of interest mostly to the illiterate section of the population. This had resulted in huge indebtedness amongst the poor people. With our renewed efforts under financial inclusion we have now advised banks to ensure that all the financial needs of the customers are met by offering, at the minimum, four basic products to customers, viz.

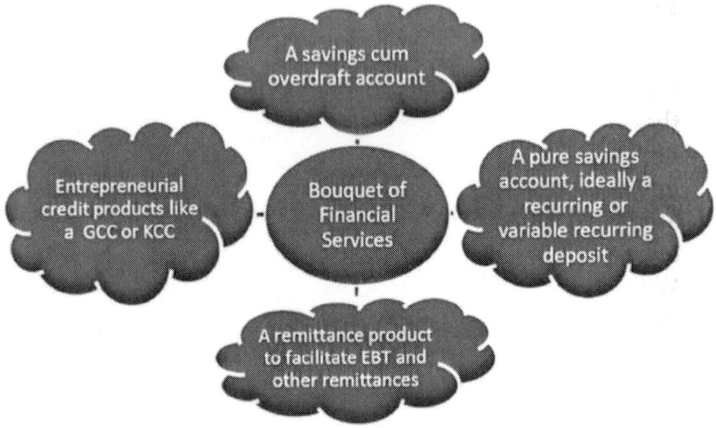

The idea is to ensure that customers who are linked to the banking system are provided with all the basic financial products that are required to enhance their income generation capacity thus helping them to come out of poverty. Such an initiative is expected to be a win-win situation for both banks as well as the large section of poor people residing in the rural areas.

Combination of Branch and BC Structure

We are advocating a combination of Brick and Mortar structure with Click and Mouse technology for extending financial inclusion, especially in geographically dispersed areas. Banks have to make effective use of technology to provide banking services in remote areas. In addition to creating a large network of small branches in rural areas, the Reserve Bank has permitted banks to utilise the services of intermediaries in providing banking services through the use of business correspondents. The BC model allows banks to do 'cash in - cash out' transactions at a location much closer to the rural population, thus addressing the last mile problem.

Leveraging on Technology

Penetrating banking services through the traditional brick and mortar model was expensive for banks. It was realised that the task of Financial Inclusion was gigantic and would not be possible without actively leveraging on technology. We have therefore encouraged banks to leverage on technology to attain greater reach and penetration for minimizing the cost of providing financial services in far flung areas of the country. With adoption of technology it has been possible for banks to deliver banking products and services to the doorsteps of villages.

Engaging Business Correspondents: The Reserve Bank has permitted banks to engage Business Facilitators (BFs) and Business Correspondents (BCs) as intermediaries for providing financial and banking services. The BC Model allows banks to provide doorstep delivery of services especially to do 'cash in – cash out' transactions, thus addressing the 'last mile' problem. The list of eligible individuals/entities who can be engaged as BCs are being widened from time to time and we have adopted a test and learn approach to this process. Now, even for profit organisations excluding NBFCs and Telcos have been permitted to operate as BCs of banks.

Relaxation of KYC Norms: The strict KYC norms inhibited linkage of common people with the Banking System. Know Your Customer (KYC) requirements for opening bank accounts have been relaxed for small accounts. Further, in order to leverage on the initiative of UIDAI, we have allowed 'Aadhaar' as one of the eligible document for meeting KYC requirements and very recently have also allowed banks to provide e-KYC services provided through the Aadhaar platform.

Simplified branch authorisation: To address the issue of uneven spread of bank branches, branch licensing norms have been relaxed considerably and banks are now free to open branches in centres with population less than 1 lakh under general permission, subject to reporting.

Opening of branches in unbanked rural centres: To further step up the opening of branches in rural areas, banks have been mandated to open at least 25 per cent of the branches in unbanked rural centres. To help facilitate achieving this mandate, banks have been advised to open small intermediary brick and mortar structures between the base branch and the unbanked villages. The idea is to create an eco-system for ensuring efficient delivery of services, efficiency in cash management, redressal of customer grievances and closer supervision of BC operations. This is expected to facilitate quicker branch expansion in unbanked rural centres.

Financial Inclusion Plan of Banks

We have encouraged banks to adopt a structured and planned approach to financial inclusion with commitment at the highest levels, through preparation of Board approved Financial Inclusion Plans (FIPs). The first phase of FIPs was implemented over the period 2010–2013. The Reserve Bank has used the FIPs to gauge the performance of banks under their FI initiatives. In this direction we have put in place a structured and comprehensive monitoring mechanism for evaluating banks' performance vis-a-vis their targets. To ensure support of the Top Management of the Bank to the Financial Inclusion process and to ensure accountability of the senior functionaries of the bank, one on one annual review meetings are held with CMDs/CEOs of banks.

A snapshot of the progress made by banks under the Financial Inclusion Plan during the period from April 2010 to March 2013 are as follows:-

- Banking outlets in villages have increased to nearly 2, 68,000 from 67,694 outlets in March 2010.
- About 7,400 rural branches have been opened during this 3-years period compared with a reduction of about 1300 rural branches during the last two decades.
- Nearly 109 million Basic Savings Bank Deposit Accounts (BSBDAs) have been added, taking the total

number of BSBDA to 182 million. The share of ICT-based accounts has increased substantially. The percentage of ICT accounts to total BSBDAs increased from 25 per cent in March 2010 to 45 per cent in March 2013.

- With the addition of nearly 9.48 million farm sector households during this period, 33.8 million households have been provided with small entrepreneurial credit as at the end of March 2013.
- With the addition of nearly 2.24 million non-farm sector households during this period, 3.6 million households have been provided with small entrepreneurial credit as at the end of March 2013.
- About 490 million transactions have been carried out in ICT-based accounts through BCs during the three-year period.

Banking Outlets

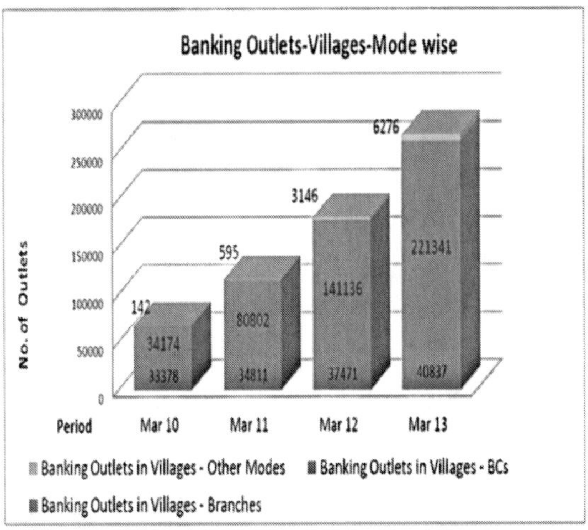

Source: FIP Monthly return.

We have now created a large banking network and have also managed to open a large number of small accounts. The focus under the FI plan has now shifted towards leveraging

BSBDA (No. in Lakh)

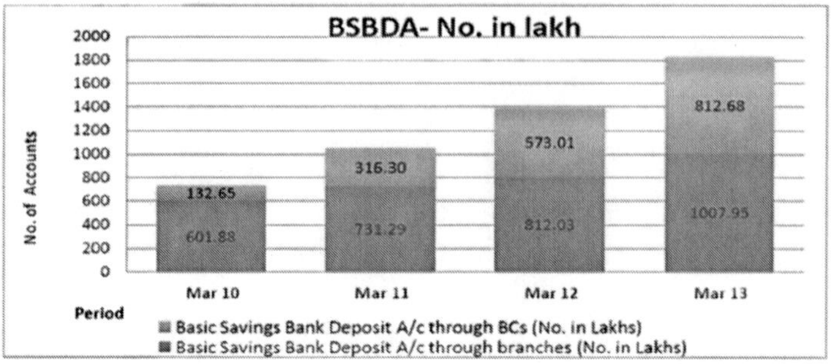

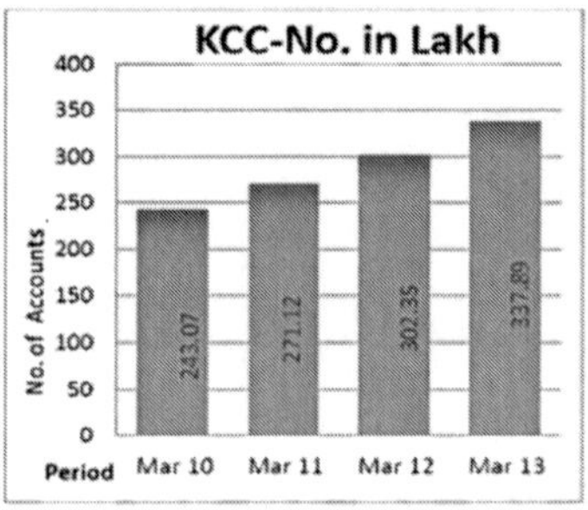

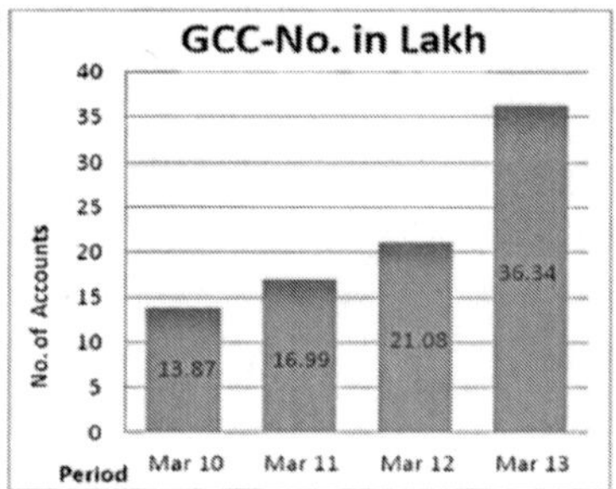

No of ICT based Transactions (No. in Lakh)

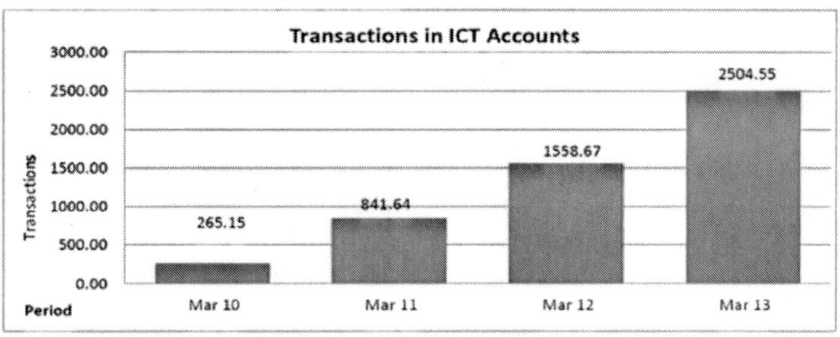

Source: FIP Monthly Return.

the banking network created for extending other products viz. credit, etc. which will help make the business more viable for banks. This would also ensure that with the large number of accounts opened and large volume of transactions taking place and people should reap the benefits of getting linked to the formal financial institutions.

Roadmap for providing Banking Services in unbanked villages: With financial inclusion gaining increasing recognition as a business opportunity and with all banks geared to increase presence, we adopted a phase-wise approach to provide banking services in all unbanked villages in the country. On completion of the first phase where nearly 74000 villages with population more than 2000 were provided with a banking outlet, we are now in the second phase where the remaining unbanked villages, numbering close to 4,90,000, have been identified in villages with less than 2000 population and allocated to banks, for opening of banking outlets by March 2016. Under the roadmap for provision of banking facilities in villages with less than 2000 population, SLBC, Madhya Pradesh has identified and allotted 47660 unbanked villages among various, out of which 18986 unbanked villages are required to be covered by March 2014.

Direct Benefit Transfer – The GoI has plans to route the social security payments through the banking network by leveraging on the Aadhaar Enabled Payment System based platform. In order to ensure smooth roll out of the Government's Direct Benefit Transfer (DBT) initiative, banks have been advised to open accounts of all eligible individuals and to seed the existing and new accounts with Aadhaar numbers.

Financial Literacy – We have realised that Financial Literacy is an important adjunct for promoting financial inclusion. We have adopted an integrated approach, wherein our efforts towards Financial Inclusion and Financial Literacy go hand in hand. Through Financial literacy and education, we disseminate information on the general banking concepts to diverse target groups, including school and college students, women, rural and urban poor, pensioners and senior citizens to enable them to make informed financial decisions. To support this we have nearly 800 financial literacy centres set up by banks. We have designed a mass scale Financial Literacy Program with an objective to integrate the financially excluded population with low level of income and low literacy level with the formal financial system. Financial Literacy Centres organise Outdoor Literacy camps which are spread over a period of three months and delivered in three phases wherein along with creating awareness, accounts are also opened in the literacy camps.

Way forward - Issues and Challenges

Structure

With adoption of new branchless delivery channels by banks, there is a need for banks to revamp the structure for carrying out banking operations. There cannot be a fixed structure defined which can be adopted by all the banks. Each bank has to based on its current architecture and develop a structure that can enhance its financial inclusion efforts. This would entail the following:—

- Review of the HR policies with respect to recruitment of staff in view of the FI requirements. Separate cadre of staff can be thought off for catering to the needs of providing banking services in far flung rural areas.
- Banks have to think and act differently and make themselves more flexible so as to meet even the smallest requirements of the rural population.

BC Model

There are many challenges being faced while implementing BC model. Sustainability and scalability of the BC model is essential. More and more innovative products would have to be introduced which would benefit both banks as well as the rural people and at the same time make the BC model more viable. Review of the cash management practices for delivery of banking services through the branchless modes need to be done for ensuring scaling up of the various models.

Transactions

During the first phase of our FI initiative, we have had success as regards to opening of banking outlets by banks and also in opening bank accounts for large number of individuals. Going forward our idea is to enable more transactions in these accounts by providing more credit products, which will not only help rural people to avail of credit at comparatively lower rates of interest but at the same time also make the BC model viable for banks. Banks have been advised to leverage upon the Direct Benefit Transfer initiative of the Government of India for linking all the individuals to the banking system and for utilising the large amounts likely to be credited in these accounts for encouraging issue of deposit and credit products.

Collaboration

Finally, financial inclusion cannot be achieved without the active involvement of all stakeholders like RBI, other financial regulators, banks, governments, NGOs, civil society, etc. The current policy objective of inclusive growth with financial stability cannot be achieved without ensuring universal financial inclusion. Banks alone will not be able to achieve this unless an entire support system would be partnering with them in this mission. All the stakeholders need to join hands and make it possible.

References

1. *www.rbi.org.in* › Publication,
2. *Report on Trend and Progress of Banking in India*
3. *Annual Report-Reserve Bank of India*

11

The Indian Model : Challenges and Prospects

India is one of the largest countries in the world with 7th largest geographical area, 2nd largest population, 10th largest economy in the world comprising of 29 States and 6 Union Territories, 644 districts, 600,000 Villages with Multilingual and multiethnic society. However, there is low level of General Literacy – (74 per cent in 2011; Female-65 per cent), large no. of Financially excluded people (more than 50 per cent)

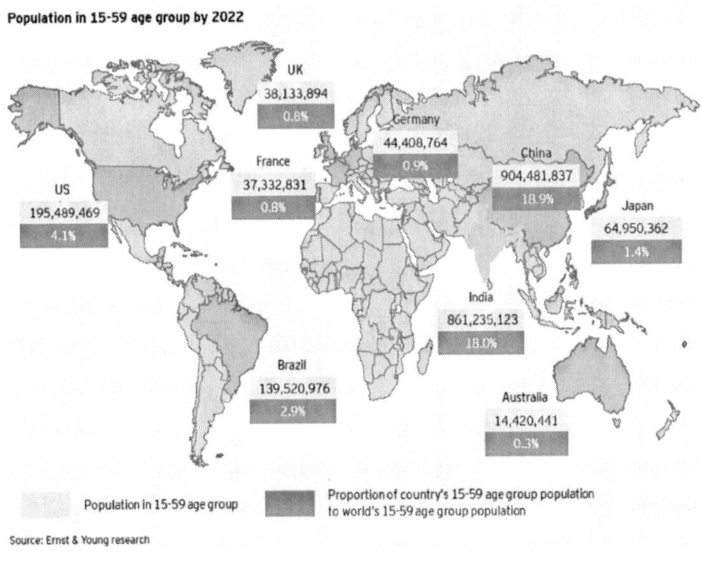

According to Planning Commission Report 2008 & ILO

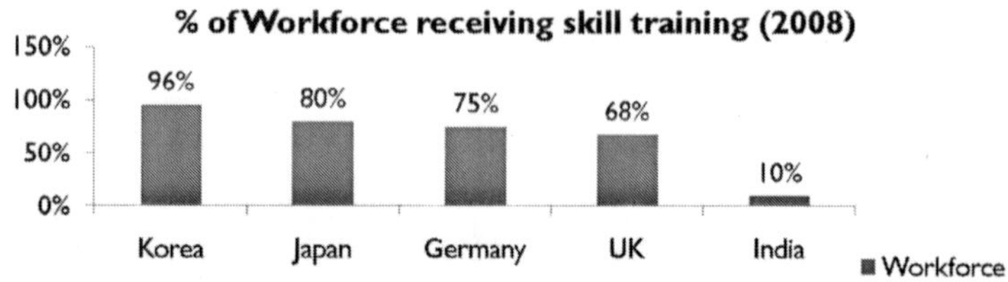

India has adopted multi-dimensional approaches for achievement and promotion of Financial Inclusion ranging from nationalisation of banks to SHG-Bank linkages. Banks were nationalised in India first in 1969 and later in 1980 with a view to bring formal financial sector within the reach of common people. With this several other initiatives have been taken like Lead Bank Scheme started in 1969, Priority Sector Guidelines were issued in 1980, Regional Rural Banks (1976), Service Area Approach(1989), SHG- Bank Linkage(1992).

The earlier approaches adopted in India were mainly Subsidy Based Approaches like interest subvention scheme, Target Oriented Banking etc. Policy intent was to help the poor but it was not directed towards making them self sufficient. Banking was never treated for poor as a commercial business but a social obligation. Besides, there was absence of suitable technology to reach large geographies economically.

The new approach is based on comprehensive definition of Financial Inclusion and adoption of technology with focus on from growth to inclusive growth, sustainability, viability, scalability, branchless mode of delivery with a view that poors are bankable.

To achieve financial inclusion our strategy is to connect people to mainstream financial institutions. It means bringing all 6 lakh villages and unbanked urban pockets in mainstream financial institutions by leveraging on network of bank branches with ICT based cost effective and user friendly delivery model for the unbanked through proper regulatory guidelines with development perspective.

We have adopted bank led model given low literacy level and past experience of high risks from non banks. Sound regulations, consumer protection to vulnerable customers and strong KYC compliance make banks financially stable. Other features of banks are like only banks are able to offer a suite of basic products-Saving, Credit, Remittances etc. Besides, No charges for safe custody of savings, interest paid on deposits and deposit Insurance upto Rs 100 thousand also make them attractive to the poor.

Institutional framework

- Government of India & Reserve Bank of India.
- Financial Stability Development Council (FSDC), Separate Technical Group on Financial Inclusion and Financial Literacy
- Financial Inclusion Advisory Committee of RBI, Public and Private sector Banks, Regional Rural Banks, about 100 Thousand branches
- 35 State Level Bankers Committees
- 671 District Consultative Committees
- Partnership with other stakeholders

Integrated Approach

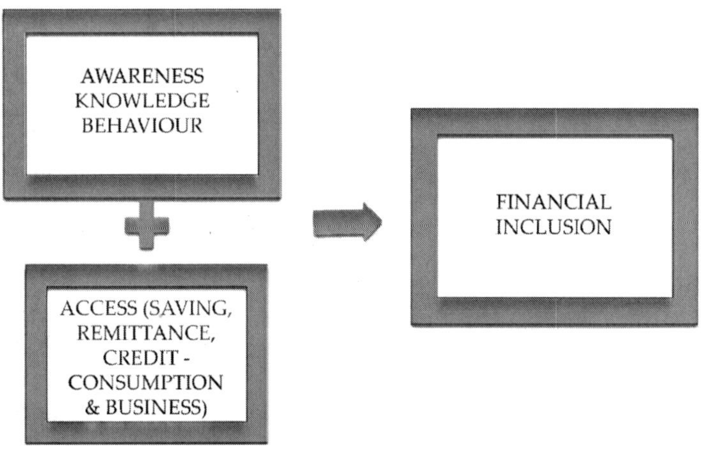

Implementation of the integrated approach of financial inclusion is based on four pillars.

- **Reach** which includes Engaging BCs as Agents, Phased Approach – Roadmap – more than 2000 & less than 2000 population unbanked centres, Relaxing branch authorisation, 25 per cent of new branches in unbanked villages.
- **Access** aiming at Saving Bank Account for every eligible individual, simplified KYC- Aadhaar as KYC and account opening in camp mode.
- **Products,** we have introduced standardised basic products, Saving Bank (S.B) accounts with inbuilt Over Draft (O.D.) and Revolving business credit. Encouraging innovation in customised products
- **Transactions,** schemes like door step delivery of services, Direct benefit Transfer, P2P payments, Migrant Remittances have been introduced.

Financial Inclusion Plan of banks

We have encouraged banks to adopt a structured and planned approach to financial inclusion with commitment at the highest levels, through preparation of Board approved Financial Inclusion Plans (FIPs). There is a emphasis on Self-set targets – 46 Parameters-FIPs to be integrated with Business plan of the banks. Coverage of unbanked villages, with more than 2000 & less than 2000 population through Brick and Mortar branches as well as by deployment of BCs. Basic Accounts, EBT, KCC, GCC accounts to be opened including through BC-ICT, Specific products to be designed to cater to the financially excluded segments.

Reserve Bank of India closely monitors progress through monthly progress and annual comprehensive review of financial inclusion plan. Financial Inclusion Plan is disaggregated for the Regional Office of RBI to review state level Financial Inclusion Plan.

Financial Inclusion has achieved tremendous success as between April 2010 to March 2013 About 2,68,000 banking outlets opened in villages with around 7400 rural branches, 27143 Urban Location covered through BCs, 182.06 million Basic Savings Accounts (NFAs), out of which BC-ICT based – 81.27 million, OD facility extended in about 3.95 million Accounts, 33.79 million KCCs and 3.63 million GCC accounts.

Penetration

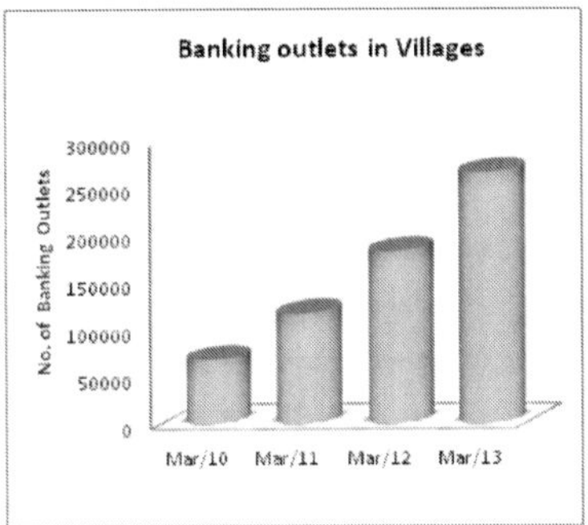

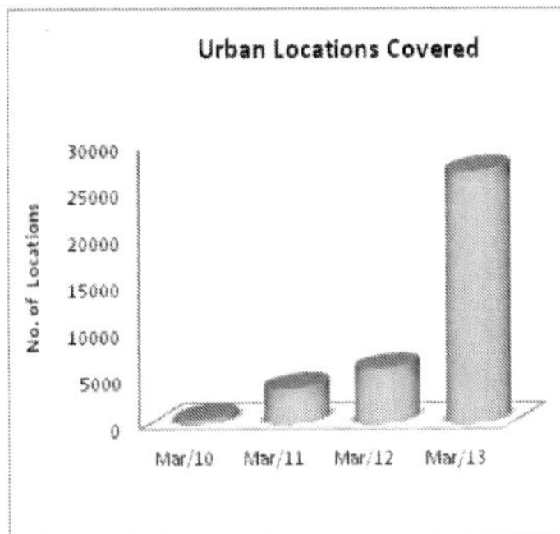

ATM Penetration

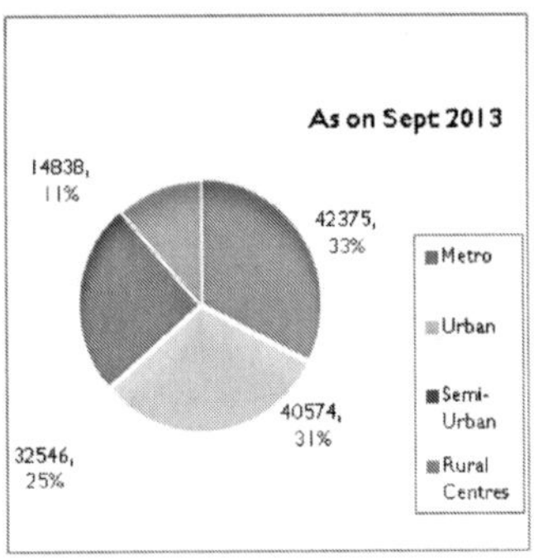

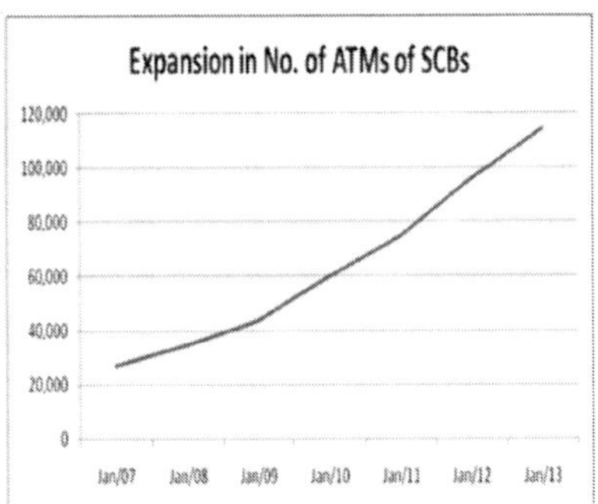

Source : Monthly Bulletin Table Payment System Indicators.

Direct Benefit Transfer

Government of India has initiated the Direct Benefit Transfer scheme with the objection of transfer subsidies directly to the people living below poverty line. DBT subsumes 28 schemes and covers 121 districts. 1st phase began in

BSBDA (No Frill accounts)

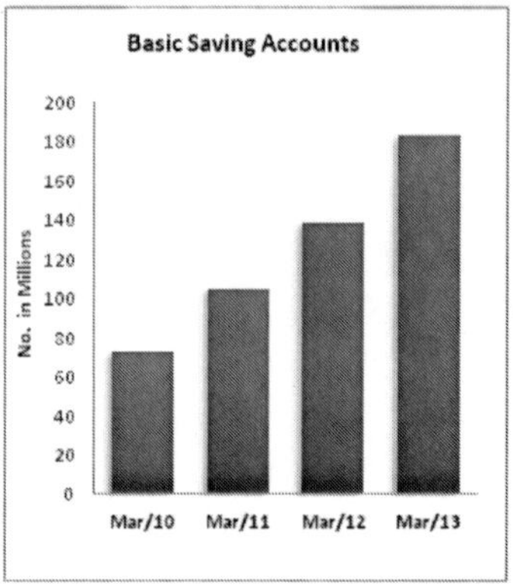

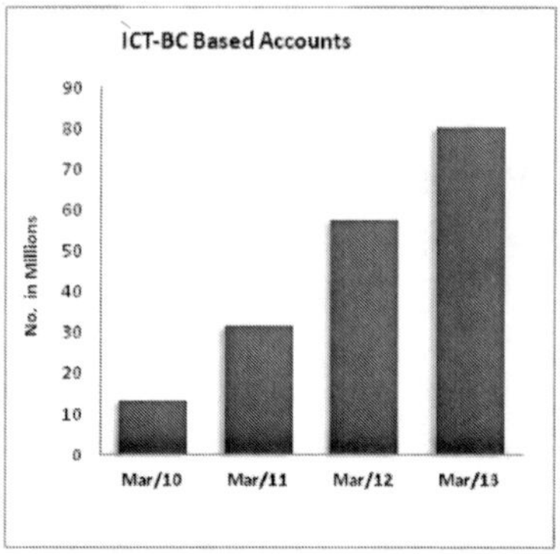

Source: FIP Monthly Return.

Entrepreneurial Credit

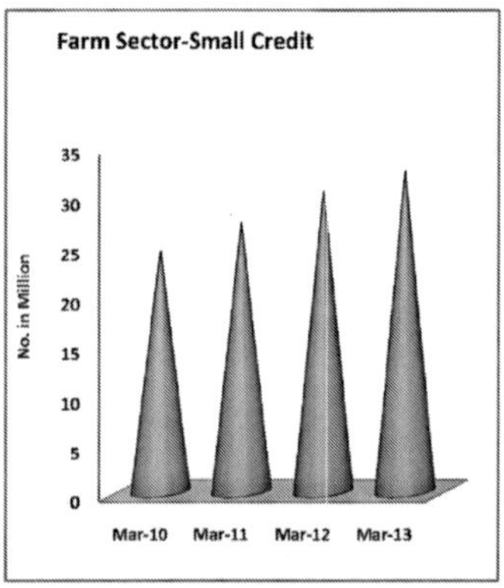

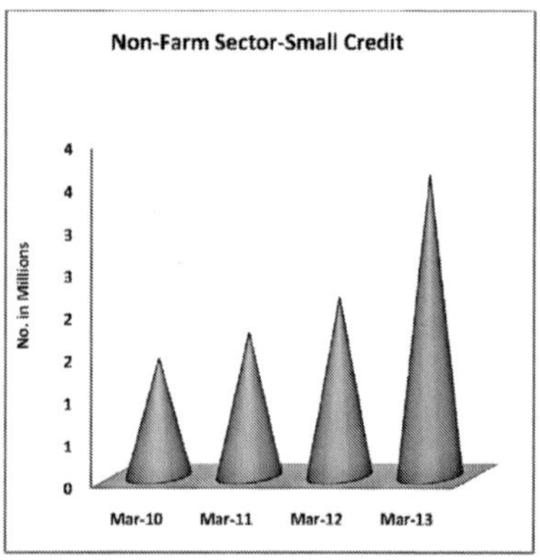

January 2013 wherein 43 districts were covered and in 2nd phase 77 districts have been covered since July 2013.

LPG subsidy – 289 Districts by Jan 14

- 1st Phase- June 13- 20 Districts
- 2nd Phase- Sept 13- 34 Districts
- 3rd Phase- Oct 13- 44 Districts
- 4th Phase- Nov 13- 46 Districts

- 5th Phase- Dec 13- 40 Districts
- 6th Phase- Jan 14- 105 Districts

DBT - RBI Guidelines

August 2011: Comprehensive operational guidelines issued.

October 2012 : SLBC convenor banks and Lead banks of selected districts are advised to coordinate with the State Administrator and field level implementing agencies to ensure smooth rollout.

May 2013: Banks advised to open accounts of all eligible individuals in camp mode, seed the accounts with Aadhaar numbers, progress to be reviewed in SLBC and DCC meetings.

July 2013: Banks to facilitate seamless rollout of Aadhaar based DBT of Government benefits including LPG subsidy. DBT Co-ordination Committee at district level, complaint Grievance Redressal mechanism in each bank.

National Strategy for Financial Education

Under the aegis of the FSDC, a National Strategy for Financial Education (NSFE) for India had been prepared. National Centre on Financial Education has been set up to ensure coordination among all financial sector regulators. NCFE conducted a nationwide baseline survey i.e. NCFE-Financial Literacy and Inclusion Survey (NCFE-FLIS) for assessing the state of financial literacy and financial inclusion. We have also developed standard contents as part of financial literacy material. Financial Education is recommended to be included in the School Curriculum –to be integrated into existing subject of Class VI to Class X. A Core Committee constituted for implementation with representation from all regulators.

Financial Literacy Material

- **Standardised Financial Literacy Material:** explaining basic concepts for unbanked audience available in

Hindi and English has been recently released in regional languages Available on RBI Website *http://www.rbi.org.in/financialeducation/Financial Literacy Guide. aspx.*

- **Financial Literacy Guide:** consisting of 5 Sections and 50 Questions on Money Management, Savings, Saving with banks, Borrowings, Borrowing from banks is developed.
- **Financial Diary:** has been distributed among target audience to make them aware of financial planning. This has sections for Record income and expenses- Weekly/ Monthly/Yearly.
- **Set of 16 posters:** Pictorial Communication- Appealing Slogans.

Mass Scale Awareness : Several steps have been taken to increase awareness among masses through existing and newly created institutions like Public, Private and Regional Rural Banks etc. 822 financial literacy centres and over 4000 rural branches conduct Literacy Camps once in a month.

Self Help Groups: This scheme was started in 1992 with the aim to deliver financial services to the poor in a sustainable manner. It is a sustainable and scalable model of financial inclusion. This scheme has been at the forefront in the promotion of women SHGs.

Rural Credit Market Penetration

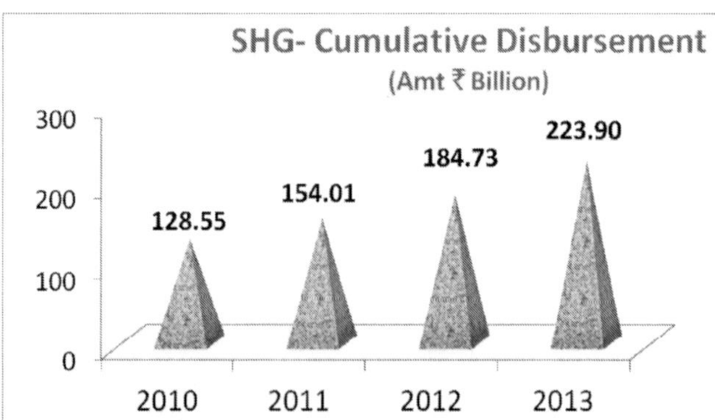

	SHGs linked (No. Million)	*Credit linked (No. Million)*	*Loans disbursed (million)*	*Loan O/S (million)*
Mar 10	6.95	1.58	128555.8	280382.8
Mar 13	7.31	1.22	223901.7	393753.0

Payment System – Initiatives

- National Payments Corporation of India (NPCI)- Umbrella organisation for retail payments.
- National Electronic Fund Transfer facilitating one-to-one funds transfer.
- Real Time Gross Settlement facilitating continues (real-time) fund transfer.
- Immediate Payment Service (IMPS) – Mobile based payment system initiative by NPCI.
- Aadhaar Bridge Payment System (ABPS) facilitating the credit transfers and Aadhaar Enabled Payment System facilitating withdrawal from account.

Mobile Banking: it provides a unique opportunity to leverage the mobile platform to meet the objectives and challenges of financial inclusion as it can reach 870 million subscribers. The IMPS was introduced in 2010 to facilitate immediate fund transfer. Mobile wallet was introduced for non-banks including MNOs. So far 69 banks approved to provide mobile banking. During Sept 13 ~ 71.69 lakh transactions amounting to approx. Rs 1565 crore took place.

Payment System Initiatives in pipeline

- **Remittances :** Fund transfer from bank-account holders to non-account holder through the use of ATMs.
- **Cash-out by non-bank** : Issued prepaid payment instruments with necessary safeguards.
- **Mobile Banking** : Technical Committee on Mobile Banking. Providing mobile banking services in a seamless and secure manner.

- **MSME Financing** : Scoping to leverage on technology and changed business processes, for the purpose of setting up a trade receivables exchange based on reverse factoring model.

Challenges

Scaling Financial Inclusion: Appropriate Business Model yet to evolve. Need for moving from a cost centric model to a revenue generating model by offering a bouquet of deposit, credit and other products and services.

Trinity to make Financial Stability Possible

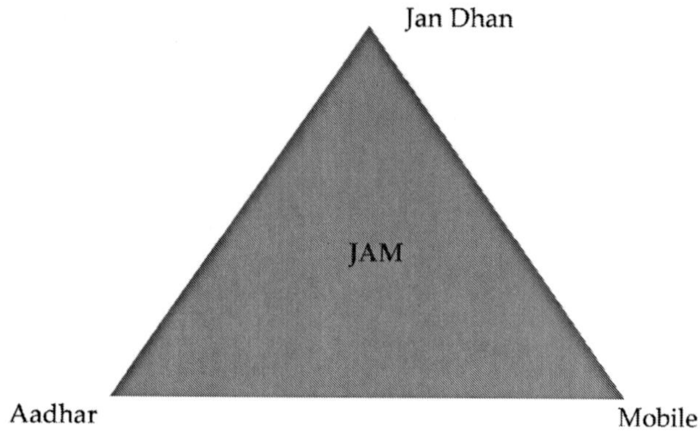

References

1. E & Y report
2. Planning Commission Report 2008 & ILO
3. Ministry of Labour and Employment, Government of India
4. http://www.rbi.org.in/financialeducation/FinancialLiteracyGuide.aspx
5. Ministry of Finance, Government of India
6. Economic Survey 2014-15

Financial Literacy

12

Financial Literacy – Some Thoughts

In the wake of the financial crisis, our financial literacy efforts had gathered greater salience. The equation of financial literacy from the demand side and financial inclusion from the supply side work in tandem. For achieving financial inclusion we identified numerous challenges in the Indian context and liberalised Know Your Customer norms with a unique identity number that would help spur financial inclusion. Banks however must treat it as a business opportunity and not an obligation thrust on them.

Financial literacy, financial education and financial stability are inextricably linked and form part of a continuum. We need to understand the seminal work of the World Bank in addressing issues of building financial capability through financial education and also the work of the RBI in this regard.

In October 2011, G 20 Finance Ministers agreed to new principles on financial consumer protection developed by an OECD led task force integrated with financial inclusion and financial education policies.

During the Financial crisis, people who did not know any better, borrowed beyond their means, not in Africa, not in Nigeria, Papua New Guinea, Japan, India but in the USA because appraisers inflated the value of properties that prospective buyers were interested in. Borrowers were led to believe that they had undertaken a standard fixed rate mortgage only to learn later that their mortgage was a complicated variable rate contract which with their income streams they could not honour. Brokers, mortgage companies etc., took the financially illiterate borrower for a ride and risky lending practices proliferated.

There was no consumer protection and different jurisdictions had their own sets of lending policies. A large part the financial crisis was a result of financial illiteracy and lack of financial capability. We are focusing on these problems to ensure that this does not happen again this is the first commitment we must make and pledge ourselves to. Appropriately our introductory session dwelt on developing National Strategies for Financial education OECD/INFE principles and practical examples from Asia and the Pacific.

It is a truism that whatever gets measured gets done and that statistics and empirical experience alone hold certitudes the rest are platitudes. Surveys as a diagnostic tool can inform policy. It is very difficult to prepare the questionnaire in different languages but in India we managed with 22 official languages and 398 living languages, mind boggling task but we did it. RBI has a series of hands on sessions that provided us a valuable and insightful Introduction to the program Knowledge Products and website of the Financial Literacy and Education Trust fund. There is currently limited evidence and little consensus on the types of programs which are effective in raising the capacity for and level of financial capability.

Effective impact evaluation is essential but often serves as a forgotten half in this context. The presentations on High Level Principles for evaluation of financial education programs were particularly valuable. Adele Atkinson-Policy Analyst of the OECD presented the OECD High Level Principles for the evaluation of financial education programs and Joanne Yoong from the National University of Singapore presented a toolkit for evaluation of financial capability Programs in Middle and Low Income countries.

The session on Youth Developing financial skills and Competencies OECD /INFE guidelines on Financial Education in schools and PISA financial literacy. Financial education in schools, innovative tools, examples and evaluation findings gave us extremely valuable insights.

The Session on Women empowerment through Financial Education was especially close to the heart. There was valuable experience sharing through presentations of the UNWOMEN. The session on Innovative methods for financial capability enhancement, in which Doorstep Banking and Financial education in India were presented was very useful.

Thus acquainting us with the range of evaluation of new methods and tools to enhance financial awareness and capability. Evidence suggests that innovative methods can bring positive outcomes on the target audience, the hardcore and asset less poor are hard to reach due to low literacy levels and geographical locations. In sum, through the cross country experience sharing we have learnt a lot.

We have covered a lot of ground but with distance still to go. Building financial capability through financial literacy is a key component of the financial Inclusion process. On this we are all agreed, every country has to tread its own path to financial inclusion and literacy depending on its particular situation literacy levels, per capita income, levels of financialisation of the economy.

We have all reached consensus on the need for financial literacy and on National Strategies engaging all stakeholders including Central and State Governments, financial regulators civil society, public private partnerships etc., We have agreed that financial literacy, financial education lead to customer protection which leads to financial stability. As you have come to India to the mystic East so I will give you a mantra, Our collective global goal is higher growth leading to inclusive and sustainable development. This is the 'mool mantra' of Growth.

Economic growth is essential but growth with equity is an imperative. We must unhesitatingly embrace the need to build financial capability which leads to growth as the highest goal. It is growth that will lead to inclusive development. Without growth there will be neither development nor inclusiveness. There is a compelling moral case for equity but it is also necessary if there is to be sustained growth. A country's most important resource is its people. You will all agree it must be financially literate, financially educated and financially included people. At the end of the day, there will be no dissent that it has been a great conference. We have indeed covered a lot of ground but several challenges remain, with distance still to go.

Our first Prime Minister Jawaharlal Nehru often recalled the words of Robert Frost "The woods are lovely dark and deep but I have promises to keep and miles to go before I sleep and miles to go before I sleep". "A part, indeed an important part, of the mandate of Central Banks is financial stability and an essential pre-requisite for financial stability is financial literacy and the Central Bank has unique leverage in providing financial literacy". We all agree on the need to build financial capability of our people. We need to empower people. Now it is the time to get down to do it and together we know we can.

References

1. Youth Developing Financial Skills and Competencies OECD /INFE Guidelines on Financial Education in schools and PISA
2. *Financial education - OECD, www.oecd.org/finance/financial-education*
3. *www.rbi.org*, Speeches

13

Financial Education Key to Promoting Financial Inclusion and Customer Protection

Financial Education is not a new idea but the enabling environment in terms of policy focus on inclusive growth and availability of technology for cost effective delivery of both banking services and financial education is of recent origin. There is a strong view that the financial crisis occured because many of the NINJA, No Income No Job or Asset borrowers in the United States were clueless as to the terms of the adjusted rate mortgage contracts they were signing-leading to the global economic crisis and this has led to serious concern on the need for financial education, financial inclusion, consumer empowerment. This was also the backdrop for the passage of the Dodd Frank Act in the United States which is a fareaching Wall Street reform in history. Dodd-Frank is expected to prevent the excessive risk-taking that led to the financial crisis. The law also provides common-sense protections for American families, and creates a new consumer watchdog to prevent mortgage companies and pay-day lenders from exploiting consumers. The law focuses on consumer protection. It is designed to make sure that everybody follows the same set of rules, so that firms compete on price and quality. It demands accountability and responsibility from everyone. It provides certainty to everybody, from bankers to farmers to business owners to consumers. If you've ever applied for a credit card, a student loan, or a housing loan you know the feeling of signing your name to pages of barely understandable fine print. What often happens as a result is that many people are caught by hidden fees and penalties, or saddled with loans they can't afford. They are then, hit with a massive rate increase on their credit card balances even though they paid bills on time. Contracts which are simpler – will put an end to many hidden penalties and fees in complex mortgages -- so common people are aware of what they're signing. Students who take student loans should have clear and concise information about their obligations. Ordinary investors -- like you and me, seniors saving for retirement -- should be able to receive and understand information about the costs and risks of mutual funds and other investment products, so that they can make better financial decisions as to what will work for them.

Today we have to recognise that the greatest threat arises from the asymmetries of information and power between financial institutions and poor consumers, an imbalance which grows as customers are less experienced and the products they can choose are more sophisticated, an imbalance which holds real potential for negative outcomes due to institutional abuses or ill-informed client decisions. Financial education is an important tool to address this imbalance and help consumers both, accept and use the products to which they increasingly have access. Because it can facilitate effective product use, financial education is critical to financial inclusion. It can help clients to both, develop the skills to compare and select the best products for their needs and empower them to exercise their rights and responsibilities in the consumer protection equation. Financial Education spans the informal and formal financial sectors, supporting clients' access to, and more importantly, use of, diverse financial services. When we speak about financial education as a lay person, we are usually referring to a set of skills that allow people to manage their money wisely, some understanding of essential financial concepts and an appreciation of the trade-off between risk and return. But let us ponder a bit deeper for a while, is it only this? Let us think from the point of view of a poor person who does not have any regular income, who is not actually literate and who has never accessed any formal source of banking services. Do we mean that such persons, and surely they form a significant part of our population, have no financial literacy. Financial diaries studies, as presented in Portfolios of the Poor (Collins et al, 2009) in Cash-in, Cash-out: Financial Transactions and Access to Finance in Malawi (Stuart et al, 2011), have demonstrated that most poor people are good financial managers in familiar environments where a majority of financial transactions occur either informally or involve money stored at home. Money has its own language and to understand it you need not necessarily be literate. It is almost like any other basic need such as hunger, sleep, etc., the understanding of which comes naturally to all. This is possibly the reason that we feel confident to impart financial literacy to all those are not formally literate.

More formally, financial education and awareness can take many forms, which include, instruction in personal finance concepts, the financial services landscape, the development of the skills, attitudes and behaviors needed to make the right decisions for the individual. Financial Education primarily relates to personal finance, which enables individuals to take effective action to improve overall well-being and avoid one's business. Financial Education is not about just markets and investing, but also distress in financial matters. It is the ability to know, monitor and effectively use financial resources to enhance the well- being and economic security of oneself, one's family and savings, budgeting, financial planning, basics of banking and most importantly about being "Financially Smart". To understand financial planning, a person should be financially literate to understand the importance of preparing household budgets, cash-flow management and asset allocation to meet financial goals.

In India, a large section of population still lack access to basic financial services from the formal financial sector and hence moving towards universal financial inclusion is both a national commitment and a policy priority. Financial Literacy is considered an important adjunct for promoting financial inclusion, consumer protection and ultimately financial stability. Financial Inclusion and Financial Literacy need to go hand in hand to enable the common man to understand the need and benefits of the products and services offered by formal financial institutions. The RBI defined financial inclusion as the access to appropriate financial products and services needed by vulnerable groups, such as weaker sections and low income groups, at an affordable cost, in a fair and transparent manner by mainstream institutional players. So, from the financial literacy perspective, it essentially involves two elements, one of access and the other of literacy which enables usage.

The most fundamental reason why people should strive to become financially literate is to help them reach their personal financial goals. Whatever the specific goal, the payoff from financial literacy is an improved standard of living and a sense of confidence about the future. Financially literate individuals are more likely to engage in sound financial planning early in their lives. This enables them to plan for retirement, fund the education of their children, and accumulate more assets. From a national perspective, the payoff is large.

Which is the target group?

Everyone in the system, be it the users or the providers of financial products/services, need to be financially literate. In the Indian context, the users are broadly categorised as the financially excluded resource-poor, the lower and middle income groups and the high net worth individuals. For the resource-poor largely excluded population, financial literacy would invariably involve addressing deep entrenched behavioral and psychological factors that are major barriers to participating in the financial system. For the purpose, financial literacy efforts are primarily directed towards dissemination of simple messages of financial prudence, in vernacular languages, through large awareness campaigns across the country combined with vigorous roll out of financial inclusion plans by banks, insurance and pension funds, and others. However, as briefly mentioned earlier, it is important to note that being literate is not a necessary prerequisite for attaining financial literacy as the basic financial messages can be conveyed through various alternate means without relying on written inputs. Some of the basic messages sought to be delivered through our financial literacy drives are:

- Why Save
- Why save regularly and consistently
- Why save with banks
- Why borrow within limits
- Why borrow from banks
- Why borrow for income generating purposes
- Why repay loans
- Why repay loans in time
- Why do you need insurance
- Why you will need regular stream of income post working life – pension
- Why you should keep money aside regularly and consistently during your earning life for pension in old age
- What is interest ? How moneylenders charge very high interest rates ?

For the middle and lower-middle income groups that are participating in financial markets as either savers or borrowers or both, i.e. the financially included, financial literacy efforts should aim at enhancing their knowledge about the market and new products/services. For instance, there is a large section of our population that has a bank account but refrains from participating in the capital market on account of lack of knowledge. Financial literacy, in such cases, would focus on creating awareness about the way the capital market functions and also about the fact that the equity market may at times provide relatively higher returns coupled with higher risks as compared to other investments.

For the high net worth individuals, better knowledge of the financial markets, new and innovative products and instruments is important as it helps them in making better use of the available avenues in the financial markets. This knowledge is also useful for taking more informed decision in their quest for greater returns from their investments in the market and to avail credit at relatively cheaper rates. Whether saving or investing, the basic lesson that "higher return implies higher risks" should not be lost sight of. Sometimes we have a tendency to feel that high net worth individuals or resource rich corporate or bankers do not need financial education. Nothing could be farther from truth. To quote an example, many corporates have incurred losses because they had not hedged their foreign currency exposures.

Similarly, in these times of financial uncertainty and risk, the importance of educating our people about the advantages of Life and Non-life insurance products cannot be underestimated. In our country even so called financially educated people, including many of us, still look at insurance, at least partly, as an investment avenue. It is difficult to convince a large number of us that insurance is risk coverage for our life and we should not expect any returns after the insurance policy has expired. Our insurance penetration is far lower than expected. For a poor person not just life, health but livestock insurance are equally important but insurance penetration continues to be poor.

While financial literacy for the users of financial services/ products is of paramount importance, financial education is also a must for financial service providers. Banks, financial institutions and other market players too need to be literate about their risk and return framework. Every bank, in order to expand its customer base, needs to understand the requirements of its customers and the market, credit and operational risks involved in its operations. They need to understand that for their business to survive, their customers must survive and for that, they need to understand the appropriateness of the products themselves to be able to explain it to their customers. Very often the frontline counter staffs of banks do not know all the features of the products being offered to the bank customers.

Institutional Framework in India

Now coming to the institutional framework created in India for the spread of financial literacy, I would like to mention that we are among the very few countries where an apex body namely the FSDC chaired by the Union Finance Minister with heads of all financial sector regulators as members has been mandated, *inter alia* to focus on spread of financial inclusion and financial literacy. Under the aegis of the FSDC, the National Strategy for Financial Education (NSFE) for India has been prepared. The Strategy envisages ways of creating awareness and educating consumers on access to financial services; availability of various types of products and their features; changing attitudes to translate knowledge into responsible financial behavior; and making consumers of financial services understand their rights and obligations. The Strategy calls for active involvement of individuals, financial sector regulators, educational institutions, NGOs, financial sector entities, multilateral international players and the Government at both Centre and State.

Our National Strategy envisages a time frame of five years for its massive financial education campaign and aims at establishing initial contact with 500 million adults, educating them on key saving, protection and investment related products so that they are empowered to take prudent financial decisions. It also seeks to create awareness about the consumer protection and grievances redressal machinery available in the country. Basic financial education is aimed to be included in school curricula up to senior secondary level. This is based upon the premise that the most effective way is to weave financial education into the normal content of school curricula. Accordingly, we are engaging with the curriculum setting bodies like the National Council of Educational Research and Training (NCERT), Education Boards like the Central Board for Secondary Education (CBSE), Central and State Governments to try and embed such concepts in the school curriculum.

One of the objectives of the NSFE is to standardise the messages that various stakeholders seek to disseminate through their financial education initiatives. The NSFE document identifies certain simple messages to reiterate such as why save; why invest; why insure; why save with banks; why borrow within limits; why repay loans in time; why borrow for income generating purposes, what is interest and how moneylenders charge very high interest rates, etc. It is a well recognised fact that the standardisation will help in ensuring consistency in the messages reaching the target audience from various sources and making them more focused and powerful.

Some work has been done in this direction. In order to ensure consistency in the messages reaching the target audience of financially excluded people during the Financial Literacy Camps, RBI issued comprehensive Financial Literacy Material containing Guidance Note for Trainers, Operational Guidelines for Conduct of Financial Literacy Camps, Financial Literacy Guide, Financial Diary and a set of 16 posters. Banks have been advised to use it as a standard curriculum to impart basic conceptual understanding of financial products and services.

Role of Banks in spreading financial literacy

RBI has adopted a planned, structured and integrated approach of achieving Financial Inclusion through Financial Literacy by advising banks to setup FLCs with a view to scale up the Financial Literacy efforts throughout the country. Banks have been advised to setup Financial Literacy Centres (FLCs) in the 630 plus offices of the lead district managers (LDMs).These offer face to face money advice Further we have mandated the 35,000 plus rural branches of SCBs including RRBs to undertake outdoor financial literacy activities at least once a month with focus on financially excluded population. In order to link the financially excluded segment with the banking system, RBI has devised model architecture to conduct the financial literacy camps in three stages starting with awareness in first stage, account opening in second stage and monitoring the usage of accounts in the third stage.

As at the end of June 2013, 750 Financial Literacy Centres (FLCs) have been set up by banks and a total of 2.8 million people have been educated through indoor education in FLCs and by organising outdoor activities like awareness camps/ choupals, goshtis, baithaks, seminars, lectures etc.

In Conclusion

We have discussed that financial education is the key to promoting financial inclusion and customer protection. In the paradigm of the post crisis world at the current global economic conjuncture the synapses between financial education, financial inclusion and customer protection assume great salience. The G20 discourse is increasingly focused on financial inclusion and consumer protection as integral to achieving financial stability and integrity. This forms part of the Global Economy Concerns and the G20 Framework for Strong, Sustainable and Balanced Growth. The World Savings Bank Institute, 2010 has recognised Financial Access as a 'key accelerator' to meet the Millennium Development Goals. We have discussed that Financial education is the process of building knowledge, skills and attitudes leading to become financially literate. Financial Education introduces people to good money management practices with respect to earning, spending, saving, borrowing, and investing. The role of financial education is to enable people to determine their financial goals and shift from reactive to proactive decision-making and work towards fulfilling these goals. By broadening an understanding of financial products, options and principles, financial education builds skills to use financial products and services, and promotes attitudes and behaviors that support more effective deployment/use of scarce financial resources. When linked to the financial inclusion agenda the implicit argument is that financial education will motivate the learner to understand the advantages of transactions with mainstream financial institutions and adopt available formal financial services.

Financial Inclusion is thus the process of bringing people from the margin to the mainstream, linking them to mainstream financial institutions so that they become customers of Banks and are able to access the full range of services - Savings, Deposits, Loans which the Banks offer.

Financial Education is key to promoting Financial Inclusion which is a step towards customer protection as it ensures linkage with mainstream financial institutions so that the hapless borrower is not at the mercy of the informal service providers who charge notoriously high rates of interest. Building financial capability is a very great challenge — the combination of knowledge, skills and attitudes with the opportunities to apply them - requires input from multiple sources including those that educate the consumer and those that sell the products. As a result, the responsibility for wise decisions regarding financial strategies and tools does not lie solely with the individual client. Building financial capabilities is not a undirectional process while Customers have a responsibility to be informed about the products they are 'purchasing', financial service providers have a responsibility to understand their market and respond with a range of appropriate and affordable services, including savings and credit accounts, payment services, insurance products and the ability to send and receive remittance payments cheaply. In sum, the Banks need to address the needs of the customer and tailor products and services customised to their requirement without adopting a one size fits all approach. They need to apply principles of transparency in a way that facilitates clients' decision-making, and verify assumptions about what clients understand and don't understand about their products and the fine print in the contracts they sign. We at RBI have embraced financial education to protect consumers from fraud and abuse. The RBI has a Banking Ombudsman Scheme which enables grievance redress in an expeditious and inexpensive manner and there is a provision of appeal against the decisions of the Banking Ombudsman. The power of appeal vests with the Deputy Governor in charge of the Department.

Thus, financial education and the financial literacy it builds leading to wider Financial Inclusion and greater customer empowerment comprise a win-win proposition at multiple levels, for several stakeholders. At the micro level, financial literacy helps poorer households to use scarce resources more effectively, choose the financial products that best meet their needs and become proactive decision makers. At the macro level, the institutional level, informed customers definitely make for better clients; they help lower institutional risk and contribute to a stronger bottom line. At the market level, financially literate consumers are a key element in effective consumer protection; placing pressure on financial institutions for services that are both appropriately priced and transparent. Public agencies such as Central Banks, must ensure the consumer voice is heard thus aligning Financial Inclusion, financial stability integrity and consumer protection policies. Inclusion, stability, integrity and protection ISIP are core objectives.

References

1. www.bis.org/review/r120606c.pdf
2. www.rbi.org

14

Financial Education and Customer Protection

The paradigm in the post crisis world is characterised by recognition of Asymmetry of information between Customer and Service Providers. Financial disintermediation; Increasing competition among banks and other financial service providers, Aggressive marketing of Para-banking activities – card, insurance, portfolio management, advisory services, Increase in the depth of markets; new financial services, thereby, recognising providers need for financial education.

Financial education is aimed at empowering clients with knowledge of–Product features / processes/precautions, Regulatory stipulations, Bank commitments-Standards and codes, Recourse to internal and external redress mechanisms etc.

India is one of the largest countries in the world as it has 7th largest geographical area and 2nd largest population. India is a union of 35 States, 659 districts, 600 thousand villages with multilingual and multiethnic society with low level of general literacy and large number of financially excluded people. In India there is very low demand to join the formal financial institutions as more than quarter of the population of India lives below poverty line; about 50 per cent population until

2007-08, did not have a deposit account; less than 15 per cent had availed credit from banks; less than 10 per cent had insurance of any kind. Besides, availability of the institutions is also inadequate as there are only 30,000 branches for half a million villages bringing the ratio to one branch for 16000 persons. To bridge the demand-supply gap– Financial education and financial services must be made available.

Institutional Framework

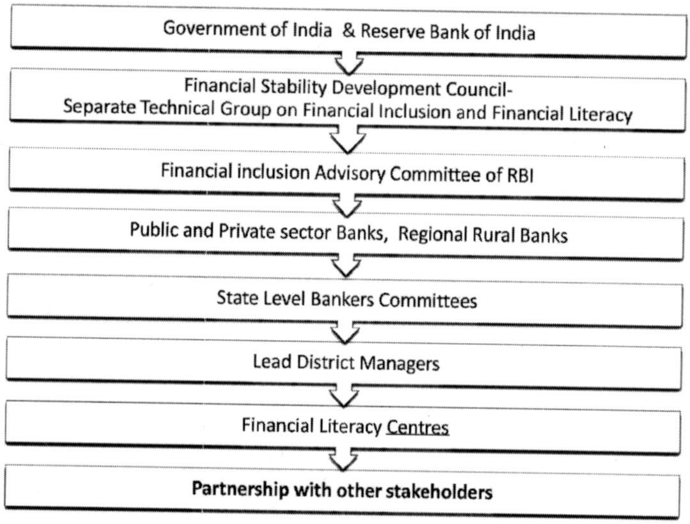

Financial Literacy Centers

Financial literacy centres have been opened by banks to reach out to the poor in rural and urban areas creating awareness of deposit, credit, other financial products and services– at least once in a month-with a standardised curriculum to provide information in organised manner. We have also prepared Financial Diary, 16 posters to impart financial literacy. This whole exercise is monitored by RBI on quarterly basis. Initiatives under financial literacy are:

- FLCs – Annual Calendar, advance publicity
- Progressive learning/follow up sessions

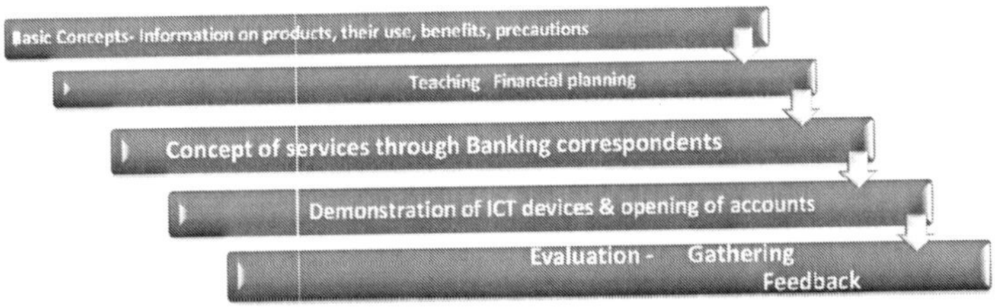

Financial Education–Broad Methodology

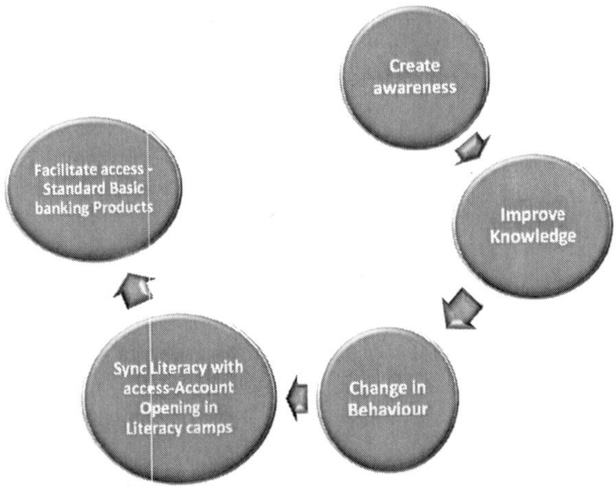

Financial education–Becoming aware of issues and choices

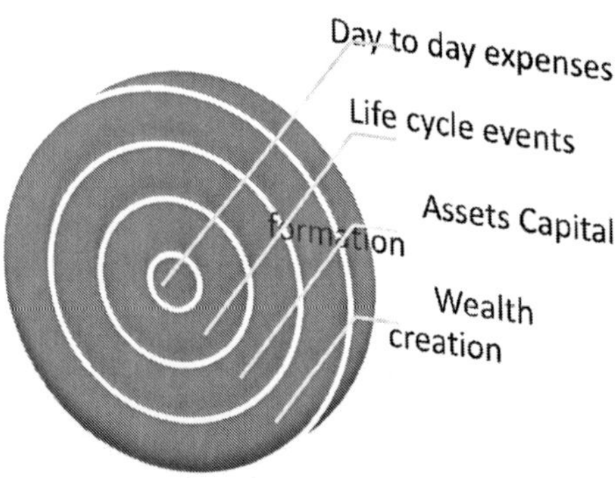

Money Wise Be Wise

Financial Education–Key to Prosperity

Reserve Bank of India has provided financial literacy material in English, Hindi and 11 vernacular languages on its website including Comic books on money and banking, Films, messages on financial planning, Games on financial education, Explaining Resolution and grievance redress framework, Link for accessing the Banking Ombudsman Scheme. FAQs on important products and services, regulatory departments, regulatory developments, schemes–Banking, Currency, Forex, Govt. Securities Market, Non-banking Finance Companies, Payment System.

RBI regularly issues advisory/warning against phishing attempts, lottery/prizes, inheritance notices, fraudulent e-mail enquiring about PIN number and other fraudulent attempts. RBI also conducts outreach visits to villages by the top management, setting up stalls in local fairs (Melas), exhibitions, distributing pamphlets, comic books, setting up, enacting street plays and skits, conducting quizzes in schools (RBI Q), Take part in information/literacy programs, Engage with other stakeholders Civil Society, Launch of print and electronic Mass media campaigns – Awareness drives- FM radio, TV, print media.

Expectations from Banks

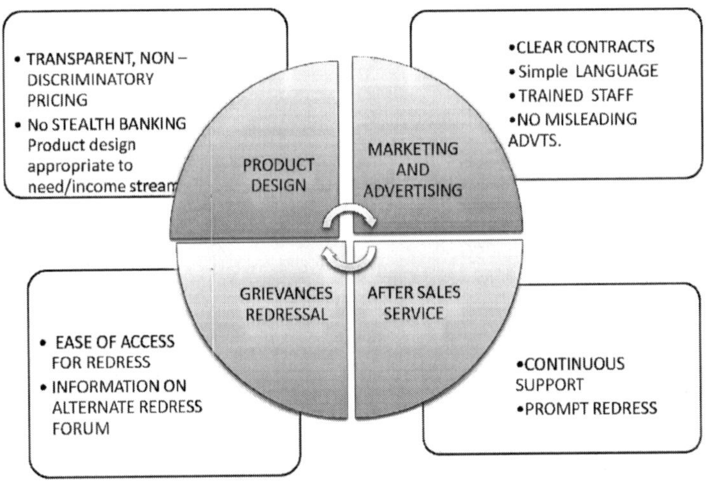

Several statutes and regulatory institutions have also been set up to maintain the integrity and robustness of the financial system: Banking Regulation Act, 1949 and Reserve Bank of India Act,1934 to protect the depositor's interest, Securities Exchange Board of India Act, 1992 to protect investors, Insurance Regulatory and Development Authority Act, 1999 for protecting insured's interest and Pension Funds Regulatory and Development Authority (soon to be enacted as an Act of Parliament) for protecting beneficiaries.

Reserve Bank of India has issued guidelines on customer protection in banking services. Guidelines on Customer Service, Deposit interest rates, loans and advances, remittances/ fund transfers, electronic banking, KYC etc. Banking Ombudsman Scheme and Banking Codes and Standards Board of India. RBI has directed banks to constitute– Board level committees, Standing Committee-for ongoing improvement and monitoring; Branch level customer service committees – formal channel of communication, Nodal officers– single point of contact for complaints, Frame internal redress and complaints escalation mechanism

Why Customer needs protection

Banking Ombudsman Scheme

The Banking Ombudsman Scheme (BOS) – notified by RBI in 1995 – under Section 35A of the BR Act. At present there are 15 Banking Ombudsman Offices covering entire country – 28

States and 7 UTs. This scheme was initially funded by participant banks and staffed by SLBC convener bank in the State and RBI. Since 2006 the Scheme is fully funded and administered by RBI and the Customer Service Department (CSD) was set up at Central Office on July 1, 2006 to oversee the implementation of BOS.

Scheme covers–customers of Commercial Banks, Urban Cooperative Banks, Regional Rural Banks. There are 27 grounds of complaints covering all banking services (*Exceptions – complaints against commercial decision of credit sanction/pricing / recovery, non-funded exposures, forex,, cases requiring elaborate examination, cases already decided earlier at Banking ombudsman office and those decided or under attention of courts / tribunals*). This is a Quasi-judicial body set up to settle disputes through conciliation/mediation adjudication if bank does not redress it. In the event of failure of conciliation, provision for issuing 'Awards' which are binding on banks subject to acceptance by complainant. Right to appeal is there and vests with the Deputy Governor in charge of Customer Protection.

Banking Ombudsman–Complaint Handling Process

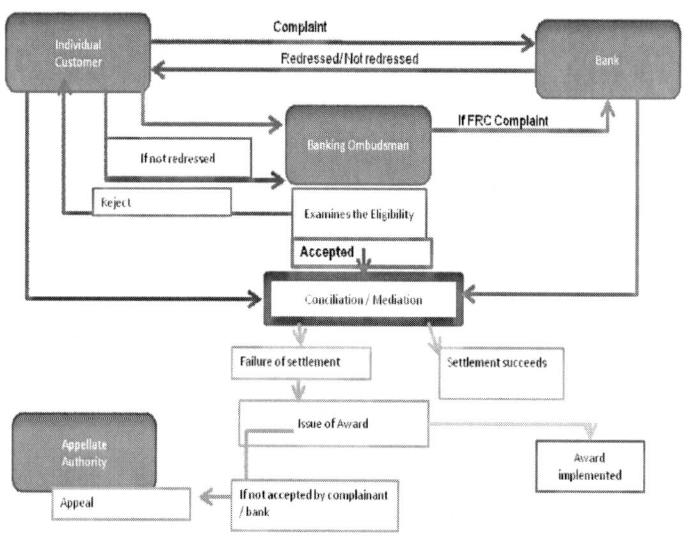

Trends of complaints received at offices of banking ombudsman

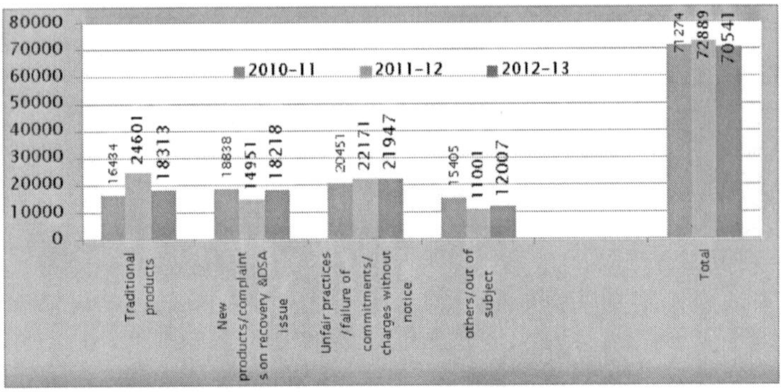

Percentage of complaints on Unfair practices/non-fulfillment of promised services

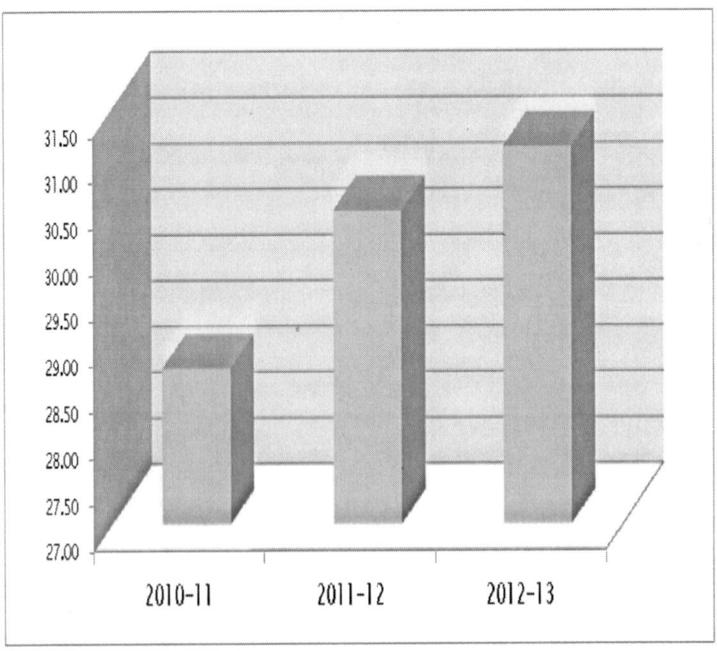

Complaint category-wise receipt & disposal by BO Offices-2012-13

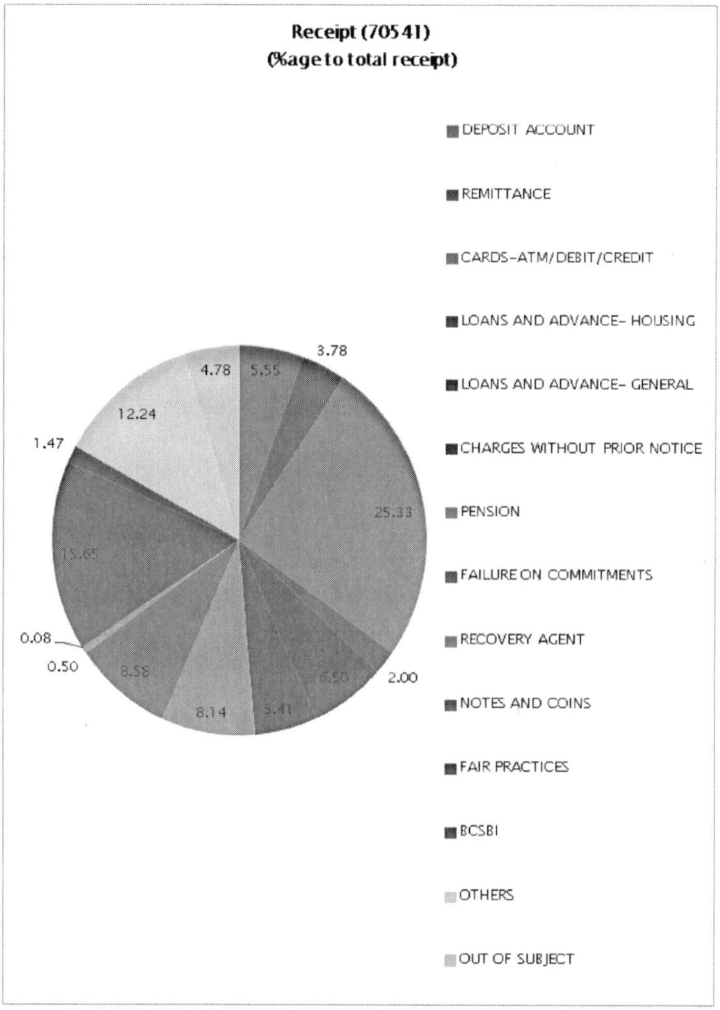

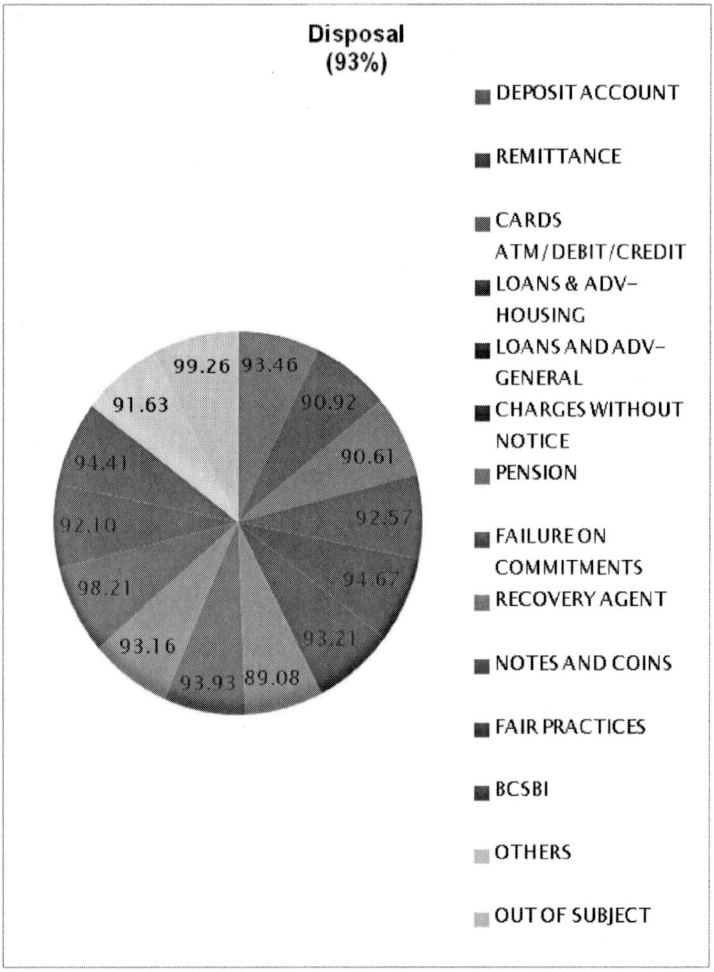

Reserve Bank of India as an apex regulator has taken several initiatives for customer protection as follows:

RBI Initiatives:

- Reasonableness of charges/fees imposed
- Guidelines on credit card operations and recovery agents,

- Norms on outsourcing services,
- Safety stipulations in electronic banking services (authentication, alerts),
- Compensation for losses due to fraud, delayed credit/ refund of NEFT transactions, delayed pension updation/payments
- Abolition of pre-payment charges on floating home loans,
- Abolition of the concept of home and non-home customers–equal inter sol charges
- Zero balance accounts–basic savings bank accounts
- Relaxed KYC norms for small accounts,
- KYC authentication based on Aadhar documents,
- Portability of accounts within bank - fresh KYC not required.

However, several issues and challenges still being addressed are: Formulating clear customer protection code; Evolving a mechanism to measure effectiveness of customer service/grievance redress in banks and in RBI, Building culture of Treating Customers Fairly; Policy on redress of grievances outside the scope of the Banking Ombudsman Scheme needed; Improving awareness, access and effectiveness of the Grievance Redress Mechanism; Ensuring skill adequacy of staff deployed for grievance redress; Benchmarking complaints handling and management systems of banks/RBI against internationally approved standards.

Trinity to make Financial Stability Possible

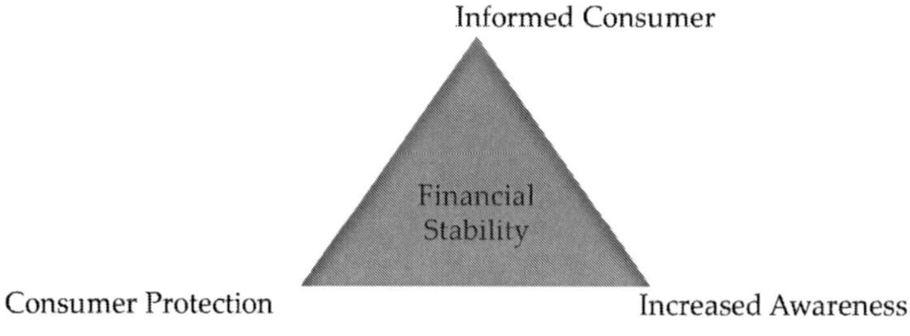

References

1. www.rbi.org.in › Index To RBI Circulars
2. rbidocs.rbi.org.in/rdocs/Speeches/PDFs/DGWB240212KC.pdf
3. Annual Report on Banking Ombudsman Scheme, 2009-10
4. National Strategy for Financial Education

15

Moving Financial Capability Forward: Innovation Scale and Impact

Financial literacy means different things to different people. We in India understand financial literacy differently depending upon the underlying objective to build greater financial inclusion through financial literacy, for maximising welfare, both individually and for society generally. Although, we have progressively promoted financial literacy, many challenges remain. These include : (i) the large excluded sections many of whom may be illiterate especially in the rural or remote areas with difficult physical access; (ii) the need for better supervisory capacity among financial regulators; and (iii) addressing the pervasive "informal" markets that handle lending, insurance, and remittances for those unable to tap into the formal system.

As we know, we have a large banking system which comprises besides Public Sector Banks, Private Sector Banks, Regional Rural Banks and Cooperatives with significant penetrative outreach. Well, these banks are now all on interoperable Core Banking System platforms which enables us to significantly leverage technology to leapfrog the barriers of geography and distance and tackle issues of voluntary access. We have significantly liberalised our rules on bank branching, we have enabled the use of Banking Correspondents (BCs), some of the mobile companies, such as, AIRTEL and VODAFONE, partner with banks as BCs. We have also liberalised the dreaded KYC norms to make it easier for a poor person or a migrant to open a bank account. We have enabled E-KYC. Our unique identity card, the Aadhar, is enabling digitisation of social benefit transfers which will also lead to steady revenue streams for service providers and we have a big push on building financial capability.

Role of Financial Education in India

Greater financial access combined with financial education creates financially responsible citizens. This mix of financial access and financial education provides a foundation for appropriate market conduct and prudential regulation. Improving individuals' financial behaviour is a long-term policy priority. Financial education needs to commence early and continue through adulthood.

In order to achieve the objective of financial inclusion, our financial literacy efforts are primarily directed towards dissemination of simple messages of financial prudence, in vernacular languages, through large awareness campaigns across the country combined with vigorous roll out of financial inclusion plans by banks, insurance and pension funds, and others. It is important to note that being literate is not a necessary pre-requisite for attaining financial literacy as the basic financial messages can be conveyed through various alternate means without relying on written inputs. Some of the basic messages we seek to deliver through our financial literacy drives are:

- Why Save
- Why save regularly and consistently
- Why save with banks
- Why borrow within Limits
- Why borrow from banks

- Why borrow for income generating purposes
- Why repay loans
- Why repay loans in time
- Why do you need insurance
- Why you will need regular stream of income post working life –pension
- Why you should keep money aside regularly and consistently during your earning life for pension in old age
- What is interest? How moneylenders charge very high interest rates?

Since the challenge in India is to link a larger number of financially excluded people to the formal financial system, the focus of our strategy at the base level is to create awareness of basic financial products. Some of the steps that have been taken by the Reserve Bank of India and other stakeholders to promote financial literacy in India are:

Outreach visits by Senior Executives of Reserve Bank of India to remote villages: The objective of these visits is to understand the ground level position, spread awareness about benefits of being connected to the formal financial system and disseminate information about the functioning of RBI.

RBI website : We have created a link for Financial Education on the RBI website, containing material in English, Hindi and 11 vernacular languages, which includes comic books on money and banking for children, films, messages on financial planning, games on financial education and link for accessing the Banking Ombudsman Scheme for customer grievance redress. Some of the popular comic books brought out by the department of communication are Money Kumar, Raju and the Money Tree and some films which very simply impart messages on financial education to children. The department of communication also hosts groups of school children and explains the working of RBI to them and imparts simple financial concepts to them.

Inter School Quiz: In line with the 'catch them young' strategy for our financial education initiatives, the Reserve Bank launched the RBIQ, an all India inter school quiz competition, in 2012. The quiz seeks to be an effective platform for disseminating financial education by creating awareness and sensitisation about the history and role of the Reserve Bank, about banking and finance, economics, current affairs, etc., besides seeking to build a 'connect' between the Reserve Bank and the young student community enrolled in schools across the country.

Financial Literacy Centres: (FLCs) have been opened by various banks with a sharp focus on the spread of Financial Literacy, to create awareness about financial products and provision of counselling facilities for customers of banks. There are more than 800 FLCs in the country as on September 30, 2013. Use of mobile Financial Literacy vans is done by banks in the difficult terrains.

Town Hall events: These are conducted across the country, including in Tier II and smaller cities, bringing together commercial banks and other stakeholders.

Mass media : The campaign are launched through tie ups with educational institutes, financial awareness workshops/ helplines, books, pamphlets and publications on financial literacy by NGOs, financial market players, etc.

Capacity Building : Is attempted through the Conduct of Financial Literacy programs by Rural Self Employment Training Institutes.

Awareness Campaigns: By distributing pamphlets, comic books, enacting plays and skits, arranging stalls in local fairs, exhibitions, participating in information/literacy programs organised by Press. Similarly, in these times of financial uncertainty and risk, the importance of educating people about the advantages of Life and Non-life insurance products is important.

Institutional framework in India for spreading Financial Education

Now coming to the institutional framework created in India for the spread of financial literacy, it should be known that we are among the very few countries where an apex body namely the Financial Stability and Development Council (FSDC) chaired by the Union Finance Minister with heads of all financial sector regulators as members has been mandated, *inter alia* to focus on spread of financial inclusion and financial literacy. So we have a buy in of our strategies at the highest levels under the aegis of the FSDC, a National Strategy for Financial Education (NSFE) for India has been prepared. The Strategy envisages ways of creating awareness and educating consumers on access to financial services; availability of various types of products and their features; changing attitudes to translate knowledge into responsible financial behaviour; and enabling consumers of financial services understand their rights and obligations. The Strategy necessitates active involvement of individuals, financial sector regulators, educational institutions, NGOs, financial sector entities, multilateral international players and the Governments both at Centre and State levels.

National Strategy for Financial Education

Our National Strategy envisages a time frame of five years for its massive financial education campaign and aims at establishing initial contact with 500 million adults, educating them on key saving, protection and investment related products so that they are empowered to take prudent financial decisions. It also seeks to create awareness about the consumer protection and grievances redress machinery available in the country. Basic financial education is aimed to be included in school curricula up to senior secondary level. This is based upon the premise that the most effective way is to weave financial education into the normal content of curriculum. Accordingly, we are engaging with the curriculum setting bodies like the National Council of Educational Research and

Training (NCERT), Education Boards like the Central Board for Secondary Education (CBSE), Central and State Governments to try and embed such concepts in the school curriculum.

One of the objectives of the NSFE is to standardise the messages that various stakeholders seek to disseminate through their financial education initiatives. The NSFE document identifies certain simple messages mentioned earlier such as why save; why invest; why insure; why save with banks; why borrow within limits; why repay loans in time; why borrow for income generating purposes, what is interest and how moneylenders charge very high interest rates, etc. It is a well-recognised fact that standardisation will help in ensuring consistency in the messages which reach the target audience from various sources and making them more focused and powerful.

Integrated approach–Financial Inclusion through Financial Education

We have already done some work in this direction. We have designed a Mass Scale Financial Literacy Program to integrate the financially excluded population with low level of income and low literacy level with the formal financial system. The program is run through our Financial Literacy Centres set up by banks, nearly 800 in numbers. About 40,000 rural branches of the banks would scale up these efforts by conducting one outdoor literacy camp in a month. In addition to this we leverage the infrastructure created at the state level, comprising of State Level Bankers Committee (SLBC) at the Apex which is ably supported by the Lead District Managers (LDMs) at the District level. Financial Literacy Centres organise Outdoor Literacy Camps which are spread over a period of three months and delivered in three phases wherein along with creating awareness, accounts are also opened in the Literacy camps. The program has been received well on the ground as an integrated approach of financial inclusion through creating awareness and providing access simultaneously.

In order to ensure consistency in the messages reaching the target audience of financially excluded people during the Financial Literacy Camps, we have issued comprehensive Financial Literacy Material containing a financial literacy Guide, Financial Diary and a set of 16 posters which contain very simple messages of How To Save. For instance, we are a nation of tea drinkers. So we just explain graphically that everyone can drink two cups of tea less! Walk into a bank walk into prosperity and so on and so forth.

Conclusion

While it is important to begin teaching financial skills at school level, achieving and maintaining financial know-how is a lifelong undertaking. The types of financial decisions that people have to make vary through the course of their lives, and thus we are trying to ensure that access to financial education is readily available at all stages of life with the help of other stakeholders. Moreover, relevant, accurate, and reliable financial information must be readily available to consumers at the time they are making their decisions.

Through financial education, we try to provide individuals with the knowledge and skills they need to make better choices about finances. Through consumer protection, we can safeguard individuals against harmful practices and bad information that lead to poor financial choices. Accomplishing these two goals we believe will result in economic empowerment for all concerned.

While a number of measures have been taken and are being taken in India, given the enormity of the task, a lot of ground still needs to be covered. Apart from the Government and the regulatory bodies, there is a need for involving the civil society and all other stakeholders in spreading financial literacy. The widespread existence of financial illiteracy indicates that we need to do a lot more. There is a lot of skepticism on whether Financial literacy actually leads to changes in behaviour and some recent papers which suggest that this does not and it is the classic conundrum of being able to take the horse to the water but not being able to make him drink! Bilal Zia our world Bank researcher and colleague discussed this thoroughly and we concluded that the trick vests in the right delivery model so targeted interventions do work.

References

1. www.rbi.org.in › Index To RBI Circulars
2. rbidocs.rbi.org.in/rdocs/Speeches/PDFs/DGWB 240212KC.pdf
3. National Strategy for Financial Education

16

Ethics and Corporate Governance

Who will guard the guards?

Over the last two decades, corporate governance has attracted a great deal of public interest, it is now widely appreciated that this is critical for the economic health of Corporations and of larger society. The headlines of newspapers of the past few years in particular, portray a dismal story of lack of corporate ethics: Satyam, Enron, falling stock markets, corporate failures, dubious accounting practices, abuses of corporate power, criminal investigations reflect that the entire economic system on which investment returns depend is showing signs of infirmity and stress that have undermined investor confidence. Almost as if checks and balances that should protect our interests are pushed to one side, driven by the overwhelming need to move fast in relentless pursuit of profits. Notably some failures were the result of fraudulent accounting and other illegal practices, others were just bad governance.

Company Boards or Old Boy's Clubs?

Company Boards often deteriorate to being a cosy club, friends of the boss, who just met to rubber stamp his decisions. of the economist (7th December 13), and the turn of phrase (on page 67) was interesting. Critics have compared directors to "parsley on fish", decorative but ineffectual; or honorary Colonels, ornamental in parade but fairly useless in battle. Ralph Nader calls them "cuckolds" who are always the last to know when managers have erred.

The corporate scandals of the early 2000s forced boards to take a more active role. The Sarbanes-Oxley Act of 2002 and the New York Stock Exchange's New Rules in 2003 obliged directors to take more responsibility for preventing fraud and self-dealing. This led to a big increase in the quality of boards. But it also wasted a lot of talent on form-filling and box-ticking. Many of the same companies exhibited actual corporate governance risks such as conflicts of interest, inexperienced directors, overly lucrative compensation, or unequal share voting rights. In the face of such scandals and malpractices, there has been a renewed emphasis on corporate governance.

OECD Definition of Corporate Governance

"Corporate governance is the system by which business corporations are directed and controlled. The corporate governance structure specifies the distribution of rights and responsibilities among different participants in the corporation, such as, the board, managers, shareholders and other stakeholders and spells out the rules and procedures for making decisions in corporate affairs. By doing this, it also provides the structure through which the company objectives are set and the means of attaining those objectives and monitoring performance".

Thus, corporate governance includes within its ambit, the relationship of a company to its shareholders and to society; the promotion of fairness, transparency and accountability; reference to mechanisms that are used to "govern" managers and to ensure that the actions taken by them are consistent with the interests of key stakeholder groups. The salient features span issues of transparency and accountability, the legal and regulatory environment, appropriate risk management measures, information flows, the responsibility of senior management and the board of directors.

The Banking Regulation Act:

Section 10A of the Banking Regulation Act lays down stipulations for the Board of Directors. They must have special knowledge of the following :

- Accountancy

- Agriculture and Rural Economy
- Banking
- Cooperation
- Economics
- Finance
- Law
- Small Scale Industry
- Or any other matter, the special knowledge of, and practical experience in which, in the opinion of the Reserve Bank, would be useful to the Banking Company. Provided that out of the aforesaid number of Directors, not less than two shall have special knowledge of, practical experience, with respect to agriculture and the rural economy, cooperation or small scale industry and shall not –

(i) have substantial interest in, or be connected with, whether as an employee, manager or managing agent, -
    - Any company, not being a company registered under Section 25 of the Companies Act, 1956 (1 to 1956), or
    - Any firm, Which carries on any trade, commerce or industry and which, in either case, is not a small scale industrial concern, or

(ii) be proprietors of any trading, commercial or industrial concern, not being a small scale industrial concern.

Voting rights will be distributed amongst the Board of Directors in a manner such that no more than three Directors are entitled to exercise voting rights in excess of twenty per cent of the total voting rights of all the shareholders to the Banking Entity.

The tenure of Directors except the Chairman or the whole time director is limited to eight continuous years.

The Chairman of the Board (appointed on a whole time basis) or the Managing Director of the Banking entity and any Director (appointed by the Reserve Bank under Section 10A of the Banking Regulation Act) will not be required to hold qualification shares in the Banking Entity.

The RBI has the power, from time to time, to appoint one or more persons to hold office as additional director of any Banking Company, if it is of the opinion that the same is in the interests of banking Policy/public interest/banking company depositors, it may also require the banking company to elect or appoint any other person as the Chairman in case it is of the opinion that the current elected Chairman is not a fit and proper person to hold such office.

Requirements of Corporate Governance as per the RBI guidelines on Corporate Governance.

RBI issues guidelines on corporate governance for public sector banks which serve as a base for the Corporate Governance framework in Banks.

Banks must perform due diligence of the directors with regard to their suitability for appointment to the Board by way of qualifications and technical expertise. The Government should also be guided by certain "fit and proper" norms for the appointment of Directors representing the Government on the Boards of Public Sector Banks.

Banks need to elect shareholder nominees in proportion to the shares issued to public subject to a maximum of six nominees in respect of banks which have issued capital to public up to 40 per cent of the Banks paid up capital.

Executive Directors (EDs) are eligible for appointment as Chairman of the Board of Directors on fulfillment of the following criteria vesting in having served in the position and residual tenure.

Guidelines on the number of EDs – Small Banks with business of less than INR 1.5 lakh crore may have two EDs with the responsibilities of the second Director including human resource development and technology. Large banks with business of more than 3 lakh crore may have three EDs, the third with responsibility for HRD and Technology.

As a Director on the Board a Public Sector Bank found that the Boards of Banks are hedged with innumerable Committees – there are Management Committee, Credit Approval Committee, Audit Committee, Risk management Committee, Special Committee to monitor large Value Frauds/ Anti-Fraud Committee, Asset Liability Committee, Customer Service Committee, Shareholders Investors Grievance Committee, Share Transfer Committee, Remuneration Committee, and so on and so forth and yet the state of Management and Corporate Governance in public sector banks remains a cause of grave concern.

If restructured assets show further deterioration surely the appraisal mechanisms were weak RAROC Risk Adjusted Return on Capital was not correctly computed. The mechanisms of Corporate Governance surely merit much greater attention.

Regulator as Supervisor

Banks constitute the largest financial intermediaries globally and possess stupendous powers of leverage. The RBI plays a direct role in Bank governance through the regulation and supervision of Banking Institutions. This role assumes greater salience viewed in conjunction with the need to ensure systemic and financial stability. Banks enjoy the benefit of high leverage with the downside protection of deposit insurance which weakens their incentives for strong management. They also remain 'Too Big to Fail' (TBTF).

The current Basel Accord lays even greater stress on risk measurement and management. Bank Supervisors must make the Boards of banks the main locus of accountability and assess board effectiveness. Regulatory and supervisory systems that foster more accurate information disclosure and empower private investors, legal rights, substantially boost banking system and profitability. Large investors may manipulate the firm contrary to the broad interests of Banks and other shareholders.

The task of the Bank supervisor is indeed onerous. Information asymmetries plague all sectors but this is even more tangential in finance; in product or other service markets, purchasers' part with money in exchange for something new. In finance, money is exchanged for a promise to pay in the future. In many product or service markets, if the product sold - a car or a haircut is defective, the buyers often find out relatively soon. However, loan quality is not readily observable for quite some time and can be hidden for extensive periods. Banks can also alter the risk composition of their assets more quickly than most non-financial industries. Banks can also sweep problems under the carpet by extending further loans to clients that cannot service previous debt obligations. In most sectors where there is an inventory pile up, be it cars or computers, it is generally a negative sign about the company's performance but when inventories of money pile up in a bank, it becomes more liquid.

It is much harder to sort out whether this is a negative signal or a prudent response by management to a risky environment. Corporate governance of Banks is an essential element of sound regulatory architecture. The regulatory response is an imperative of ethics.

Is the Business of Business just Business?

Milton Friedman had a view that corporate executive's responsibility generally will be to make as much money as possible while conforming to the basic rules of the society, both, those embodied in law and those embodied in ethical custom. The objective is the maximisation of consumption and production. "The business of business is just business". This is not an axiom one can concur with. If you consider the business of Companies historically, it has embraced colonialism and slavery! So the element of ethics must always underlie necessity of both business personal and organisational conduct.

Formal Codes of Ethics

While many of the governance issues that organisations face are not new, the environment in which they confront them today is more challenging than ever. Many companies are adopting legal compliance mechanisms which address ethics or conduct issues in formal documents.

RBI ethics@work- code of conduct

The RBI, Code of Conduct for itself, which we term ethics@work. You may well ask, why an ethics manual and I quote from the ethics manual

"An Ethics Manual promotes:

- Solidarity among colleagues;
- Pride and commitment to working for the Organisation;
- Personal Aspirations that are aligned with organisational goals."

The ethics manual is expected :-

To define and clearly set out what will be deemed to be acceptable behaviour.

We hope that this will promote and ensure high standards of practice

And also establish a benchmark for self-evaluation

Lay down the mainframe for professional behaviour and responsibilities

Enable a sense of occupational identity Ideals we can clearly ascribe to.

The written code of ethics will be useful for socialisation of our new recruits in the organisation, serve as an implement of employee training. Be a benchmark transgression of the same, will invite disciplinary action. It will also help in dispute and conflict management. The moral dilemmas, the approach conflicts will be more easily resolved with reference to the touchstone of the code of ethics. It clarifies the organisation's expectations from the employee and vests on enshrining complete transparency. This is a formal code of business conduct and ethics, to be ascribed to and strictly adhered to by all employees. It is morally incumbent upon them to do so.

Some organisations also have ethics officers but in the ultimate analysis, the foundations of ethical behaviour go well beyond corporate culture and policies. These are rooted in one's moral training, lessons parents and school teachers have taught from early childhood on which affect not just individual behaviour the competitive business environment and indeed society as a whole.

Conclusion

From an ethical dimension, at a fundamental level, the key issues of corporate governance involve questions concerning relationships and building trust (both within and outside the organisation. Aristotle, in the *Nichomacnean Ethics* explained that it is 'in justice' that the ordering of society is centered.

Ethics comes from the Greek ethos and embraces both work ethics and 'mores'–the conduct and culture of the organisation. It is therefore all encompassing and must be all pervasive.

References

1. www.oecd.org › Corporate governance
2. OECD Principles of Corporate Governance - 2004 Edition
3. www.rbi.org.in › Speeches
4. Banking Regulation Act, 1949 (AACS) – Reserve Bank of India

17

Cooperative Bank

Strengthening and Revitalising Rural Cooperative Credit Delivery System

Since inception the Indian Cooperative movement was initiated by the Government to align the rural credit system with the objectives of development planning. The RBI played an important role. The RBI's concern and involvement in the sphere of rural credit stemmed from its very statute of incorporation. Specific provisions were made in the Reserve Bank of India Act, 1934 for the establishment of an Agricultural Credit Department and for extending refinance facilities to the cooperatives. RBI laid emphasis on strengthening and ensuring viable provincial cooperative bank, central cooperative banks, marketing societies and primary agricultural credit societies in each province for seasonal agricultural operations.

Role of cooperatives

The cooperative movement in the country, originated as a measure against rural poverty, agrarian disturbances in 1875 in the Deccan against moneylenders led to the enactment of Taccavi legislation in 1892. Sir Frederick Nicholson recommended the establishment of cooperative societies on the Raiffeisen Model popular in Germany. Thus, cooperatives as people's institutions have a long legacy and a rich tradition in India. The founders of Planning in India considered cooperation an instrument of economic development combining the advantages of private ownership with public good.

Rural credit cooperatives in India were originally envisaged as a mechanism for pooling the resources of people with small means and providing them access to cheap and cost-effective financial services. Democratic in features, the movement was also an effective instrument for development of degraded waste lands, increasing productivity, providing food security, generating employment opportunities in rural areas and ensuring social and economic justice to the poor and vulnerable. In light of this, the cooperatives occupy an important position in the Indian financial system.

Cooperatives were the first formal institutions to be conceived and developed to purvey credit to rural India and have been a key instrument of credit delivery to enable farmers to meet their production needs and so increase production and productivity in the rural areas.

Evolution of Cooperatives in India

In the first Phase (1900-1930), the cooperative movement originated due to the initiative of the colonial government in the early twentieth century. The idea of establishing cooperatives of the type that worked successfully in Germany was mooted in the late nineteenth century. These cooperatives were seen as a means to liberate the poor farmers from the clutches of usurious money-lenders. The Government passed the Cooperative Societies Act in 1904 followed by a more comprehensive Cooperative Societies Act later in 1912. In 1915 the Maclagan Committee advocated that "there should be one cooperative for every village and every village should be covered by a cooperative." The Royal Commission made the observation "if cooperation fails, there will fail the best hope of rural India".

In the second Phase (1930-1950), by virtue of the provisions of the RBI Act, the Reserve Bank was given a mandate to closely associate with matters relating to rural credit and banking. RBI Act provided for both the establishment of an Agricultural Credit Department in the bank and extension of refinance facilities to the cooperative credit system. RBI introduced credit facilities to provincial cooperative banks for seasonal agricultural operations and marketing of crops from 1942.

In the third Phase (1950–1990), a major initiative for pursuit of the mandate given to the Reserve Bank was taken with sponsoring of All India Rural Credit Survey in 1951-52. The study recommended an integrated approach to cooperative credit and emphasised the need for viable credit cooperative societies by expanding their area of operation, encouraging rural savings and diversifying business. The Committee also recommended government participation in the share capital of the cooperatives. The National Commission on Agriculture (1976) recommended setting up of Farmers Service Cooperative Societies with the active collaboration of the nationalised banks. The involvement of commercial banks was institutionalised through nationalisation of major commercial banks in 1969, causing unprecedented penetration of commercial banks in the rural sector. The State has used co-operatives to channel its development schemes, particularly subsidy-based programs for the poor. As these institutions have a wide reach in the rural areas and also deal with finances, the choice was natural.

By 1982, to consolidate the various arrangements made by the RBI to promote/supervise institutions and channel credit to rural areas, NABARD was established based on the recommendation of the CRAFICARD (Sivaraman Committee 1981). The Agriculture Credit Review Committee (Khusro Committee, 1989) stressed the importance of encouraging members' thrift and savings for the cooperatives. It also emphasised the need for better business planning at the local level and for strategies to enable cooperatives to be self-sustaining. To this end, the Committee was in favor of serving non-members, if it made business sense. The 1990s witnessed more concerted attempts by both the government and non-official organisations and cooperators, to explore ways to revitalise the cooperatives.

In the Fourth Phase (1990s and onwards), there has been an increasing realisation of the deleterious impact of intrusive State patronage, politicisation, and the consequent impairment of the role of cooperatives in general, and of credit cooperatives in particular, leading to a quest for reviving and revitalising the cooperative movement. Several Committees were set up to suggest cooperative sector reforms during this period.

Short-term Cooperative Credit Structure (STCCS)

Since inception, cooperatives have made available institutional credit at affordable cost particularly to the agricultural sector. The Short-term Rural Cooperative Credit Structure (STCCS) provides mainly short-term and medium-term production credit besides other financial services. At present, there are nearly 92,432 Primary Agricultural Credit Societies (PACS), 371 District Central Cooperative Banks (DCCB) with 13,233 branches and 32 State Cooperative Banks (SCB) with 992 branches. On an average, there is one PACS for every 8 villages. These societies have a total membership of more than 120 million rural people making it one of the largest rural financial systems in the world. 60 per cent of population still depends upon agricultural income.

Performance of rural cooperative banks in extension of agriculture credit

Institutional lending to agriculture and allied activities has recorded a significant growth during the last two decades due to the aggressive policy of the government in expanding credit to agriculture. The following figure depicts the growth in agricultural credit distributed by the STCCS:

Performance of STCCS under Agricultural Credit

(Rs. in crore)

Years	*StCBs*	*DCCBs*	*PACS*
2002-03	35052	52820	33996
2007-08	53314	95974	57642
2008-09	51866	97207	58787
2009-10	59784	104997	74938
2010-11	68481	122795	91304
2011-12	81523	144761	107300

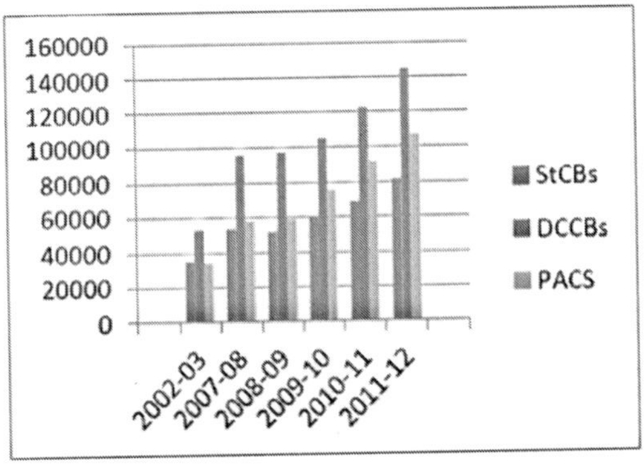

Lending by cooperative credit institutions grew much faster than that by other banks during the 1990s. Thereafter, their share has been declining since 2007-08. Despite this fall, cooperatives clearly remain the major source of agricultural credit to small and medium farmers in terms of the number of borrowers and size of individual loans.

Agricultural Loans Disbursed during the Year

(Rs. in crore)

Agency	*2006-07*	*2007-08*	*2008-09*	*2009-10*	*2010-11*	*2011-12*
Coops.	42,480 (18)	48,258 (19)	46,192 (15)	63,497 (17)	78,121 (17)	87,963 (17)
RRBs	20,435 (9)	25,312 (10)	26,765 (9)	35,217 (9)	44,293 (9)	54,450 (11)

(Contd...)

CBs	1,66,485 (73)	1,81,088 (71)	2,28,951 (76)	2,85,800 (74)	3,45,877 (74)	3,68,616 (72)
Total	2,29,400	2,54,658	3,01,908	3,84,514	4,68,291	5,11,029

Figures in brackets indicate percentage share of different agencies to total agricultural credit.

Problems of cooperatives

Despite the phenomenal outreach and volume of operations, the health of a very large proportion of rural credit cooperatives has deteriorated significantly. The institutions are beset with problems like poor governance, infrastructural weaknesses, operational inefficiencies and the consequent impairment of their financial health. Several factors such as low borrowing membership, low resource base, lack of democratisation and professionalism, high incidence of overdues and almost stagnant recovery performance have led to the deterioration in the financial soundness of cooperatives. There is an urgent need to find ways for strengthening the cooperative movement to meet the credit needs of rural India, especially the resource-poor and resource-less poor farmers. The revitalisation and strengthening of cooperative institutions at all levels should therefore be considered not only desirable but expedient. The thrust has to be four-fold, financial, operational, organisational and systemic.

Poor Governance

Cooperatives operate within the legal framework formulated by state governments. However, compliance with the legal provisions of the State Cooperative Societies Acts has not been ensured. Governance, connected lending, transparency in grant of loans, audit, internal checks and control, recovery of dues, recruitment of qualified persons are issues trammeling the efficient functioning of cooperatives.

As dominant share holders, state governments interference in the management of cooperatives. Supervision and guidance by the elected Boards is lax. Delay in conduct of elections, frequent supersession of the Boards, lack of participation by members in the management and decision-making process have impaired functioning of cooperatives on sound business lines. In the absence of professional management, accountability and uncertain tenures, the Board members are not able to provide dynamic leadership to the organisation. Restoring and strengthening autonomy, mutual help and self governance are the cornerstone of the cooperatives.

Absence of prudent interest rate policies

Cooperatives have access to huge deposits from public but there is no system to ensure prudent deployment of these funds. They have not taken advantage of the freedom given to them to decide on the interest rates on deposits and advances. While deposits are accepted at unsustainably higher rates, loan pricing is done in imprudent manner without factoring in cost of funds. Many cooperatives are unable to generate enough revenue or surplus to sustain their operations and boost capital formation on account of very thin or negative margins. As a result, there are frequent demands for recapitalisation which causes pressure on the limited resources of governments which could have been used for productive investments benefitting the society at large.

Lack of HR Policies and professionalism

The quality of human resources is an important determinant of the success of any organisation. This aspect, however, has not received due importance in the cooperative institutions. The cooperative banks are headed by a committee of elected members who are not professionals and do not possess sound knowledge banking functions. The Committee takes crucial business decisions involving sanction of loans, investments, interest rates on deposits and loans, etc. which require a minimum degree of skill and expertise. Often, the role of Chief Executive Officers in these areas is minimal.

Cooperatives do not have well defined capacity building and HR policies in crucial areas like recruitment, placement, training, career progression, succession planning, etc. Recruitments are done without any objective and systematic manpower assessment. All these have led to inefficiency and lower productivity. Though there is a system of training in place in many cooperative banks, there is no need-assessment to align training with the current and future staff requirements. Training programs should be designed to achieve skill upgradation in areas related to audit and expenditure, management and aptitude development. It is also necessary to keep the staff sufficiently motivated through periodic job rotation, job enrichment and recognition of performance.

Poor Recovery Performance

Frequent loan waiver announcements by governments aimed to garner electoral support have vitiated the credit discipline among the borrowers and affected the recovery atmosphere. The resultant weak finances, growing NPAs and poor resource base have contributed to the declining performance of the cooperatives, particularly at the grass root level. Since these grass root institutions depend on liquidity support from higher financing agencies like State and Central Cooperative Banks, non-payment of dues impairs the financial health of the entire chain.

Inadequate Internal control and audit

Cooperatives do not pay attention to implementation of adequate and foolproof internal checks and control. Balancing of books and reconciliation of entries are in arrears for unduly long periods. As a result, there is frequent incidence of frauds involving the staff who game the system. Very often, these cases are held up due to protracted litigation in Courts of law and the guilty are not brought to book. There is absence of effective audit mechanism. There are delays in the conduct of audits and submission of reports. Quality of audit leaves much to be desired in as much as it fails to address the gaps in the systems and processes and improve efficiency of operations of the cooperatives.

Lack of Member Participation

The cooperative structure should be member-driven. However, members having a voting right do not take active part or show interest in the affairs of the cooperatives since the control and management is vested in a few members. Besides, depositors, whose money is intermediated by the cooperatives, have no voting right or any say in the management.

Not keeping pace with changes

Cooperatives have been unable to adapt themselves to the rapid pace of changes in the financial sector. Cooperatives have lagged behind in designing of new products and services and in adoption of technology and advanced management practices that have changed the face of financial sector in the post economic-liberalisation era. As a result, they are unable to cope with the stiff competition posed by other banks in rural finance and retain their market share.

Equality of Control

Under the Constitution, 'Cooperation' is a state subject governed by the respective State Cooperative Societies Acts. Registration, incorporation, management, election, and audit are governed by the State Acts. Some aspects relating to banking activities are regulated and supervised by the Reserve Bank of India / NABARD under the Banking Regulation Act, 1949 (As Applicable to Cooperative Societies). There is an urgent need to remove the overlapping controls and endowing functional autonomy and operational freedom to cooperatives. Banking functions should be brought completely under the Banking Regulation Act. The provisions of the Banking Regulation Act should override the provisions of the State Acts/ bye-laws/rules which run counter to it. This will lead to clear demarcation of the areas of activities of cooperative banks.

Need for Revival of the Cooperative Credit Institutions

It is pertinent to mention that in the first place, India is a country with a population of more than 125 crore, of which around 70 crore reside in a little over 6 lakh villages. As there are a little over ninety two thousand PACS in the country, every 8th village, on an average, has an existing cooperative credit outlet. It is in this context that the role of cooperatives assumes importance. A number of Committees were set up to suggest reforms in the sector. Based on the recommendations of the Vaidyanathan Committee, the Government of India rolled out in January 2006, a package for revival of the Short-Term Rural Co-operative Credit Structure. The Task Force also suggested wide-ranging reforms in the governance and management of STCCS including crucial amendments to the respective State Cooperative Societies Acts that were to precede the recommended one-time capitalisation jointly by the Central government, the state governments and the STCCS of the state itself.

Twenty-five state governments signed the MoU with Government of India and NABARD to participate in and implement the package. As on December 2012; 21 states had amended the respective State Cooperative Societies Act. An amount of Rs 9,002 crore was released by NABARD as the Government of India's share, while the state government released Rs 856 crore as their share for recapitalisation of 53,202 eligible PACS in 17 States. Recapitalisation assistance could not be released in many cases as the states did not complete all the necessary benchmark activities within the stipulated period.

Licensing of Rural Cooperative Banks

The Committee on Financial Sector Assessment set up by the Government of India in September 2006 to look into the financial health of all the banks including the cooperative banks and made recommendations for improvement of financial health and systems for attaining and maintaining financial stability. A major recommendation of the Committee was to prohibit unlicensed banks from functioning beyond March 2012.

As there were a large number of cooperative banks (17 out of 31 State Cooperative Banks and 296 out of 371 District

Central Cooperative banks) functioning without license, the Reserve Bank of India relaxed the licensing norms to grant license to these banks. The relaxed norms were:

Progress in licensing of State and Central Cooperative Banks

Position as on	*StCBs*			*DCCBs*		
	Licensed	*Unlicensed*	*Total*	*Licensed*	*Unlicensed*	*Total*
31 March 2006	13	18	31	73	298	371
31 March 2009	14	17	31	75	296	371
31 March 2012	30	01	31	329	42	371
30 September 2012	31	-	31	330	41	371
30 November 2012	31	-	31	345	26	371
31 March 2013	31	-	31	348	23	371
31 December 2013	32*	-	32	348	23	371

* The Jharkhand State Coop. Bank was issued license on 26 August 2013.

(i) Capital to Risk-weighted Assets Ratio (CRAR)– Minimum 4 per cent, and

(ii) Compliance with CRR and SLR for the last one year (default on one or two occasions were permitted).

Consequent upon relaxation of licensing norms, 50 banks qualified for issue of license reducing the number of unlicensed banks from 73 as on February 29, 2012 to 43 as on March 31, 2012 and further to 23 as on June 30, 2013.

Recent Policy Initiatives

Implementation of Core Banking Solution

The Reserve Bank of India has granted permission to StCBs and CCBs to participate in the payment system and offer RTGS/ ECS/NEFT facilities to their customers/members. Since IT infrastructure is the prerequisite for offering these services, Core Banking Solution (CBS) is being implemented in StCBs and CCBs. Several banks have joined the NABARD assisted project and made significant progress in implementation of CBS. Some banks have undertaken implementation of CBS on their own. Full implementation is expected to be achieved by March 31, 2014.

Progress in implementation of CBS as at January 31, 2014							
No of banks		CBS completed		CBS in progress		Yet to commence	
StCBs	DCCBs	StCBs	DCCBs	StCBs	DCCBs	StCBs	DCCBs
32	371	28	294	4	55	-	22

Prudential norms on capital adequacy

Rural Cooperative Banks have been kept out of Capital to Risk-weighted Assets Ratio (CRAR) framework for a long time on the grounds that there is an in-built accretion to capital every time a loan is availed of by a member. In view of the high level of default characterising the STCCS and the risk posed by higher concentration of loan portfolios of these banks in a single sector with defined areas of operation, the Vaidyanathan Task Force recommended for bringing all tiers of the STCCS under the CRAR framework. The Reserve Bank of India recently reviewed the position of CRAR in StCBs and CCBs and has introduced the minimum CRAR requirement for these banks. A roadmap has been laid down for achieving CRAR of 7 per cent by March 31, 2015 and 9 per cent by March 31, 2017.

Since these banks have limited avenues of mobilising additional capital resources, permission has been granted for issue of Long-term (Subordinated) Deposits and Innovative Perpetual Debt Instruments. State/Central Co-operative Banks (StCBs/CCBs) are now allowed to issue Long-term (Subordinated) Deposits (LTD) with the prior permission of the respective Registrar (RCS) granted in consultation with the Reserve Bank. LTD can be issued to members and non-members, including those outside the area of operations of the StCBs/CCBs concerned. There is no prohibition on existing shareholders subscribing to LTD. The amounts raised through LTD will be eligible to be treated as lower Tier II capital, subject to certain conditions.

State/Central Co-operative Banks are also allowed to issue Innovative Perpetual Debt Instruments (Innovative Instruments). The instruments may be issued as bonds or debentures to qualify for inclusion as Tier I capital for capital adequacy purposes. Banks are required to obtain prior approval of the Reserve Bank of India, on a case-by-case basis, for issue of innovative instruments. Innovative instruments shall not exceed 15 per cent of total Tier I capital. Innovative instruments in excess of the above limits shall be eligible for inclusion under Tier II, subject to limits prescribed for Tier II capital. However, investors' rights and obligations would remain unchanged.

Membership of Credit Information Companies

Under the Credit Information Companies (Regulation) Act, 2005, all Co-operative Banks are credit institutions and every credit institution has to be a member of at least one Credit Information Company (CIC). State and Central Co-operative Banks are required to take membership of at least one CIC. In developing economies, lending, especially to retail, has been made possible by credit information companies, which perform the vital task of collating and distributing reliable credit information to the specified users. Reports from CICs contain information about the payment behaviour of consumers and commercial entities, including data on timely fulfillment of or delinquency in meeting the financial obligations. It helps credit institutions in making an informed decision about a credit applicant.

State Cooperative Banks–Guiding Role

State Cooperative Banks are the apex level institutions in the federal structure of STCCS. They accept huge deposits from the affiliated/member societies and also from non-members. They provide liquidity support and financial accommodation to the member societies down the chain. Large volume of funds in the form of governmental assistance under various welfare and subsidy schemes, grants and refinance from higher refinance agencies are channeled through state cooperative banks to the lower tier institutions. Hence, it is the responsibility of the state cooperative banks to provide guidance and direction to the member societies and ensure that the valuable resources are not frittered away and diverted to investments in risky assets. Weaknesses in lower tier institutions would eventually move up the chain and bring down the entire edifice of the federal cooperative credit structure. Even strong state cooperative banks would face threat to their survival if the structural weaknesses are not addressed in a timely manner.

State cooperative banks have a larger role in the development of the state economy. They should rise above the self-interest and work for serving the economic interests of the society at large. It need to be emphasised that these banks should keep their own house in order and conduct themselves with unquestionable integrity and social responsibility.

Way forward

Co-operatives have inherent advantages as member-owned and member-controlled institutions. Successive governments have acknowledged their role in improving the productivity and eradication of poverty among the rural masses and contribution to development of rural economy and provided support and assistance as a part of State-promoted policies. However, cooperatives have to make sustained efforts to address the constraints and inadequacies discussed above.

To sum up, cooperatives should practice good corporate governance and social responsibility. These institutions should be purely 'member-driven' keeping the principle of cooperation in letter and spirit. Professionalism should be introduced in staffing and adequate training opportunities should be provided to the employees of cooperatives for skill upgradation. They should frame sound and prudent policies for loans and investments and conduct themselves in the larger interests of the depositors and the general public. Cooperatives should overcome their inertia and resistance to change and emerge as technology-driven, well-managed institutions to inspire confidence in the public and secure their survival.

References

1. *Banking Regulations Act*-NABARD
2. *www.rbi.org.in* › Publications

18

Regional Rural Banks (RRB)

Interface with the Chairmen of RRBs. This becomes especially important as we all accept that the quality of customer service and the bank's treatment of customers depend on guidance of its Top Management in the building of an organisational culture committed to high levels of customer service with an ethical value system.

The Banking Codes and Standards Board of India (BCSBI) was set up seven years ago, since then it has prepared and published voluntary comprehensive Codes and Standards for banks for providing fair treatment to customers.

It functions as an independent body to monitor and to ensure that the Codes voluntarily adopted by banks are adhered to, in true spirit in delivering the services, as promised.

BCSBI had evolved two Codes for Member Banks to implement:

Code of Bank's Commitment to Customers

Code of Bank's Commitment to Micro and Small Enterprises

These Codes are periodically updated keeping in view the recent changes.

Regional Rural Banks RRBs:

The RRBs are now treated on par with other commercial banks and as banks, they must focus on customer empowerment and extending customer service.

Establishment of RRBs

The Narasimham Working Group (1975) conceptualised the creation of RRBs in 1975 as a new set of regionally oriented rural banks, which would combine the local feel and familiarity of rural problems characteristic of cooperatives with the professionalism and large resource base of commercial banks. Regional Rural Banks (RRBs) were established under the Regional Rural Banks Act, 1976 to create an alternative channel to the cooperative credit structure and to ensure sufficient institutional credit for the rural and agriculture sector. RRBs are jointly owned by the Government of India, the concerned State Government and sponsor banks, with the issued capital shared in the proportion of 50 per cent, 15 per cent and 35 per cent, respectively. As per the provisions of the Regional Rural Banks Act, 1976 the authorised capital of each RRB is Rs 5 crore and the issued capital is a maximum of Rs 1 crore.

From a modest beginning of 6 RRBs with 17 branches covering 12 districts in December, 1975 the number of RRBs increased to 196 RRBs with 14,446 branches in 1991 operating in 518 districts across the country. After a phase of consolidation starting from September, 2005 the number of RRBs was reduced from 196 to 82. In the current phase of consolidation which began in October, 2012 by amalgamation of RRBs across sponsor banks within a State, the number of RRBs has further reduced to 61 RRBs as on date with over 18000 branches in 638 districts.

Reforms in the RRB Sector have taken place in three phases:

First Phase: 1993–2000

Based on the recommendations of the Narasimham Committee Report (1992), reforms were initiated in 1993 with a view to improve the financial health and operational viability of RRBs. Various measures including recapitalisation, rationalisation of branch network, providing better access to non-fund business, expanding avenues of investment and advances, upgrading the level of technology and taking up select RRBs for comprehensive restructuring. Further, they were permitted to lend to non-target group borrowers upto 60 per cent of new loans. From January, 1995 the investment avenues for RRBs were broadened to improve their operational efficiency and profitability. In December, 1996 the investment policy was further liberalised, to accord parity with commercial banks, permitting RRBs to invest in shares and debentures of corporates and units of Mutual Funds with a ceiling upto 5 per cent of the incremental deposits of the bank during the previous year. Prudential accounting norms of income recognition, asset classification, provisioning and exposure, were implemented during this period to provide durability to the reform process. In April 2000, RRBs were allowed to apply for permission to maintain non-resident accounts in rupees.

Second Phase: 2004—2010

The next Phase of reforms started in 2004-05 with the structural consolidation of RRBs by amalgamation of RRBs of the same sponsor bank within a State. Capital support aggregating Rs 1796 crore was provided during the period 2007-08 to 2009-10 as part of this process. In October, 2004 RRBs were permitted to undertake insurance business without risk participation and in May, 2007 they were allowed to take up corporate agency business for distribution of all types of insurance products without risk participation. In December, 2005 to further extend support to RRBs for accelerating the flow of credit to the rural areas, the resource base of RRBs was expanded to include lines of credit from sponsor banks; they were also permitted to access the term money markets and CBLO/Repo markets. Issuance of credit/debit cards, setting up of ATMs, opening of currency chests, undertaking government business, as subagents, were allowed to enhance business opportunities. In March, 2006 RRBs were permitted to apply for AD-Category II licence to undertake non-trade related current account transactions for certain specified purposes to further enhance the scope of business. In June, 2007 to increase their exposure to foreign exchange business they were allowed to accept FCNR deposits. RRBs were also allowed to participate in consortium lending with sponsor banks, DFIs and other banks within the area of operation. The capital adequacy standards were introduced in December, 2007 in the context of financial stability and RRBs were required to disclose the level of CRAR in their balance sheets.

Third Phase: 2010 onwards

Based on the recommendations of Dr K. Chakrabarty Committee (2010), 40 RRBs have been taken up for recapitalisation to enable them to achieve and sustain a CRAR of 9 per cent. In November, 2010 the branch licensing policy was liberalised which allowed RRBs to open branches in Tier 3 to Tier 6 centres (with population of upto 49,999 as per 2001 Census) without prior approval from the Reserve Bank, subject to certain conditions. This policy was further liberalised in August, 2013 to also include Tier 2 centres. The second phase of consolidation commenced from October, 2012 with amalgamation of RRBs across sponsor banks within a State.

Performance of RRBs Post Amalgamation:

It can be seen from the data on performance of RRBs post amalgamation that there has been consistent progress in the operations of RRBs.

	2005-06	*2006-07*	*2007-08*	*2008-09*	*2009-10*	*2010-11*	*2011-12*	*2012-13(P)*
No of RRBs	133	96	90	86	82	82	82	64
No of branches	14489	14563	14790	15524	15475	16024	16914	17867
Net profit (cr)	617	625	1027	1335	1884	1785	1886	2384
Profit/loss making RRBs	111/22	81/15	82/8	80/6	79/3	75/7	79/3	63/1
Deposits (cr)	71329	83144	99093	120189	145035	166232	186336	211457
Loans & Advances (cr) 38520	47326	57568	65609	79157	94715	113035	133098	

(Contd...)

CD ratio (per cent)	55.7	58.3	59.5	56.4	57.6	59.51	63.3	66.13
Share of CASA in deposits (per cent)	59.14	61.21	59.63	58.35	57.90	60.35	58.51	57
Share of PSA in total	81	82.2	82.9	83.4	82.2	83.5	80	86
Share of agri adv to total (per cent)	54.2	56.6	56.3	55.1	54.8	55.7	53	63
Gross NPA (per cent)	7.3	6.55	6.1	4.2	3.72	3.75	5.03	5.65
Net NPA per cent		3.46	3.36	1.81	1.62	2.05	2.98	3.40

Source: Reports on Trend and Progress of Banking in India and NABARD

Post amalgamation, in terms of total business 2 RRBs are larger than some private sector commercial banks as can be seen from the graph below:

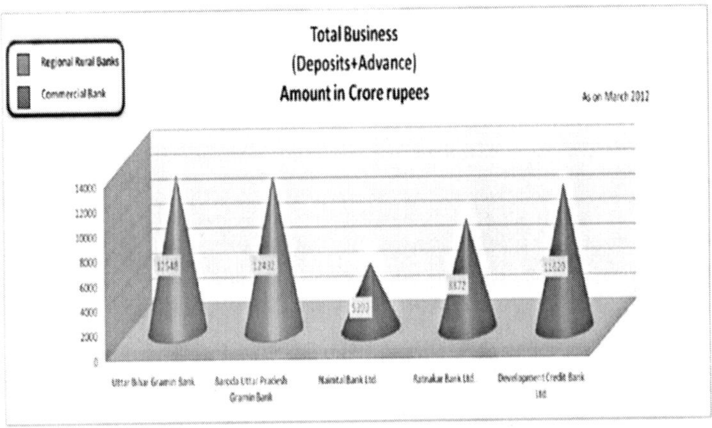

In terms of owned funds Andhra Pragathi Grameena Bank is much larger than some of the private sector commercial banks.

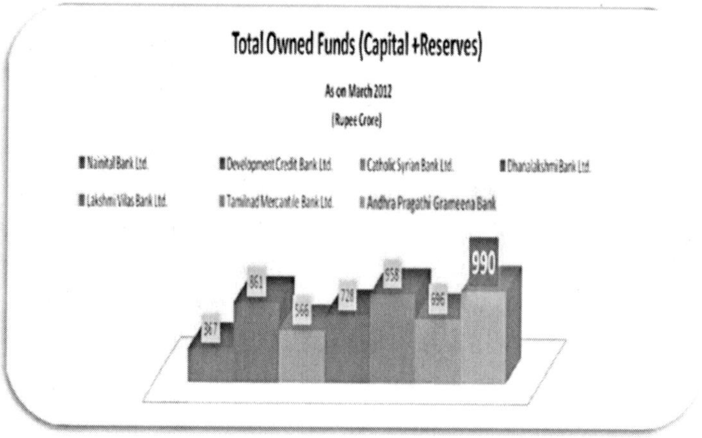

Financial Inclusion by RRBs

In order to achieve the objective of universal financial inclusion, RRBs have been directed to use a combination of strategies, which include: (a) provision of basic banking products; (b) introduction of the Business Correspondent/ Business Facilitator (BF) model; (c) adoption of the relaxed regulatory Know Your Customer (KYC) guidelines; (d) enhanced use of technology; and (e) setting up financial literacy centres in districts to achieve greater outreach. Though the share of RRBs in aggregate deposits and gross bank credit is only around 2.5 to 3 per cent, they play a critical role in financial inclusion. RRBs are required to prepare Financial Inclusion Plans which are to be integrated with their business plans. The major highlights of their performance under the first FIP for the period April, 2010–March, 2013 are as under:

1. Banking Outreach

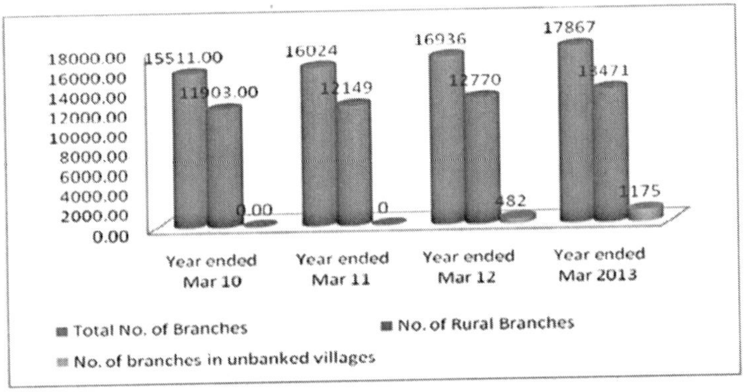

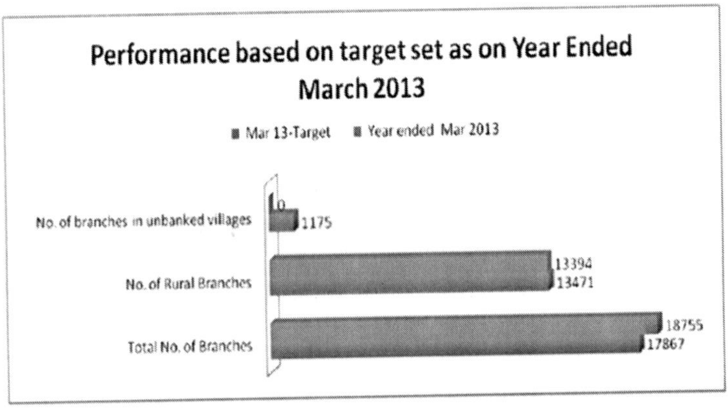

The number of rural branches has increased by 15 per cent. The self set FIP targets have almost been met. At the same time number of branches in unbanked villages has grown from 0 in 2011 to 1175 as on year ended March, 2013. However, they could not completely fullfill their targets of opening up the total number of branches. The target was set around 18,755 branches while they were able to open close to 17,867 branches only as on year ended March 2013.

2. Type of Banking Outlets-Based on Size of Population

a. Population > 2000

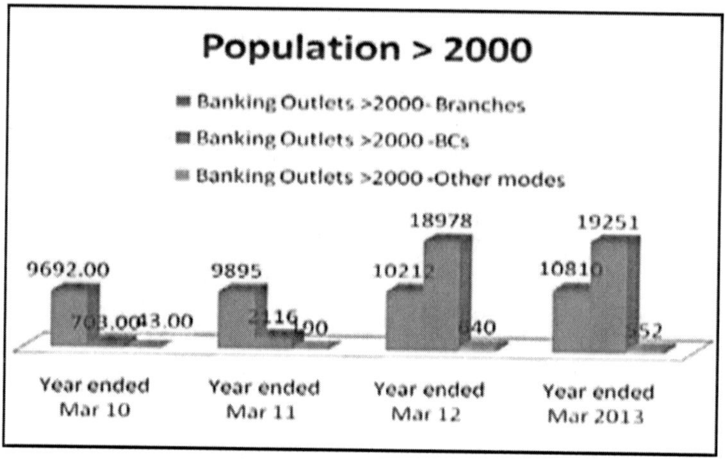

The total number of banking outlets can be viewed in terms of Bank Branches, Business Correspondents (BCs) and Other Modes. For villages with population of more than 2,000 there has been a considerable increase in the number of BCs. There was a steep rise from mere 703 BC outlets (year ended March, 2010) to close to 19,000 BC outlets (year ended March, 2012).

b. Population < 2000

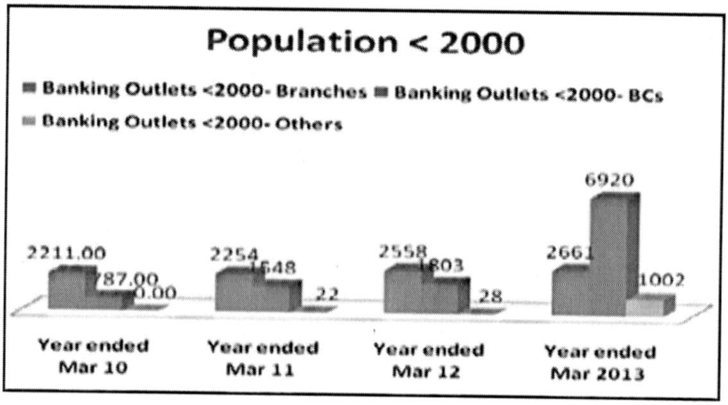

For villages with population less than 2000, the number of BCs registered a sharp growth. However, the RRBs failed in achieving the set target for BC outlets for the year ended March, 2013.

3. Basic Savings Bank Deposit Account

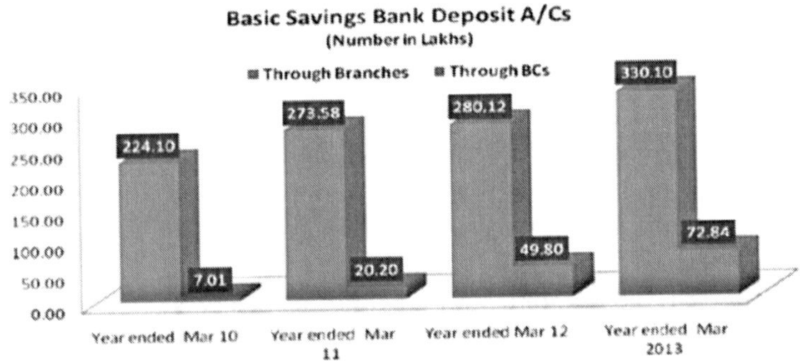

It is observed that most of the Basic Savings Bank Deposit Accounts (BSBDA) were opened through branches. The number of accounts opened through branches stood at 330.10 lakh, while only 72.84 lakh accounts were opened through BCs (year ended March 2013).

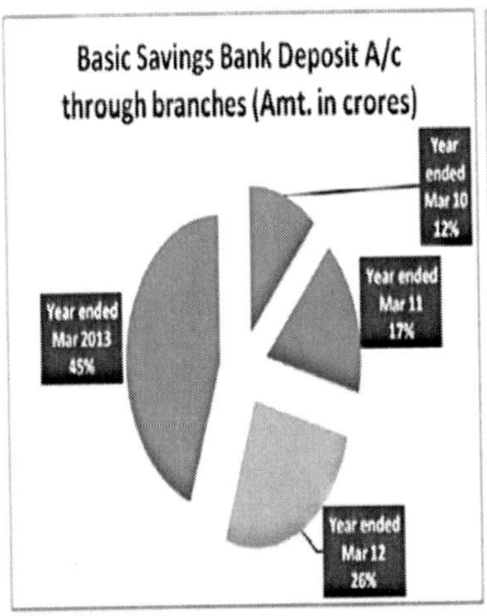

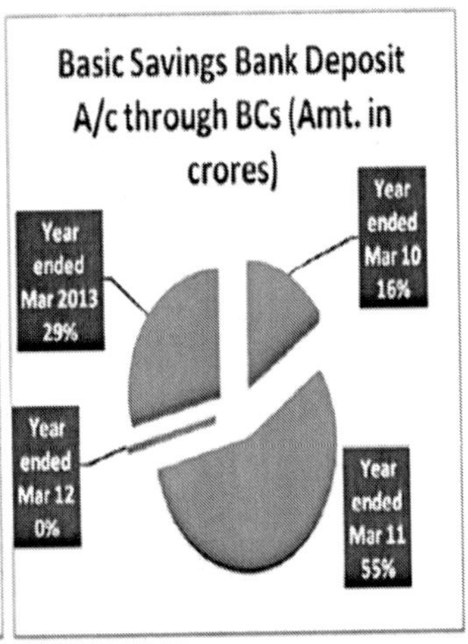

The graphs show the amount mobilised each year (in percentage) in Basic Savings Bank Deposit Account (BSBDA) through branches and BCs. In the year 2012, there was a sharp fall in the amount mobilised through BCs but it has again picked up in 2013.

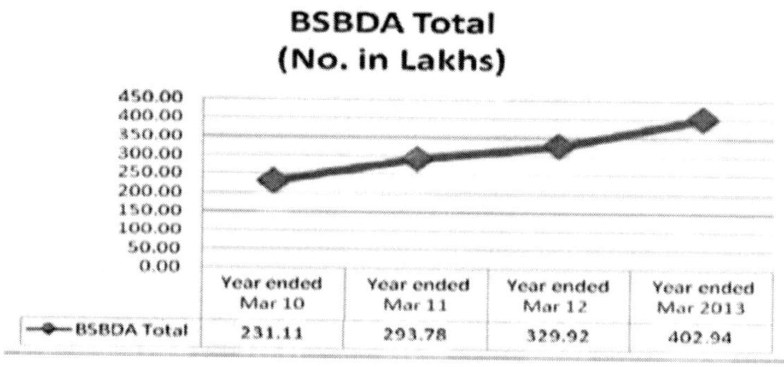

The total number of Basic Savings Bank Deposit Accounts has increased considerably. From around 230 lakh accounts (year ended March, 2010) to more than 400 lakh accounts (year ended March, 2013), the growth rate has been equal to 74 per cent.

4. Kisan Credit Cards

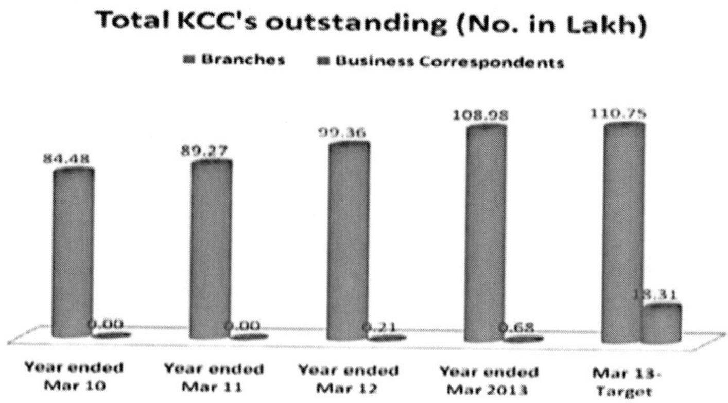

The branches were successful in achieving their target number of KCCs (year ended March, 2013). No KCCs were sourced through the BCs for the years ended 2010 and 2011.

5. General Credit Cards

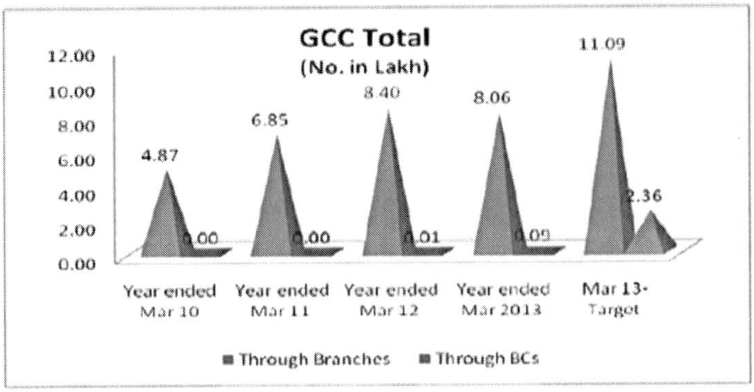

The BC is utilised to externalise part of the credit cycle. He has to work towards spreading awareness of the availability of the bank's products and services. BCs can be better leveraged by the RRB branches. They are in need of greater handholding and necessarily of close and continuous supervision.

Though there has been reasonable progress with regard to extending the penetration of banking services and opening of basic bank accounts, the number of transactions through the ICT based BC outlets are poor. During the period of the next 3 year Financial Inclusion Plan i.e. 2013-16 RRBs should endeavour to leverage technology to the optimum. Technology enables the bank to transcend the barriers of geography and to provide services at the borrower's doorstep. Though the initial cost is high over time it pays for itself. Regional Rural Banks should through financial innovation try to focus on mezzanine finance, on the creation of customised products linked to the income streams of the poor borrowers and geared to meet the specific needs of the rural clientele. Mobile technology can be harnessed to improve access and usage of banking services.

The Codes and RRBs

All banks offer the same products with variants but what distinguishes and sets apart and gives the competitive edge to a bank is the quality of customer service extended by the bank.

The Codes are the RRBs mandate, adopted by RRBs with the specific approval of the Board of Directors. RRBs must take full ownership of these Codes and facilitate their adoption ensuring complete adherence.

RRBs have undergone a sea change. They are now almost treated on par with other commercial banks. The customers of the RRBS are illiterate and poor; there is also an asymmetry of information. Hence, the adoption of standards of behaviour and codes of conduct framed by BCSBI for dealing with customers is an imperative.

At some point we are all customers of banks. What are the ingredients of treating customers fairly? Transparency, proper disclosure, non-discriminatory and non-exploitative pricing, building a robust and responsive grievance redressal mechanism within the bank and also making the customer aware of redressal available through the Banking Ombudsman Scheme. Transparency does not mean bombarding the illiterate customer with humungous amount of information which she is neither able to understand or use. It merely means no hidden charges. The customer must up front understand what she is letting herself in for; the terms and conditions of the contract should be clearly understood.

The codes need to be clearly understood and fairly implemented by Regional Rural Banks. Banks are commercial establishments. They are not philanthropic organisations. However, they enjoy great leverage and an oligopolistic position simply as the borrower in the rural areas may lack choice which his urban counterpart enjoys. This casts a much greater responsibility upon the RRBs. Knowledge and general awareness about the Codes of the BCSBI needs to be increased.

Despite valiant attempts knowledge of and appreciation of the BCSBI codes was spreading very slowly and this was a cause of concern. The Chairmen of the RRBs must appreciate that the poor borrower who comes to the door step of the Bank is highly unlikely to meet the Chairman of the bank. For him the frontline manager is the Bank. The frontline manager needs to be sensitised to the importance of the Code of Bank's Commitment to Customers. He must understand and believe in them. This affirmation will then translate to increased sensitivity and in empathetic behaviour towards the special niche clientele of the RRBs. The pay off in terms not just of profitability but in terms of job satisfaction assuredly, will be tremendous.

To close with a few clear messages for easy recall:

- Please ensure that all the RRB staff are aware of, clearly understand and committed to the BCSBI Codes.
- The Codes are evident in precept and practice and in the actual business of the Banks.
- Customer empowerment occurs as knowledge and awareness of customer rights is enhanced.

References

1. https://www.nabard.org/English/rrbs.aspx
2. *www.rbi.org.in/commonman/English/scripts/banksinindia.aspx*

Glossary

Basic Saving Bank Deposit Account (BSBDA) – Basic Savings Bank Deposit Accounts' offers minimum common facilities as stated therein. Banks have been required to convert the existing 'no-frills' accounts into 'Basic Savings Bank Deposit Accounts'.

Banking Ombudsman – The Banking Ombudsman is a senior official, appointed by the Reserve Bank of India to address grievances and complaints from customers, regarding deficiencies in banking services. It covers all kinds of banks – PSU Banks, Private banks, Rural banks and Co-operative banks.

Business Correspondents – Under the 'Business Correspondent' Model, NGOs/ MFIs set up under Societies/ Trust Acts, Societies registered under Mutually Aided Cooperative Societies Acts or the Cooperative Societies Acts of States, Section 25 Companies, registered NBFCs not accepting public deposits and Post Offices may act as Business Correspondents. In the light of the announcement made in paragraph 92 of the Budget Speech 2008-2009 by the Hon'ble Finance Minister, Govt. of India, it was decided to permit banks to engage retired bank employees, ex-servicemen and retired government employees as **Business Correspondents (BCs)** with immediate effect, in addition to the entities already permitted, subject to appropriate due diligence.

Capital to Risk weighted Asset Ratio—CRAR framework, as advocated by Basel Accord, has been adopted by most of the regulatory authorities as the basis of measurement of capital adequacy, which takes into account the element of risk associated with various types of assets reflected in the balance sheet as well as in respect of off-balance sheet items and the level of capital held by the banks.

CD Ratio—Credit-Deposit ratio is proportion of loan created by banks from deposits it receives. In other words, its capacity of banks to lend.

Core Banking Solution– Core Banking Solution (CBS) is networking of branches, which enables Customers to operate their accounts, and avail banking services from any branch of the Bank on CBS network, regardless of where he maintains his account. The customer is no more the customer of a Branch. He becomes the Bank's Customer. Thus, CBS is a step towards enhancing customer convenience through anywhere and anytime Banking.

District Consultative Committee (DCC)– It is conceived to be a common forum for bankers as well as government agencies/departments to come to a common platform to find solutions to the problems arising hindering the smooth functioning of the various developmental activities under the Scheme at the district level.

District Level Review Committee– In addition to bankers MP–MLA and other non-official members are invited to find solutions to the problems arising hindering the smooth functioning of the various developmental activities under the Scheme at the district level.

Direct Benefit Transfer– Direct Benefit Transfer or DBT is an anti-poverty program launched by Government of India on 1st January 2013. This program aims to transfer subsidies directly to the people living below poverty line.

Financial Inclusion– The process of ensuring access to financial services and timely and adequate credit where needed by vulnerable groups such as weaker sections and low income groups at an affordable cost.

Financial literacy– It is the ability to understand how money works in the world: how someone manages to earn or make it, how that person manages it, how he/she invests it (turn it into more) and how that person donates it to help others.

General Credit Card- It is to increase flow of credit to individuals for entrepreneurial activity in the non-farm sector.

Gross Domestic Product- is the market value of all officially recognised final goods and services produced within a country in a year, or other given period of time.

Lead Bank Scheme - Lead Bank Scheme (LBS) was introduced in 1969, based on the recommendations of the Gadgil Study Group. The basic idea was to have an "area approach" for targeted and focused banking.

Naional Skill Development Policy- The objective of this policy is to empower all individuals through improved skills, knowledge, nationally and internationally recognised qualifications to gain access to decent employment and ensure India's competitiveness in the global market.

National Rural Livelihood Mission-National Rural Livelihood Mission was launched by the Ministry of Rural Development (MoRD), Government of India in June 2011. Aided in part through investment support by the World Bank, the Mission aims at creating efficient and effective institutional platforms of the rural poor enabling them to increase household income through sustainable livelihood enhancements and improved access to financial services.

No Frill Account- These accounts are offered without having any obligation of minimum balance.

Microfinance- A type of banking service that is provided to unemployed or low-income individuals or groups who would otherwise have no other means of gaining financial services. Ultimately, the goal of microfinance is to give low income poor an opportunity to become self-sufficient by providing a means of saving money, borrowing money and insurance.

Organisation for Economic Cooperation and Development - The OECD Forum is a public fora bringing together leaders from all sectors of society to debate the most pressing social and economic challenges confronting society.

Priority Sector Lending- Priority sector refers to those sectors of the economy which may not get timely and adequate credit in the absence of this special dispensation. Typically, these are small value loans to farmers for agriculture and allied activities, micro and small enterprises, poor people for housing, students for education and other low income groups and weaker sections.

The State Level Bankers' Committees (SLBCs)—have been constituted, following instructions from Government of India in April 1977 as an inter-institutional forum for co-ordination and joint implementation of development programmes by all financial institutions operating in a State. It comprises the representatives of commercial banks (including RRBs), State Cooperative Banks (SCB), Land Development Banks (LDB), NABARD, RBI, etc.

Swarn Jayanti Shahari Rojgar Yojana : The Swarna Jayanti Shahari Rozgar Yojana (SJSRY) was launched on 1st December 1997 after subsuming the earlier three schemes for urban poverty alleviation, namely Nehru Rozgar Yojana (NRY), Urban Basic Services for the Poor (UBSP), and Prime Minister's Integrated Urban Poverty Eradication Programme (PMIUPEP). The key objective of the Scheme was to provide gainful employment to the urban unemployed or underemployed through the setting up of self-employment ventures or provision of wage employment.

District Level Review Committee–In addition to bankers MP–MLA and other non-official members are invited to find solutions to the problems arising hindering the smooth functioning of the various developmental activities under the Scheme at the district level.

Direct Benefit Transfer–Direct Benefit Transfer or DBT is an anti-poverty program launched by Government of India on 1st January 2013. This program aims to transfer subsidies directly to the people living below poverty line.

Financial Inclusion–The process of ensuring access to financial services and timely and adequate credit where needed by vulnerable groups such as weaker sections and low income groups at an affordable cost.

Financial literacy–It is the ability to understand how money works in the world: how someone manages to earn or make it, how that person manages it, how he/she invests it (turn it into more) and how that person donates it to help others.

General Credit Card–It is to increase flow of credit to individuals for entrepreneurial activity in the non-farm sector.

Gross Domestic Production–is the market value of all officially recognized final goods and services produced within a country in a year, or other given period of time.

Lead Bank Scheme–Lead Bank Scheme (LBS) was introduced in 1969, based on the recommendations of the Gadgil Study Group. The basic idea was to have an "area approach" for targeted and focused banking.

Naional Skill Development Policy–The objective of this policy is to empower all individuals through improved skills, knowledge, nationally and internationally recognized qualifications to gain access to decent employment and ensure India's competitiveness in the global market.

National Rural Livelihood Mission–was launched by the Ministry of Rural Development (MoRD), Government of India in June 2011. Aided in part through investment support by the World Bank, the Mission aims at creating efficient and effective institutional platforms of the rural poor enabling them to increase household income through sustainable livelihood enhancements and improved access to financial services.

No frill Account–These accounts are offered without having any obligation of minimum balance.

Microfinance–A type of banking service that is provided to unemployed or low-income individuals or groups who would otherwise have no other means of gaining financial services. Ultimately, the goal of microfinance is to give low income people an opportunity to become self-sufficient by providing a means of saving money, borrowing money and insurance.

Organisation for Economic Cooperation and Development- The OECD Forum is a public event bringing together leaders from all sectors of society to debate the most pressing social and economic challenges confronting society.

Priority Sector Lending- Priority sector refers to those sectors of the economy which may not get timely and adequate credit in the absence of this special dispensation. Typically, these are small value loans to farmers for agriculture and allied activities, micro and small enterprises, poor people for housing, students for education and other low income groups and weaker sections.

The State Level Bankers' Committees(SLBCs)- have been constituted, following instructions from Government of India in April 1977 as an inter-institutional forum for co-ordination and joint implementation of development programmes by all financial institutions operating in a State. It comprises the representatives of commercial banks (including RRBs), State Cooperative Banks (StCB), Land Development Banks (LDB), NABARD, RBI, etc.

Swarn Jayanti Shahari Rojgar Yojanas: The Swarna Jayanti Shahari Rozgar Yojana (SJSRY) was launched on 1st December 1997 after subsuming the earlier three schemes for urban poverty alleviation, namely Nehru Rozgar Yojana (NRY), Urban Basic Services for the Poor (UBSP), and Prime Minister's Integrated Urban Poverty Eradication Programme (PMIUPEP). The key objective of the Scheme was to provide gainful employment to the urban unemployed or underemployed through the setting up of self-employment ventures or provision of wage employment.

Index